Peace & Freedom

12556

$9.99

6.50

Y0-BDH-945

Peace & Freedom

FOREIGN POLICY FOR A CONSTITUTIONAL REPUBLIC

TED GALEN CARPENTER

CATO INSTITUTE
Washington, D.C.

Copyright © 2002 by Cato Institute.
All rights reserved.

Library of Congress Cataloging-in-Publication Data

Carpenter, Ted Galen.
   Peace & freedom : foreign policy for a constitutional republic /
      Ted Galen Carpenter.
         p. cm.
   Includes bibliographical references and index.
   ISBN 1-930865-34-1 (cloth : alk. paper)—ISBN 1-930865-33-3
   (paper: alk. paper)
      1. United States—Foreign relations—2001- I. Title: Peace and
   freedom. II. Title.

E895.C37 2002
327.73′009′0511—dc21

2002074013

Cover design by Amanda S. Elliott.
Cover photography © Zigy Kaluzny/Stone.
Printed in the United States of America.

CATO INSTITUTE
1000 Massachusetts Ave., N.W.
Washington, D.C. 20001
www.cato.org

To Professor Robert A. Divine, for all his encouragement and guidance during the early years of my career.

Contents

Preface

During my 17 years as a scholar at the Cato Institute, I have written on a wide range of foreign policy topics for newspapers, magazines, and policy journals. *Peace and Freedom: A Foreign Policy for a Constitutional Republic* is a representative sample of those writings. Taken as a whole, they present a comprehensive view of what I believe should be America's strategy for dealing with the rest of the world. That approach, which I call "strategic independence," emphasizes a vigorous defense of America's vital interests and a rigorous adherence to America's fundamental values. Strategic independence rejects the notion that the United States should intervene militarily when vital interests are *not* at stake. Promiscuous global interventionism places needless burdens on American taxpayers, entangles the United States in an assortment of irrelevant quarrels, and ultimately puts the lives of all Americans at risk.

Most of my conclusions have stood the test of time. My prediction that the drug war in Latin America would prove to be an endless, futile crusade seems even sounder today than when I first made it in the mid-1980s. Likewise, my warnings that Washington's victory in the Persian Gulf War would be merely the beginning of a long and frustrating mission in that region, that nation-building enterprises in such places as Somalia and the Balkans would prove disappointing, and that America's NATO and East Asian allies would continue to free ride on the U.S. security guarantee have been borne out. Most notably, my argument that the United States needed a more coherent and effective strategy to deal with the threat of terrorism seems all too evident in light of the events of September 11.

A few other conclusions were less accurate. I overestimated the determination of Russian leaders to resist NATO's expansion eastward, overestimated the likelihood that disaffected factions in Bosnia would target U.S. and NATO peacekeeping troops, and overestimated (at least so far) the willingness of U.S. administrations to use military personnel to wage the international war on drugs. No one bats a thousand in the policy analysis field, and I am no exception to that rule. Any policy expert who contends that he managed to get every issue right is either deceiving himself or trying to deceive others.

On still other issues, it is too soon to tell whether my conclusions are correct or incorrect. For example, I have articulated a "hedging strategy" for dealing with China, but it may be another decade or two before it will be possible to determine whether that is the best approach. I've also expressed the view that America's intervention in Kosovo will ultimately make the southern Balkans less rather than more stable, but only time will tell whether that prediction is accurate.

Gratitude is owed to several individuals for making this book possible. I am especially grateful to Ed Crane, president of the Cato Institute, for his consistent and enthusiastic support of my work over the past 17 years. He has chosen to make a critique of U.S. foreign policy a core component of the Institute's program even when it might have been easier (and more rewarding in terms of fundraising) to have ignored the topic. That decision reflects both courage and integrity. I am grateful as well to David Boaz, Cato's executive vice president, for his support and helpful comments.

Finally, I want to express a special thanks to Jennifer Assenza for her work in preparing the manuscript. Without her able and diligent efforts, it would simply not have been possible for me to complete such a complex undertaking in a timely fashion.

Introduction: U.S. Security Strategy after 9-11

The horrific events of September 11 underscore the need for a shift in the focus of America's security policy. Prior to September 11 it would have been nearly impossible to find a U.S. policymaker or high-ranking military officer who believed that the highest priority of the U.S. armed forces was to respond to an attack on the American homeland. For more than half a century, the principal mission of the U.S. military had been to serve as an instrument of Washington's foreign policy in far-flung regions of the world. As a military mission, homeland defense was barely on the radar screen.

Now, that has all changed. U.S. forces have fought al-Qaeda terrorists in the mountains of Afghanistan and helped to overthrow the Taliban government that made that country a haven for Osama bin Laden and his followers. Speculation is rampant about where the next phase of the war against the perpetrators of the September 11 attacks will be conducted. Those Americans who believe that Iraqi dictator Saddam Hussein has links to anti-U.S. terrorists (including, perhaps, al-Qaeda itself) want the next stage to be an attack on Iraq to remove his regime. Other Americans believe that dangerous cells of al-Qaeda fighters are hunkered down in such countries as Yemen, Somalia, and Pakistan and that the war should be taken to those locales. An attack on Iraq, in their view, is inappropriate and potentially counterproductive.

There is also disagreement about the proper scope of America's anti-terrorist mission. The Bush administration has added to the confusion by making inconsistent, even contradictory, statements. At times, the administration seems to focus on the people responsible for the September 11 attacks. (The congressional resolution authorizing the use of force also is restricted to those adversaries.) But on other occasions, administration officials have implied that America's goal is a war against terrorism per se, whether specific terrorist organizations target the United States or only other countries. In his

1

2002 State of the Union address, President Bush went even further, singling out Iraq, Iran, and North Korea as an "axis of evil" and indicating that the acquisition of weapons of mass destruction by those countries was part of a global terrorist threat.

America badly needs to clarify its objectives. A war against al-Qaeda and any other organization or government that targets the United States for attack is different from a general crusade against all organizations that use terrorist tactics against some adversary. The latter would be an extraordinarily broad and difficult mission. Yet even that mission is narrower than a crusade against all terrorist organizations plus all evil regimes that might possess weapons of mass destruction. One of the prime requirements of any good security strategy is that its objectives be realistic and attainable. There are serious doubts about whether either the second or the third mission can meet that test.

Equally troubling is Washington's failure to adjust its overall security strategy to meet the new threat. There has been no discernible willingness to rethink old commitments and obligations even though America now confronts a dangerous new adversary. Instead, all of the old missions are preserved and the new one is simply added to the list. That is a terribly myopic approach. The United States should have used the end of the Cold War to conduct a detailed audit of its security commitments around the globe, determine which ones were no longer relevant, and develop a security strategy appropriate for the post–Cold War era. The refusal to undertake such a reassessment was a major failing of U.S. foreign policy in the 1990s.

With the events of September 11, such a reassessment is no longer merely desirable, it is imperative. It is clear that even a narrowly defined anti-terrorist campaign will be a major concern of the United States for several years. Obsolete or nonessential commitments are a distraction that the United States can ill afford—financially or otherwise. September 11 should be the catalyst for creating a wholly new security strategy for the United States in the 21st century. If conducted properly, a detailed audit will produce a policy that will enhance America's security at less cost and risk.

An appropriate security strategy for the United States should be based on an assessment of current and prospective conditions in the international system, an appreciation of America's exceptional geostrategic position within that system, and an unemotional calculation of the most cost-effective and risk-averse methods of protecting the Republic's vital interests. Because of the vast changes that have occurred in the past decade or so in the international system, the United States can exploit its unique geostrategic advantages (unparalleled military capabilities, markedly superior economy, and lack of powerful, hostile neighboring states) in ways that would have been difficult during the atypical era of Cold War bipolarity. Specifically, since there is no looming hegemonic threat, Washington can be far more selective in its political and military commitments. The United States can play the role of balancer of last resort rather than intervener of first resort.

Unfortunately, post–Cold War U.S. policymakers have reflexively sought to preserve the principal features of the strategy the United States pursued during the Cold War—high levels of military spending, an emphasis on U.S. global leadership, and a hypersensitive reaction to "aggression" anywhere in the world—despite the vastly altered strategic environment. There has been no willingness to jettison or even downgrade Washington's Cold War–era security commitments. NATO and the bilateral alliances with such countries as Japan and South Korea are deemed as vital as ever, as is the strategy of forward deployment of U.S. forces to underscore the seriousness of America's commitments. Where substantive policy changes have occurred, the result has been an even more interventionist tendency. For example, the United States is now undertaking security obligations in Central and Eastern Europe through an expanded NATO and has become the would-be stabilizer of the perennially turbulent Balkans.

That approach is fundamentally wrong-headed. The United States should not construct its 21st-century foreign policy around slightly remodeled components of its Cold War policy. A radically altered global political, economic, and strategic environment calls for rethinking all assumptions and building a new policy from the ground up. A new, more relevant U.S. policy should emphasize three features.

Encourage Multiple Centers of Power

One of the major components of a security strategy ought to be a willingness to encourage the emergence of multiple centers of power, that is, a global environment with several economic and military great powers and an assortment of mid-sized regional powers. Rather than resist the international system's return to a more "normal" condition of multipolarity—a return that is occurring gradually in any case, regardless of U.S. preferences—Washington should accept that change and seek to turn it to America's advantage. The presence of other significant political and military players in the international system—especially if those players are stable, status quo, democratic great powers—can provide important security buffers for the United States. Ideally, such states might take the lead in forging effective regional security organizations. A more robust version of the European Union is the most prominent example of that possibility. In most cases, though, regional multipolarity would take the form of more informal balance-of-power arrangements. Even that outcome, however, would usually serve American interests. Indeed, the mere existence of multiple powers (even if some of them were not especially friendly to the United States) would make it less likely that a hegemonic threat comparable to that posed by the Soviet Union could ever emerge again.

Unfortunately, there is today a virtual obsession among U.S. policymakers with protecting America's prerogatives as the self-proclaimed indispensable nation. Almost any political or military initiative by other major countries, even democratic countries, is seen as a threat to America's preeminent status. To be sure, that is not a new phenomenon. Several scholars have argued that Washington has long sought to "smother" the ambitions of other great powers and mesh them into the U.S.-led security system and global economy.

The heart of the smothering strategy has been to prevent the rise of any political and military competitor, especially in Western Europe or East Asia. That approach at least arguably made sense when it seemed necessary for Washington to mobilize the resources and capabilities of the free (or more accurately, noncommunist) world to contain Soviet power. The rationale is far less compelling when there is no lethal common threat requiring a unified resistance effort under U.S. leadership. Yet, ironically, the objective of discouraging other powers from even aspiring to play more active political and military roles was most candidly expressed *after* the Cold War— in the preliminary draft of the Pentagon's planning guidance document that was leaked to the press in 1992.

Throughout the post–Cold War period, U.S. officials have reacted with suspicion and alarm whenever they have detected signs that another major power was seeking to become more active in the security realm. For example, when Japanese prime minister Toshiki Kaifu made a surprise proposal in the summer of 1991 for a "security dialogue" between Japan and the members of the Association of Southeast Asian Nations, Washington reacted vehemently. Secretary of State James A. Baker III warned the ASEAN foreign ministers against adopting new arrangements that would replace "tried and true frameworks" involving the United States. Privately, U.S. officials expressed strong opposition to the Japanese proposal because it might weaken the bilateral arrangements between the United States and various nations in East Asia.

The Clinton administration was more subtle in implementing the smothering strategy, but administration officials still seized every opportunity to emphasize America's determination to maintain a large military presence in East Asia and to continue the role of stabilizer. For example, Secretary of Defense William Cohen stated that the United States would hope to keep forces deployed in Korea even if reunification of the peninsula takes place—a policy that the administration of George W. Bush has also endorsed.

The Pentagon's 1995 security strategy report for the East Asia–Pacific region likewise confirmed the insistence on U.S. preeminence. That report conceded that one important reason forward-deployed U.S. forces were in East Asia was to "discourage the emergence of a regional hegemon." Although U.S. officials were vague about what rival might aspire to that status, a passage in the report suggested the cause of Washington's apprehension: "If the United States does not provide the central, visible, stabilizing force in the Asia and Pacific region," the report cautioned, "it is quite possible that another country might—but not in a way that meets America's fundamental interests. . . ." The reference to a "stabilizing" force suggests that Washington primarily fears that Japan, rather than a potentially revisionist power such as the People's Republic of China, is the potential rival for primacy.

The wary, if not hostile, attitude toward an activist security role for Tokyo is reflected in the revisions to the defense guidelines for the U.S.-Japanese alliance announced in September 1997. The principal change authorized Japanese nonlethal logistical support for U.S. military operations in "areas surrounding Japan" that are relevant to Japan's own security. Although the new defense guidelines confirmed that U.S. officials had finally accepted the need to modestly increase Japan's involvement in the region's security affairs, Tokyo was still seen as Washington's very junior partner. There is no indication that U.S. leaders ever want Japan to have a responsibility equal to America's for preserving stability in East Asia—much less that they want Japan to assume the lead role. The new defense guidelines merely allow Japan to be a slightly more active and helpful U.S. military dependent.

Washington has been just as firmly committed to the smothering strategy with regard to Western Europe. Historian Ronald Steel captures the underlying reality of the long-standing U.S. preeminence in NATO, noting that throughout the Cold War the alliance had been a kind of "Lincoln's Cabinet": every member would solemnly express its opinion, but the American president had the only vote that mattered.

With the collapse of the Soviet empire, the West European countries attempted to show greater assertiveness. Instead of encouraging such signs of initiative, however, Washington reacted with hostility to manifestations of greater European self-reliance. As early as February 1991, National Security Advisor Brent Scowcroft complained that the West European governments were meeting privately on security issues and then presenting a common front to the United States.

The Bush administration sought to undermine more recent manifestations of European military initiative, such as the EU's effort to create a common security and foreign policy. Clinton administration officials stressed that the United States would support such an initiative only if the EU's security entity did not duplicate NATO's military resources or decouple U.S. and European security interests. Even that tepid support was too much for John Bolton, who became under secretary of state in the Bush administration. Bolton (and other incoming Bush administration officials) criticized the EU's efforts as inherently threatening to NATO. In other words, U.S. policymakers insist that Europe's security structure in the 21st century be centered around NATO—the security organization in which the United States plays the dominant role.

Events in both East Asia and Europe have underscored the unpleasant side effects of the smothering strategy. The tensions between the PRC and Taiwan in early 1996, and the subsequent deployment of U.S. naval forces, produced a disturbing revelation. Washington's "friends and allies" in East Asia carefully distanced their policies from that of the United States as the Clinton administration dispatched two aircraft carriers to the western Pacific. The same lack of allied support was evident in April 2001 during the tense confrontation between the United States and China when a U.S. spy plane and a Chinese air force jet collided over the South China Sea.

That lack of support suggests that Washington's habit of discouraging independent security initiatives on the part of the East Asian countries has created a dangerous and unrewarding situation. How the East Asian countries have exploited Washington's insistence on U.S. preeminence is illustrated in a comment by former Japanese prime minister Yasuhiro Nakasone that U.S. forces stationed in Japan should be used as a watchdog to prevent conflicts in the Asia-Pacific region. Nakasone's rationale was that Japan provides money to the United States, allows it to station troops in Japan, and uses them as watchdogs. He added that he thought such an arrangement was wise.

That cynical exploitation of Washington's superpower vanity puts the United States in a precarious position, especially with regard to the PRC. If China makes a bid for regional hegemony at some point, there is no power other than the United States that would have the capability to block such a bid. That is a blueprint for a U.S.-Chinese conflict in which Japan and China's other neighbors remain on the sidelines. Unless Washington encourages Japan to become the primary strategic counterweight to an increasingly assertive China, and informs the other East Asian countries that America will not be the volunteer security watchdog for the region, the United States will end up filling the watchdog role by default.

Similarly, events in the former Yugoslavia expose the downside of the smothering strategy in Europe. As the EU stumbled in its mediation attempts (often undermined by Washington's carping, if not sabotage), the United States retook the lead role in containing the disorder. The result is that America is now mired in a seemingly interminable peacekeeping and nation-building venture in Bosnia— a mission that President Clinton promised in late 1995 would last only one year. Even worse, the United States is rapidly becoming the de facto ruling power of the entire Balkan region. That point became evident in 1999 when the United States led a NATO military intervention in Kosovo. U.S. troops have been on the ground in Kosovo ever since, leading another open-ended peacekeeping mission.

The smothering strategy is a losing proposition for the United States in another way. Just as nature abhors a vacuum, the international system abhors unipolarity and global hegemonic pretensions, even on the part of a democratic great power that regards its hegemony as benign and universally beneficial. The more the United States proclaims itself the "sole remaining superpower," the greater the incentives for other powers to seek opportunities to puncture that status. The behavior of France and Russia in systematically undermining Washington's efforts to isolate Iraq and Iran is a classic example of such an approach.

Thus, Washington's smothering strategy threatens to create the worst of all possible outcomes from the standpoint of America's best interests. When it serves their interests, other "friendly powers" can wheedle the United States into subsidizing their defense or incurring the costs and risks of dealing with messy regional problems. On other occasions, when it serves their interests, those same countries can ignore U.S. policy preferences and even sabotage U.S. policy initiatives.

Washington should abandon its smothering strategy and actively facilitate the emergence of multiple centers of power in the international system. True, there is a small risk that encouraging such countries as Japan and Germany (or a cohesive EU) to become more self-reliant and assertive might someday produce a strategic adversary. But it is an exceedingly remote risk and one well worth incurring. It is far more likely that such entities would be the principal firebreaks against disorder and aggression in their respective regions—a development that would provide significant indirect security benefits to the United States.

Reject the "Light-Switch" Model of U.S. Engagement

A second component of a new foreign policy would be to recognize that U.S. engagement in world affairs can take a variety of forms. Unfortunately, whenever critics suggest pruning Washington's overgrown global security commitments, defenders of the status quo reflexively cry "isolationism."

That reaction is a manifestation of the light-switch theory of American engagement—that there can be only two possible positions, on or off. Either the United States continues pursuing an indiscriminate global interventionist policy that requires putting American military personnel at risk in such places as Somalia, Haiti, and the Balkans, or we adopt a "Fortress America" strategy and "wall ourselves off from the world."

Such a contention is either obtuse or disingenuous. No serious analyst advocates creating a hermit republic. It is possible to adopt a security policy between the extremes of global interventionism—which is essentially the current U.S. policy—and Fortress America. Moreover, there are different forms of engagement in world affairs, of which the political-military version is merely one. Economic connections and influence are crucial—and growing in importance. Diplomatic and cultural engagement is also significant, especially in the age of the information revolution.

There is no reason why the United States must have identical positions along each axis of engagement. It is entirely feasible to have extensive economic and cultural relations with the rest of the world and to have an active and creative diplomacy without playing the role of world policeman, much less the world's armed social worker. For example, a refusal to police Europe, East Asia, or the Persian Gulf region does not imply that the United States must withdraw from the World Trade Organization. Those are separable issues. Similarly, a refusal to participate in peacekeeping and nation-building missions in the Balkans or elsewhere does not imply that the United States must spurn requests to mediate disputes. As long as the parties to a conflict understand and accept that Washington's role is that of mediator, not arbitrator and financier, it is a proper function of U.S. diplomacy to help resolve problems. It is only in the areas of security commitments and military intervention that the United States needs to reduce its level of engagement.

Focus on the Big Issues

The final component of a new foreign policy would be to recognize that even a country as large and powerful as the United States cannot dictate outcomes everywhere and on every issue. There must be a sense of limits and a greater willingness to set priorities. The United

States needs to focus its attention and energy on dealing with *large-scale* adverse changes in the international system, since those developments have the potential to pose a threat to America's own security and well-being. The United States cannot afford to become bogged down in an assortment of petty conflicts in the name of preserving Washington's global leadership.

U.S. policymakers must especially learn to distinguish between parochial squabbles and serious security threats. Interventionists invariably argue that the United States has no choice but to continue its global policing mission if it is to protect America's own security. Disagreements among interventionists are confined to the proper method for carrying out that mission: unilaterally, as the "sheriff" leading coalitions of the willing, or as a good, collegial member of a more robust United Nations.

The argument that the United States must be the global policeman is based on the premise that manifestations of international disorder per se threaten American interests. But is that a valid assumption? The best case for that proposition was made during the Cold War, when it was plausible to argue that even minor regional or internecine conflicts had larger implications, since they typically involved surrogates of the other superpower or at least could be exploited by that rival. In a strategically bipolar world, the reasoning went, there were no geopolitical peripheries; a victory by a pro-Moscow regime or movement was a corresponding defeat for the U.S.-led "free world."

That approach oversimplified complex international realities even during the worst stages of the Cold War, and it led to such foolish commitments as the Vietnam intervention. But even if the reasoning was valid in the Cold War setting, it is inapplicable in the 21st century. The United States no longer faces a would-be hegemonic rival, nor is any credible challenger on the horizon. That development should fundamentally change how we view regional or internecine conflicts. In most cases such disorders will not impinge on vital U.S. interests. Washington can, therefore, afford to view them with detachment, intervening only as a balancer of last resort when a conflict cannot be contained by other powers in the affected region and is expanding to the point where America's security is threatened. Indeed, a policy of promiscuous intervention actually increases one danger to America's security: the possibility of terrorist reprisals.

From the standpoint of long-term American interests, what matters is the conduct of the dozen or so major powers—those nations with significant military or economic capabilities, or both. As long as those states remain at peace with one another, and no menacing would-be hegemonic power emerges, the only remaining threat to America's security is the risk of terrorist attack. Events involving minor countries may create annoyances, but they do not disrupt a regional, much less the global, balance of power and the overall stability of the international system. Put bluntly, the behavior of a country like China ought to matter to the United States; whether Kosovo becomes independent, Somalia holds together, or injustices occur in Burma should not.

By exercising greater discrimination in evaluating the significance of the unsavory developments that are certain to occur from time to time around the world and abandoning the strategy of discouraging independent initiatives by regional players whose interests overlap with America's interests, America would be able to exploit its uniquely advantageous geostrategic position and other unparalleled strengths. The United States may be the most geostrategically secure great power in history. America enjoys the luxury of weak, friendly, and relatively stable neighbors on its northern and southern borders as well as vast oceanic moats on its eastern and western flanks. Such factors make the notion of a major conventional military assault on the American homeland utterly implausible. The vast U.S. strategic arsenal—in addition to overwhelming conventional military superiority—makes a nuclear attack by a hostile state scarcely more likely. In addition, America has by far the largest and most productive economy, with all the attendant influence.

Those multiple advantages make the United States an ideal candidate to play the role that scholars have described variously as minimalist realism, off-shore balancer, and balancer of last resort. Playing such a role would be an appropriate response to the redistribution of power in the world in the post–Cold War era and the international system's return to the normal status of multipolarity.

A global role based on America's strategic independence combined with a policy of selective engagement that emphasized economic, diplomatic, and cultural interaction rather than promiscuous military intervention would be an enlightened and sustainable strategy for the 21st century. It would materially reduce the bloated U.S.

defense budget. The United States currently spends more than $350 billion per year on the military—more than the expenditures of the next eight highest-spending countries combined. Moreover, the U.S. defense budget is projected to rise to more than $450 billion within five years. The huge disparity in military spending between the United States and all other countries is directly attributable to Washington's far-flung security responsibilities. Playing a more cautious global political and military role would enable the United States to decommission superfluous units and cut the defense budget even as it focuses on waging war against its terrorist adversaries. Moreover, by refusing to be on the front lines of parochial conflicts, America would reduce its risk exposure—including the risk of terrorist retaliation. All that is needed is for U.S. policymakers to have the wisdom to adopt such a restrained, nuanced approach to world affairs.

Making that change would have been wise even before the events of September 11. The terrorist attacks on America have given added urgency to the need to adjust Washington's security policy. As we confront a fanatical adversary, we cannot afford the distraction of maintaining increasingly obsolete and irrelevant security commitments around the globe. It borders on the absurd to have U.S. military leaders complaining about a lack of personnel to wage the war against al-Qaeda while 100,000 American troops sit uselessly in Western Europe, another 48,000 are deployed in Japan, and thousands more are tied down in baby-sitting missions in Bosnia and Kosovo. America must clear the decks for war against its terrorist adversaries, and that should mean jettisoning unnecessary commitments and exploiting the advantages of a multipolar world.

1. Responding to Terrorism

Introduction

The terrorist attacks of September 11, 2001, compelled the United States to confront a dire threat to its security and well-being. Virtually all of Washington's military actions in the post–World War II era have been discretionary. This one was not. America had little choice but to respond to the attacks by pursuing and eliminating the perpetrators. Cato Institute scholars were among the first to call for military action not only to eradicate the al-Qaeda terrorist network but also to oust the Taliban regime in Afghanistan that had actively collaborated with Osama bin Laden.

Yet in one important sense the September 11 attacks should not have come as a great surprise. For several years, critics of Washington's global interventionism had warned that the policy was greatly increasing the likelihood that adversaries would seek revenge by launching terrorist strikes against American targets. Indeed, long before September 11 there were ample signs of the danger. The bombing of the World Trade Center in 1993 and the bombings of two U.S. embassies in East Africa in 1998 were only the most prominent examples. By the beginning of the 21st century, Washington's habit of meddling in regional problems—especially the high-profile U.S. military presence in the Persian Gulf region and the policy of supporting corrupt, friendly autocrats in the Islamic world—had elevated the risk to catastrophic levels.

An effective policy to reduce the threat of terrorism must therefore contain two elements. The first is a crushing military response to any terrorist attack on the United States. It was important to take out the Taliban regime not only because it was at least a passive accomplice in the September 11 attacks but also to provide an object lesson to any other regime that might be tempted to sponsor or harbor anti-American terrorists. The second component must be to alter U.S. foreign policy to reduce this country's risk exposure. It is dubious enough to meddle in conflicts that have little or no direct bearing on America's security or well-being even when the risk of adverse consequences is minimal. It is even more unjustified to engage in such meddling when the consequence might be thousands or—if terrorists obtain a weapon of mass destruction—hundreds of thousands of American casualties. That degree of risk should never be incurred except in the defense of core American security interests. Dictating political outcomes in the Balkans or propping up the Saudi royal family does not rise to that level.

It is important to pursue the struggle against the September 11 terrorists to a definitive conclusion. But it is equally important for U.S. leaders not to have the war evolve into an amorphous crusade against terrorism per se, much less an even more amorphous crusade against "evil." There are numerous insurgent groups that use terrorist tactics against their adversaries, but most of those groups do not attack the United States. America must be careful not to become entangled in other countries' bitter fights. Foreign governments are already trying to lure the United States by packaging their problems with insurgents as part of the global terrorist menace. Russia portrays the conflict in Chechnya in that light, the Philippines contends that a long-standing Islamic secessionist movement is linked to al-Qaeda, India insists the insurgents in Kashmir are part of a terrorist international, and the government of Colombia argues that left-wing rebels in that country are "narcoterrorists." Those allegations are questionable at best.

U.S. policymakers must vigorously resist such efforts to entangle the United States. America has enough enemies of its own without taking on the adversaries of other countries.

Reducing the Risk of Terrorism

The sabotage of Pan American flight 103, the bombing of the World Trade Center, and (possibly) the crash of TWA flight 800 make it clear that Americans have become targets of international terrorism. Unfortunately, that danger is likely to grow rather than recede in the coming years. Moreover, the potential for thousands, rather than dozens or hundreds, of casualties in any single incident is also rising.

In a speech to a recent conference on terrorism sponsored by the Cato Institute, former CIA director R. James Woolsey noted that a terrorist attack involving chemical or biological agents instead of conventional explosives would be vastly more destructive than the terrible events that have already taken place. For example, the introduction of anthrax, a deadly but easily cultivated bacterium, into an urban environment could kill tens of thousands of people in a matter of days. The quantity of anthrax needed to produce such a catastrophe could be carried in a briefcase. It is imperative that Congress and the executive branch begin to examine ways in which to deal more effectively with the threat of international terrorism. Although it is not possible for a free society always to prevent determined terrorists from striking, there are policy changes that can materially reduce the risk that Americans will be the target of terrorist initiatives directed from abroad. Those changes will, however, require a radically different U.S. foreign policy as well as a refocused mission for the U.S. intelligence community.

What Terrorism Is—And Isn't

Most discussions of terrorism are surprisingly vague about the concept itself, and even prominent experts frequently fail to define the term. Their approach is reminiscent of Supreme Court Justice Potter Stewart's handling of obscenity. Stewart conceded that he could not define obscenity, but he assured his colleagues, "I know it when I see it." If we are to deal intelligently with terrorism, a more rigorous approach is necessary. Terrorism is best defined as violence directed against innocent people for a political purpose. Both the "political purpose" and the "innocent people" components are crucial. The political purpose requirement is needed to distinguish terrorist incidents from ordinary crimes, however brutal those crimes may be. For example, the New York City nightclub arsonist

15

and (probably) the Centennial Park bomber in Atlanta were common criminals, not terrorists.

The "innocent people" standard is more difficult to define with precision and is also more controversial. With rare exceptions, though, "innocent people" should mean civilians, not military personnel. That is especially true if targeted military forces are operating in another country and are parties to an armed struggle or ongoing political dispute. Indeed, attacks on military personnel should not be defined as terrorism even if the troops are operating in their own country, if there is no peaceful mechanism to remove the incumbent regime from power and the armed forces serve to prop up a dictatorship. Under those circumstances, attacks directed against such targets constitute guerrilla warfare, not terrorism.

The consequences of the attacks are, of course, no less terrible than terrorism would be for the victims and their loved ones. Nevertheless, it is important to make the distinction between guerrilla warfare directed against professional soldiers and wanton assaults on innocents who are in no way involved in the underlying disputes.

U.S. Foreign Policy: Making America a Target

The bombing of the World Trade Center and the other terrorist incidents that have victimized American civilians—as well as the attacks on U.S. troops in Saudi Arabia—demonstrate that Washington's foreign policy has a direct bearing on the likelihood of violence against both American military personnel and American civilians. Such acts are hardly inexplicable. Perpetrators are not randomly selecting the United States out of a directory of members of the United Nations; they have rather specific grievances against America.

It might be tempting to conclude that those who attack American targets are simply fanatics who hate American values and culture. Many experts on terrorism have advanced that argument. University of California professor Ronald Steel, for example, contends that

> the United States is the locus of power in a "new world order" that would render irrelevant traditional faiths and even whole societies. Americans pride themselves on being in the forefront of the modern, in being the world's leader. But not everyone finds that world as appealing or even as inevitable as we do. To many it is deeply threatening. Naturally, the discontented of the world hold us responsible for their plight: their poverty, their ignorance, their weakness, their irrelevance.

Steel is not entirely wrong. There are certainly some terrorists who hate America because of the values it represents: especially modernity, secularism, and individualism. Nevertheless, it would be a mistake to conclude that most attacks on U.S. targets are motivated by a blind hatred of American values. City University of New York professor Yan Sun, responding to Steel's assertion, made a crucial distinction. Steel missed the point "of why certain segments of the rest of the world may harbor resentment of the United States," Yan Sun argued. "It is not American ways and values that threaten them," but "American insistence on imposing those on others."

It is even more accurate to say that terrorism is primarily a backlash against Washington's meddlesome global interventionist foreign policy—a policy that often has little, if any, connection with the values embraced by most Americans. U.S. leaders have chosen to interfere in an assortment of regional, subregional, and even internal quarrels around the world. Whether in Somalia, Haiti, Bosnia, the Persian Gulf, or the Taiwan Strait, U.S. leaders are willing to threaten to use or actually use military might to impose "made in Washington" solutions. Such interventions inevitably work to the advantage of certain countries or factions and to the decided disadvantage of others. We should, therefore, not be surprised that aggrieved parties may want to exact revenge against the United States.

Nowhere is that tendency more pronounced than in the Middle East. Washington's pervasive support of Israel and its policies is an obvious source of anti-American sentiment throughout the Islamic world, but it is not the only one. The increasingly extensive U.S. support of an array of "friendly" Arab dictatorships also inflames groups that want to oust those regimes. Washington's friends and allies in the region—Egypt, Algeria, Jordan, Saudi Arabia, Kuwait, and the other Persian Gulf states—have three characteristics in common. They are repressive, corrupt, and faced with growing domestic opposition.

The depth and intensity of popular bitterness toward the United States for being the patron of such autocracies would probably shock most Americans. Even relatively moderate opponents of the incumbent regimes increasingly regard Washington as an enemy. Mohammed Masari, the London-based Saudi exile who heads the Committee for the Defense of Legitimate Rights, typifies that attitude. Masari advocates democracy for Saudi Arabia and repeatedly condemns terrorist acts. Nevertheless, after the bombing of the American barracks in Dhahran, Masari told BBC radio that foreign troops in his country were "legitimate targets" and that the United States should expect similar incidents as long as its soldiers stay in the kingdom propping up the House of Saud.

If Washington insists on playing the role of global policeman, violent retaliation against American targets, both inside and outside the United States, will be one of the inevitable costs of that policy. And the cost appears to be rising. Incidents such as the bombing of the World Trade Center are especially significant. Even at the height of the Vietnam War, Hanoi's agents never dared attack Americans in the United States. The World Trade Center incident indicates that terrorists are becoming bolder.

Perhaps most ironic, some of the terrorists appear to be monsters of our own making. During the 1980s the U.S. government financed, trained, and equipped the Afghan mujahideen in their armed struggle against the Soviet invader. The policy was a short-term success, as Afghan fighters tied down Soviet military units and inflicted numerous casualties. The war itself became so unpopular in the Soviet Union that it probably contributed to the political unraveling of the communist state.

Nevertheless, the policy has produced horrific side effects over the long term. Not only does the chaos in Afghanistan exceed that in such places as Somalia and Bosnia, but alumni of the Afghan war are showing up in insurgent forces and terrorist organizations throughout the Middle East and beyond. And the principal target of their animosity is their one-time patron, the United States. Such are the unintended consequences of an interventionist foreign policy.

A Policy for Dealing with Terrorism

A sustainable policy to deal with the threat of terrorism would have three key elements. First, the United States should stop meddling in conflicts and disputes that do not have a direct and substantial connection to the vital security needs of the American people. A global interventionist strategy was dangerous enough when the lives put in harm's way were primarily those of American military personnel. The strategy has now become prohibitively risky; the lives of thousands, or even millions, of American civilians could be threatened by terrorist attacks. No rational policymaker should want to run such risks except for the most crucial stakes.

Rescinding Washington's global interventionist policy would not be a case of appeasing terrorists, as proponents of interventionism habitually claim. Adopting a more restrained security strategy would be a wise move even if no terrorist threat existed. The present policy is far too expensive and entangles the United States in conflicts in strategically and economically insignificant countries such as Somalia and Bosnia. The danger of terrorism being directed at Americans is merely an additional reason for rejecting interventionism.

Second, the attention and resources of the intelligence agencies need to be focused on serious national security threats such as terrorism. They must not be distracted by inappropriate missions such as dealing with the "threat" of economic espionage. That does not mean that the budget of the intelligence community (nearly $30 billion annually) needs to be increased. The intelligence agencies do not need more money or personnel; they need to better utilize the money and personnel they now have. Indeed, a leaner, better focused intelligence apparatus might well be able to do its job on significantly less than $30 billion a year, and Congress should seriously consider that possibility.

Counterterrorism will pose a great challenge to the intelligence agencies. Monitoring terrorist organizations and assessing their capabilities and intentions is a crucial mission, but penetrating such cells will be exceptionally difficult. Many of them are small, freelance, highly decentralized operations whose members are almost pathologically suspicious of outsiders. In addition to an extreme reliance on an "old boy network"—in which service in the Afghan war is often a key feature—the personnel are typically motivated by fanatical religious or ideological agendas. Bribes and other inducements that intelligence agencies use to recruit operatives are markedly less effective with such individuals than with officials of corrupt governments.

The decentralized nature of many terrorist organizations makes retaliation as difficult as penetration. Unlike their predecessors in the 1970s and 1980s, today's terrorists often do not boast of their deeds. That makes it difficult even to identify the perpetrators of a terrorist incident, much less to locate and either apprehend or eliminate them.

Nevertheless, the intelligence agencies have a vital role to play in the campaign against terrorism. They must be America's eyes and ears in a dangerous world. The agencies have a twofold mission— to identify international terrorist organizations and plans so they can be thwarted and, whenever those efforts fail, to locate the culprits so that retaliatory measures can be brought to bear.

Third, although many (perhaps most) current terrorist organizations are relatively small, free-lance operations, there are cases in which terrorist initiatives against Americans are directed or sponsored by other governments. Countering such state-sponsored terrorism is not a matter solely for the intelligence or law enforcement agencies. As syndicated columnist Charles Krauthammer argues, the United States has every right to consider such incidents acts of war against the American people and should respond accordingly.

Krauthammer's argument is conceptually correct. Evidence indicates, for example, that two agents in Libya's intelligence service planted the bomb that brought down Pan Am flight 103, killing 189 Americans. It is difficult to believe that those agents acted without the authorization of senior officials in the Libyan government. Therefore, if the evidence of Tripoli's complicity stands up to scrutiny, that incident constitutes an act of war just as surely as if Libyan ships had shelled an American city and inflicted those casualties.

Responding to such an outrage with a declaration of war might seem drastic, but one of the prime constitutional responsibilities of the federal government is to defend the American people from external attacks. It is supremely ironic that Washington is willing to use military force for an assortment of causes around the world, most of which have little if any relevance to the security of the American people, but has treated the slaughter of 189 Americans by the Libyan government as merely an extradition issue involving the two agents.

Issuing a declaration of war does not necessarily mean that U.S. bombers must immediately launch strikes against the target country or the Marines conduct an amphibious invasion. U.S. leaders would have a full range of options for implementing such declarations at times and places of their choosing. War aims could be set at whatever level was deemed appropriate. Options might range from a demand that the perpetrators of the terrorist attack be turned over to American authorities to the complete removal of the offending regime.

A declaration of war is important as a statement of national intent. It also puts the United States in a different position under international law. Imposing a naval blockade, for example, is illegal in peacetime but legal in wartime. Washington could then inform countries trading with America's enemy that a state of war exists and that their ships must remain outside the blockade zone or be subject to boarding or attack.

Although Krauthammer is correct that a state-sponsored terrorist incident is an act of war, not a law enforcement matter, some qualifications need to be attached to his proposal. Most important, there must be clear and compelling evidence of another government's complicity in the attack. When it is a question of the direct participation of government operatives, as was apparently the case in the Pan Am bombing, the issue is simply whether there is sufficient evidence. A trickier situation arises when the allegation is of government sponsorship, rather than direct involvement. In that case, the standard should be that the accused regime must have actively sponsored an organization or individual that it knew intended to attack American civilians. General financial support of, or military training and other assistance to, organizations with political agendas (such as overthrowing the existing government in their respective countries) is not a sufficient casus belli unless the organization has already committed terrorist acts against the American people and the regime has nevertheless continued its sponsorship.

As a matter of policy, Washington should consider a declaration of war only when state-sponsored terrorism has been directed against Americans inside the United States or in another locale where they have a reasonable expectation of safety. (Passengers aboard an airliner flying in international airspace certainly qualify.) American civilians who travel to areas where there is an armed conflict are in a different category. An attack on such civilians is no less an act of terrorism, but the American government and society cannot be expected to incur the risks entailed in prosecuting wars merely to avenge the deaths of their fellow citizens who have voluntarily put themselves in harm's way. Those civilians who insist on being in such places as Sarajevo, Mogadishu, or Kabul must do so at their risk.

Finally, in addition to the requirement for clear and compelling evidence of state complicity in a terrorist act, it is imperative that the evidence be presented to Congress along with a request for a

21

formal declaration of war. A decision about whether the Republic goes to war is too important to leave in the hands of the president and his appointed advisers. The decision ought to be made—as the Constitution specifies—by Congress. Not only is that mandated by the Constitution—a fact that has largely been forgotten as chief executives have waged numerous presidential wars during the past half century—but it is an important check on rash action. The president may believe that the evidence of state-sponsored terrorism is compelling in a particular case, but others may conclude otherwise. It is important that the president's assessment be evaluated by an independent tribunal.

The policy outlined here for dealing with international terrorism is not a panacea, but it is prudent, balanced, and sustainable. We would not go around the planet looking for trouble, as Washington's current policy has us doing. But if trouble comes to us despite a policy of restraint, we will be prepared to use the intelligence agencies to identify and neutralize such threats whenever possible. We must also be willing to use the armed forces to punish those responsible for terrorist outrages that cannot be thwarted.

This article originally appeared in *The Cato Handbook for Congress*, 105th Congress, January 1997.

Exploiting the New War on Terrorism

It is regrettable but hardly unexpected that various political groups are using the Sept. 11 terrorist atrocities to boost their own pet causes. All Americans should support a vigorous war effort to locate and eliminate those responsible for the slaughter of thousands of innocents. But we must be vigilant that the war against terrorism doesn't become a convenient facade for an assortment of irrelevant and even bogus measures.

There are precedents that should worry us. America's involvement in World War I was a major factor leading to the adoption of Prohibition. In World War II, the government acquired the power to withhold income taxes from workers' paychecks—a "temporary" measure that is with us still and serves to disguise the extent of the tax burden on Americans. During the Cold War the "national defense" justification was used to pass laws that had nothing to do with that task. It is not coincidental that the legislation that gave the federal government a foot in the door on educational matters was the National *Defense* Education Act.

Already the advocates of pet causes are citing the terrorist threat as a reason for their schemes. Several pundits have argued that the attack occurred because America had allowed its military to atrophy during the 1990s, and they insist that we should increase the military budget by tens of billions of dollars per year. That argument ignores some inconvenient facts. At the time of the assault on the World Trade Center and the Pentagon, the United States was spending well over $300 billion a year on the military. That sum was six times greater than the spending of the country with the second largest budget—Russia—and was more than the spending levels of the next eight countries combined.

If such a vast military apparatus failed to deter the terrorists, is it credible that a $350 billion or $400 billion budget would have done so? The United States does not lack military resources to deal with the terrorist enemy: It needs to reallocate the resources it already has. Maintaining 100,000 troops in Europe—including an armored division in Germany—to guard against an invasion by a Warsaw Pact that no longer exists led by a Soviet Union that no longer exists is one example of wasted resources.

The advocates of ever-larger military budgets are not the only people exploiting the terrorist threat. Some of the usual suspects have used the occasion to call for a resumption of conscription. Such a proposal makes even less sense. We're not going to send mass armies against Osama bin Laden and the Taliban. That mission requires air strikes and attacks by highly trained Special Forces. Knights on horseback would be about as relevant as infantry conscripts in a war against terrorism.

Not surprisingly, anti-immigration forces have used the Sept. 11 tragedy to call for tougher measures to bar foreigners from this country. It's not clear how excluding Mexican agricultural workers or computer programmers from South Korea and India would have stopped the terrorists, but those who hate immigration aren't about to let such inconvenient details undermine their case.

And then we have the bashers of global capitalism. One pundit argued that economic globalism contributed to the rise of terrorism because it "dislocated" people. Indeed. Hundreds of millions of people from China to Chile have been dislocated from poverty by the rise of the global economy over the past two decades. Presumably, though, we should abandon that course and revert to the "enlightened" policies of trade protectionism, high taxes, and onerous regulatory regimes. That would apparently have stifled the upsurge of terrorism.

There will likely be more misuses of the terrorism issue in the coming months and years. Americans should recognize that political and ideological opportunists are not above exploiting any issue. We should also understand that not everything advertised as essential in the fight against our terrorist enemy is worthy.

This article originally appeared in the *Santa Barbara News Press*, September 23, 2001.

A Winnable War Needs a Clearly Defined Aim

The United States has committed to a war against the terrorists who committed the attacks on the World Trade Center and the Pentagon. That response is entirely justified and Americans should maintain a steadfast determination to pursue the war to victory. It is imperative, however, that the enemy be clearly and realistically identified and that the United States not launch an amorphous global crusade.

Unfortunately, some of the statements coming from Bush administration officials are not reassuring on that score. Secretary of State Colin Powell has stated that the U.S. goal is nothing less than to rid the world of the "evil of terrorism."

Agitated pundits also advocate a war against "terror states" and terrorist organizations everywhere in the world. Although such calls may be emotionally satisfying, they violate the most fundamental rule of good foreign policy: The objective pursued must be attainable.

If Powell is taken at his word, the U.S. war aims would be daunting indeed. Even if the United States confined its campaign to countries listed by the State Department as sponsors of international terrorism and organizations designated as terrorist entities, the roster of enemies would be breathtakingly long. It would include seven countries (Cuba, Iran, Iraq, Syria, North Korea, Libya and Sudan) and more than 30 organizations. A war on that scale would be far beyond what the American people have contemplated.

The list, moreover, is far from complete. Curiously, Afghanistan is not listed as a state sponsor of terrorism. Nor are such U.S.

"friends" as Saudi Arabia and Pakistan, even though both governments have funded extremely dubious organizations for years. The roster of terrorist organizations itself continues to expand steadily. Just a few weeks ago, the right-wing United Self-Defense Forces of Colombia was added.

Waging a global crusade against terrorism would require the United States to fight an assortment of organizations that, while often vile, have never seemed to regard this country as their enemy. Would the United States really want to go out of its way to take on the IRA, the Basque separatists in Spain, the Tamil Tigers in Sri Lanka or Colombia's United Self-Defense Forces? What would be the possible gain from acquiring enemies where they do not now exist?

The suspicion persists that most officials and pundits who call for a comprehensive campaign against terrorism really mean a campaign against Islamic terrorism. But that focus has its own problems. If the United States goes after only Islamic organizations and states, it will be almost impossible to convince Muslims around the world that the campaign is not a holy war by the West against their faith. That perception would have ugly ramifications that could plague the United States for decades.

International political realities will probably compel the Bush administration to abandon loose rhetoric and focus its substantive efforts on the real task: identifying and eradicating the parties responsible for the atrocities committed on Sept. 11. Those who are unsatisfied by such limited war aims should remember U.S. policy during World War II. The United States declared war on Japan and Germany; it did not declare war on dictatorship. Indeed, America did not even declare war on fascism. The United States never took military action against Spain's Francisco Franco or Argentina's Juan Perón. Both were odious rulers, and they certainly did not wish the United States well, but they did not make themselves overt enemies.

A similar approach ought to be adopted in the current crisis. Any party that attacks the United States is fair game for retaliation. But the United States should not take action against parties that, however much they might dislike the United States, have not harmed it. Achieving victory over those who have harmed us will be a difficult enough challenge.

This article originally appeared in the *Taipei Times*, September 29, 2001.

Afghans Are Their Own Best Keepers

The destruction of Osama bin Laden's al-Qaeda terrorist network and the destabilization of Afghanistan's extremist Taliban regime will be difficult enough to achieve. Recently, though, Secretary of State Colin Powell and others have begun to hint at another objective: influencing the composition of a post-Taliban government.

There are reports that U.S. leaders have slowed the pace of the U.S. military campaign lest the Taliban collapse before an alternative regime is ready. Such a flirtation with nation building is both unwise and unnecessary. One might hope that the United States had learned from the disastrous experiments in Somalia, Haiti and Bosnia. Despite years of work and billions of dollars, the efforts failed big-time in all three cases.

Afghanistan is no more promising as a candidate for nation building. For more than 20 years, it has been plagued by civil war. The fighting has created millions of refugees and destroyed what modest economy the country had. Afghanistan can hardly be called a nation at all. The three most prominent ethnic factions—the Pushtuns in the south and the Tajiks and Uzbeks in the north—barely tolerated each other during the best of times. Not surprisingly, they are on opposite sides in the current civil war. The Taliban draws the bulk of its support from the Pushtuns (the largest bloc) while the rival Northern Alliance gets most of its strength from the Tajiks and Uzbeks.

Washington apparently hopes for an effort under the auspices of the United Nations to form a broad coalition government to replace the Taliban. Reports have surfaced of negotiations to broaden the Northern Alliance by bringing in non-Taliban Pushtun political leaders. Some U.S. officials have dropped hints about enticing moderate Taliban factions to join such a coalition. The capstone to such a scheme is the proposal to invite Mohammad Zaher Shah, the Afghan king who was ousted in 1973, to return to the throne.

Such a plan is ill-conceived. First, the notion of moderates in the Taliban is absurd. The Taliban is the most bizarre, extreme movement in Islam. Even the most moderate members would be considered wild extremists in any other setting. Second, although the proposal to bring back the king has some appeal, he was an often erratic and difficult figure when he occupied the throne. At 87, he is not likely to be any easier to work with. Finally and most important, the long-standing antipathy among the Pushtuns, Tajiks, Uzbeks and assorted other tribes is not going to end because of a U.S. or UN nation-building presence.

Although the United States should not stand in the way if Afghanistan's neighbors and the UN want to conduct an experiment in nation building, the United States should not be part of it. Indeed, U.S. participation might heighten fears in the Islamic world about American imperialism.

This is the ultimatum that Washington should give to any post-Taliban rulers: Refrain from supporting anti-American terrorists and the United States will not interfere in your country's internal politics. Harbor terrorists and the United States will mete out the same treatment to you as it is now giving to the Taliban. It is a deal that any rational Afghan government would accept.

It is not necessary for the United States to step into the quicksand of nation building in Afghanistan. The United States' security does not require the existence of a stable, democratic government in Kabul. Such a regime is not likely to emerge in any case. America's security requires only that whatever government controls any portion of Afghanistan not harbor and assist terrorists the way the Taliban has.

This article originally appeared in the *Los Angeles Times*, November 2, 2001.

Don't Risk Sinking into a Quagmire with U.S. Forces Fighting on Multiple Fronts

The decision by the United States to attack targets in Afghanistan is the correct response to the terrorist assault that killed so many innocent civilians on Sept. 11. It is no small matter to take the U.S. republic into war, but a failure to respond vigorously to such an outrage would have led Osama bin Laden and his followers to assume that they could kill more innocents with impunity. A crucial responsibility of the federal government under the Constitution is to defend the American people from foreign enemies, and the United States now clearly faces a mortal enemy.

Washington seems determined to root out bin Laden's al-Qaeda network and destabilize Afghanistan's extremist Taliban regime. The Bush administration wisely is resisting the pressure exerted by some members of the international coalition to refrain from going after the Taliban government.

It should be an explicit goal of U.S. policy to bring down that regime. The Taliban has given bin Laden sanctuary for years, and the two factions have maintained an odious symbiotic relationship. At the very least, the Taliban was a passive accomplice in the Sept. 11 attacks and, therefore, deserves to meet the same fate as al-Qaeda.

In all of this, the Bush administration has enjoyed overwhelming support from opinion leaders across the political spectrum. There is less unity, however, about what the United States should do beyond its objectives in Afghanistan. Some hawkish pundits advocate much broader policy aims. American Enterprise Institute scholar Michael Ledeen, for example, proposes a "new Reagan Doctrine" to assist insurgent groups to overthrow a variety of anti-American regimes in the Islamic world. *Weekly Standard* editor William Kristol and syndicated columnist Charles Krauthammer, among others, go even further. They favor direct U.S. military action against any government that has been guilty of sponsoring terrorist movements even if those movements have directed their ire against other countries and have not attacked U.S. targets.

Following the advice of the militant hawks might be emotionally satisfying, but it would risk turning the current, relatively focused campaign against the perpetrators of the Sept. 11 outrage into an amorphous and unrealistic crusade. Destroying bin Laden's terror network and destabilizing the Taliban are difficult enough challenges without trying to pursue a goal of regime change throughout the Islamic world.

Merely providing support to insurgent groups is unlikely to get the job done in any case. Proponents of a new Reagan Doctrine would fund an aggressive U.S. information (propaganda) campaign to urge the populations in the target countries (Iraq, Iran, Syria, Libya and Sudan) to overthrow their oppressive rulers. Arms and money also would flow to anti-government forces.

Even if the Bush administration embraced such measures, the prospects for success would be dim. Joshua may have brought down the walls of Jericho with nothing more than trumpet blasts, but the regimes in question are not likely to be brought down by the trumpets of U.S.-financed propaganda. Supplying arms to insurgent groups might be marginally more effective, but the organizations opposing most of the current governments seem less than robust.

Iraq is a case in point. Some optimists argue that the so-called Iraqi democratic opposition in exile—especially the largest umbrella group, the Iraqi National Congress (INC)—can oust Saddam Hussein from power with modest assistance from Washington. That apparently was the logic motivating the U.S. Congress to pass the Iraq Liberation Act and earmark funds to support the INC's efforts.

But few knowledgeable analysts take the Iraqi opposition's prospects seriously. Gen. Anthony Zinni, former commander of U.S. forces in the Persian Gulf, noted that anti-Saddam forces are rife with factionalism and have shown little independent initiative. Indeed, the opposition is an assortment of more than 90 groups running the gamut from Marxist revolutionaries to Islamic fundamentalists. Thus far, the principal focus of the INC seems to be on extracting funds from a credulous U.S. Congress rather than waging an armed liberation struggle against the Baghdad regime.

Iran's opposition in exile shows many of the same limitations as its Iraqi counterpart. Forces dedicated to overthrowing Tehran's theocratic regime range from royalists determined to put a new shah on the Peacock Throne to avowed communists. Such a disparate, fragmented opposition has shown little ability to mount a serious rebellion. Prospects are even worse in places such as Syria and Libya. No effective, coherent political opposition exists in either case. Only in Sudan is there a serious in-country force of armed insurgents. But the Sudanese rebels draw almost all their support from the black Christian population in the south and therefore have more credibility as a secessionist movement than as a prospective government for the entire country.

Not only would U.S. military forces probably be needed to help install most of the insurgents in power, but those forces almost certainly would have to remain to protect the embryonic governments from their enemies. That would entail nation-building missions dwarfing the efforts in Bosnia and Kosovo, and it would create the widespread impression that an imperialistic America was propping up puppet regimes. An ongoing U.S. military presence certainly would inflame Islamic populations and stoke anti-American passions that are already at disturbingly high levels.

And even if all those problems could be overcome, we hardly could be confident of the long-term result. Ledeen and others who invoke the Reagan Doctrine should examine more closely the fruit of that initiative. Supporting anti-Soviet rebels around the world seemed like a good strategy and Afghanistan was hailed as the crowning success. But as we know now, U.S. aid to the anti-Soviet mujahideen inadvertently strengthened radical Islamic forces. Both the Taliban and al-Qaeda are the ultimate beneficiaries of the process that began with the original Reagan Doctrine. We should be wary about going down a similar path in an effort to help insurgents overthrow regimes we dislike. That is especially so given the dubious political and ideological credentials of some of the anti-government elements.

Attacking offensive regimes with U.S. military forces would be more effective than attempting to aid feckless rebels. But there are serious drawbacks to that option as well. If the suggestions of Krauthammer and Kristol were taken seriously, the United States would have to be prepared to wage a five- or six-front war. The logistical requirements of such an undertaking would be mind-boggling. It is perhaps not surprising that most proponents of a wider war against terrorism have never served in the military and have no appreciation of the difficulties involved.

Moreover, if the rhetoric of the advocates of wider war were taken literally, the United States would have to target more countries than those that usually are cited. If Washington were to go after all governments that have been guilty of sponsoring terrorist organizations, Saudi Arabia and Pakistan would have to be included on the list. Both countries have been guilty of funding and supporting some extremely dubious groups. Indeed, Pakistan has been the principal ally of Afghanistan's Taliban regime from the beginning. Only in response to enormous pressure from Washington has the Islamabad government finally turned against its client.

Worst of all, widening our war aims would risk transforming the current struggle into a holy war between the United States and Islam. That is, of course, precisely what bin Laden wants. Thus far, the Bush administration skillfully has portrayed the campaign as a fight by a broad, U.S.-led international coalition against terrorist outlaws. Washington has received surprisingly extensive support from most governments in the Islamic world and enjoys considerable sympathy from the populations in those countries who rightly regard bin Laden's orgy of mass murder as the ultimate perversion of Islam. All that would change if the United States adopted a general policy of seeking to overthrow regimes it considers offensive.

The Bush administration has struck the correct balance on the issue of widening the war beyond Afghanistan. Administration leaders have reserved the right to take action against other movements and governments if there is evidence of their culpability in the terrorist atrocities against the World Trade Center and the Pentagon. That may become pertinent if more evidence emerges of connections between Iraqi intelligence operatives and some of the hijackers.

But such an approach is far different from a policy to undermine or attack an assortment of countries merely because they have been hostile to the United States. A wider war is, at the very least, premature. Achieving our current goals will prove challenging enough without embarking on a holy crusade to remake the political map of the Islamic world.

This article originally appeared in *Insight*, November 12, 2001. Reprinted with permission.

Don't Fear the "Oil Weapon"

Almost every day we read another galling story in the press about our "allies" in Saudi Arabia. It's time for the United States to take the diplomatic gloves off.

The Saudi government has resisted our requests to use their bases for military operations against Osama bin Laden and the Taliban. They've dragged their heels when it came to freezing the assets of those Saudis bankrolling al-Qaeda. They've lectured New Yorkers through Crown Prince Abdullah about how it's our fault that the attacks have come in the first place. And they refuse to fully share information about terrorist suspects.

Then it comes out that the Saudi monarchy has been the principal financial backer of the Taliban since at least 1996 and that Saudi sources have channeled funds to Hamas and other groups that blow away Israeli civilians day after day in acts of terrorism that are as chilling and morally repellent as those that killed Americans last September.

That's all on top of the Saudi monarchy's long-standing policy of funding radical Islamic schools and "charities" throughout the world, fronts for incubators of Islamic revolution and anti-Western fanaticism.

The common wisdom is that we must turn the other cheek and stay on friendly terms with the Saudi autocrats because we need

31

their oil. Nonsense. They need our money more than we need their oil. Repeat after us: "There is no 'oil weapon.'"

First, let's dispel the notion that we need to worry about an oil embargo directed at the United States. Once oil is in a tanker or refinery, there is no controlling its destination. During the 1973 embargo on the United States and the Netherlands, for instance, oil that was exported to Europe was simply resold to the United States or ended up displacing non-OPEC oil that was diverted to the U.S. market.

Saudi oil minister Sheik Yamani conceded afterwards that the 1973 embargo "did not imply that we could reduce imports to the United States . . . the world is really just one market. So the embargo was more symbolic than anything else."

Second, the Saudis are hardly in a position to "punish" the industrialized nations with a major production cutback. That's because one of the main causes of instability in the region is declining oil revenues. Saudis who've gotten used to living on the state's generous oil dole are now finding that the dole is running out and that jobs are scarce. If the Saudis stopped selling oil, they'd bankrupt their economy and almost certainly trigger a revolution.

Third, if the last 30 years have taught us anything, it's that oil producers make decisions based on economic—not political—criteria. Never once in OPEC's history has the cartel or any member in it left money on the table to pursue some political objective.

When the Ayatollah Khomeini displaced the shah in 1979, the oil kept flowing. When U.S. bombs rained down on Libya's Moamar Quaddafi in 1986, the oil kept flowing. We had to impose an embargo on Iraq's Saddam Hussein to get him to stop selling oil to the world market.

In fact, there is not and has never been any correlation between OPEC "price hawks" and "price doves" and how those OPEC members felt about America or the industrialized West in general.

Of course, all that could change if bin Laden's political agents seize control of the OPEC oil kingdoms. After all, their brand of Islam leaves no room for corrupting agents such as money or economic prosperity. So if there's a case for turning the other cheek when it comes to the Saudis, it's that any regime replacing the House of Saud would probably be worse than the one we're dealing with now.

But cozying up to dictators who don't have the support of their own people is penny-wise and pound-foolish. Embracing shaky regimes doesn't extend their political life spans—it only buys us hatred from those who will sooner or later come to power over the bodies of the dictators we're cavorting with.

Propping up "friendly autocrats" is what has earned us the enmity of the Shiite revolutionaries in Iran and is why, in the eyes of the Arab "street," the United States is associated with autocracy, hypocrisy, corruption, oppression and economic stagnation.

Saudi Arabia is an oppressive regime that mocks everything this nation stands for. They helped to create and sustain the terror network that now threatens our existence. Saudi Arabia is not a reliable member of the international coalition against terrorism.

In fact, when it comes to terrorism, the Saudi regime is part of the problem, not part of the solution. American foreign policy should react accordingly and not spend a single minute worrying about the "oil weapon" that never was.

This article, coauthored with Jerry Taylor, originally appeared in the *New York Post*, November 16, 2001. Reprinted with permission.

United States Should Dump Dated Obligations

U.S. President George W. Bush has emphasized that the war against terrorism will be lengthy and difficult, despite the gratifying initial successes in Afghanistan. He is right. That's why it is imperative that the United States promptly clear the decks for war. America must jettison obsolete or unnecessary commitments and expenditures.

When a family suffers an unexpected hardship or tragedy, it does not continue with business as usual, leaving its priorities and spending patterns unaltered. Likewise, a nation must alter its priorities when facing similar difficulties. For America, the war against the terrorists who committed the Sept. 11 outrages will be the top priority for the foreseeable future. Yet instead of reducing or eliminating less essential commitments, Washington seems inclined to merely pile the new commitments on top of the old ones.

There are numerous candidates for elimination. In the realm of security affairs, three such candidates stand out.

Terminate the nation-building missions in the Balkans. Those ventures were foolish and unnecessary to begin with. Despite the exertions of America and its NATO allies, Bosnia is no closer to being a viable country today than it was when the Dayton peace agreement was signed six years ago. The NATO intervention in Kosovo is even worse. It merely strengthened the hand of Albanian nationalists who want to create a Greater Albania and who have recently stirred up trouble across the border in Macedonia. The missions in Bosnia and Kosovo cost the United States nearly US$6 billion a year. That money, as well as the military personnel tied down in useless peacekeeping tasks, could be used far more effectively to prosecute the war against terrorism.

Withdraw the 100,000 U.S. troops stationed in Western Europe. That troop presence is an utterly obsolete commitment inherited from the Cold War. The U.S. forces are apparently on duty to prevent an invasion of Western Europe by a Warsaw Pact that no longer exists led by a Soviet Union that no longer exists. How tank divisions stationed in Germany benefit the security of the United States is truly a mystery. Those units should be withdrawn and demobilized and some of the personnel reassigned to lighter, more mobile units that would be relevant in the fight against terrorism. Such a move would save billions of dollars.

Withdraw the 37,000 U.S. troops stationed in South Korea. That troop presence is another obsolete, Cold War–era obligation. South Korea faces only one adversary: communist North Korea. Yet South Korea has twice the population and an economy at least 30 times larger than its adversary. A nation with those characteristics should certainly be able to defend itself. Instead, South Korea chooses to underinvest in defense and remain dependent on the United States for major portions of its military capabilities. U.S. leaders should inform their South Korean counterparts that the days of free riding on the U.S. security guarantee are over. America has its own war to wage and can no longer afford to subsidize prosperous security clients.

It is uncertain whether the United States would need to redirect all of the savings from terminating obsolete or unnecessary overseas commitments to the war on terrorism. Clearly, some additional resources ought to be devoted to beefing up our Special Forces units and intelligence gathering and evaluation capabilities. They have both been shortchanged for years, and yet they are the front-line forces in the fight against terrorism.

But there may well be some money left over. That is not a bad thing. At the very least, such savings might head off the looming prospect of a return to large federal budget deficits. The savings might even be enough to give the beleaguered American taxpayer a modest break. But however the money is used, it would be better than the current wasteful situation.

This article originally appeared in the *Taipei Times*, January 7, 2002.

Head Straight for Pakistan

General Tommy Franks, commander of U.S. forces in Afghanistan, recently caused a stir when he hinted that U.S. forces might pursue al-Qaeda fighters across the border into Pakistan. Secretary of Defense Donald Rumsfeld has now quietly but firmly rejected that suggestion. That's too bad, because General Franks was right. Instead of sending U.S. troops to (at best) marginally relevant arenas such as the Philippines and the Republic of Georgia for training missions, the next stage of the war against terrorism needs to be fought in Pakistan.

There is overwhelming evidence that, after the initial victories last autumn by the United States and the Northern Alliance, hundreds of Taliban and al-Qaeda fighters fled Afghanistan to seek refuge in Pakistan's rugged northwest frontier province. A similar pattern occurred in response to the recent U.S. offensive, Operation Anaconda.

The reality is that al-Qaeda will never be destroyed as long as it can enjoy a de facto sanctuary in Pakistan. One of the most serious mistakes in the otherwise successful U.S. military operation in Afghanistan was the decision to trust the Pakistani government to seal the border and trap Taliban and al-Qaeda troops. It is now clear that Pakistan failed to fulfill that task.

Given the terrain, sealing the Afghan-Pakistani border would have been a daunting task even for the most capable military force. But it seems that the Pakistani authorities made something less than a wholehearted effort. Indeed, there is evidence that elements in Pakistan's military, as well as the notorious Interservices Intelligence directorate (ISI), actually helped evacuate Taliban and al-Qaeda fighters following the first U.S.-led offensive in October.

Although such treachery might seem shocking, it would be consistent with Islamabad's track record. The Bush administration likes to tout Pakistan as an enthusiastic ally in the war on terrorism, but the regime of military dictator Pervez Musharraf is a very recent convert in that struggle. Prior to the September 11 attacks, the Pakistani government—especially the ISI—was the chief patron of the terrorist Taliban regime in Afghanistan. And religious schools, the *madrassas*, in Pakistan were renowned incubators for the terrorist recruits who joined Osama bin Laden.

It would be a mistake to allow misplaced gratitude to the Musharraf regime for belatedly abandoning the Taliban to deter us from taking the war against al-Qaeda to its next logical stage. The principal nest of terrorist vipers is not in the Philippines, Georgia, Yemen, or Somalia. It is in Pakistan.

Washington should inform Musharraf that we intend to wipe out the al-Qaeda sanctuaries in the northwest frontier province, with or without Islamabad's permission. The reality is that the writ of Pakistan's central government has rarely extended to that region in any case. Typically, the local tribes exercise most of the real power. Musharraf would be wise to recognize his lack of control and give the United States permission to take military action. If he declines to do so, the United States should make it clear that from now on we will regard Pakistan as part of the problem in the struggle against terrorism, not part of the solution, and will treat the country accordingly. The recent comment by Foreign Minister Abdul Sattar that his government was prepared to discuss allowing U.S. troops to cross the border in pursuit of al-Qaeda suspects is an encouraging development and should be explored.

But whatever Musharraf's ultimate decision about granting permission, the United States should not shrink from confronting al-Qaeda in its Pakistani lair. The war against the perpetrators of the September 11 atrocities will not be successful until that mission is accomplished.

This article originally appeared in *National Review Online*, April 4, 2002.

2. Balkan Policy

Introduction

The U.S.-led NATO interventions in the Balkans have produced decidedly unsatisfactory results. Bosnia is no closer to being a viable, unified country now than it was when the three feuding ethnic factions responded to Western pressure and signed the Dayton agreement nearly seven years ago. True, NATO's intervention did bring an end to the fighting in Bosnia's civil war, and that was not a trivial achievement. Fears that U.S. troops would be targeted by aggrieved factions (primarily the Bosnian Serbs) also did not materialize.

At the same time, the assurances given by proponents of the peacekeeping mission in Bosnia that U.S. forces would be withdrawn within a year of the signing of the Dayton agreement proved ludicrously inaccurate. Clinton administration officials and their allies who gave such assurances were either naively optimistic or disingenuous. Today, Bosnia remains a Potemkin country and an international welfare case. An army of international bureaucrats runs that NATO protectorate in an increasingly autocratic fashion, making a mockery of the West's commitment to democratic norms. There is no end in sight to the NATO military occupation. From the standpoint of U.S. interests, the best hope is that the thankless peacekeeping and nation-building mission can ultimately be offloaded onto the European allies.

The outcome of the intervention in Kosovo is even worse. NATO leaders insisted that the 1999 military campaign against Serbia was necessary to prevent ethnic cleansing and genocide. Those arguments were, at a minimum, hyperbole. The counterinsurgency effort waged by the Belgrade government against the Kosovo Liberation Army was unquestionably brutal, but no more so than similar measures taken by governments in numerous other countries that confronted violent secessionist movements. Moreover, Belgrade did not begin a concerted ethnic cleansing campaign until NATO launched its air strikes.

Having justified its intervention on the grounds of preventing ethnic cleansing, NATO then stood by while a massive reverse ethnic cleansing took place. In the two years after NATO took over Kosovo, the KLA and other Albanian nationalists expelled more than 220,000 people from the province. The victims included not only Serbs but Montenegrins, Bulgarians, Jews, and the Roma (Gypsies). Ultimately, some three-quarters of the province's prewar non-Albanian population were expelled, and the remainder have huddled in a handful of heavily guarded NATO enclaves.

By intervening in Kosovo, NATO strengthened the position of the faction in the Balkans that retains the most virulently expansionist agenda. KLA leaders have openly boasted that their ultimate goal is to create an ethnically pure "Greater Albania" that incorporates not only present-day Kosovo and Albania but chunks of territory from Serbia, Montenegro, Macedonia, and Greece. The KLA has already used Kosovo as a base of operations to foment an insurgency in neighboring Macedonia. Fighting flared in that country in the spring of 2001, and the disorder subsided only when the United States and its NATO allies pressured the government of Macedonia to make dubious concessions to the militant Albanian minority.

Perhaps worst of all, Muslim extremists have gained a foothold in both Bosnia and Kosovo. There is mounting evidence that Osama bin Laden's operatives have been active in the Balkans since the early 1990s and that elements in Bosnia and Kosovo have aided them in their activities. The NATO interventions did little to prevent that development and, by tilting toward the Muslim cause in the Balkans, may even have facilitated it.

America could have and should have avoided becoming entangled in the turmoil of the Balkans. The violence that accompanied the breakup of Yugoslavia was undoubtedly tragic for the people involved, but it was indistinguishable from the parochial disorders that afflicted many other parts of the world in the 1990s—and continue to do so in the 21st century. It did not involve the rise of an aggressive great power that might have disrupted the international system. By choosing to intervene, the United States is now stuck with not one but two futile and seemingly endless missions. Those of us who opposed those interventions have seen some of our most pessimistic conclusions come true.

Who Lost Yugoslavia?

Criticizing the European Community for its handling of the Yugoslavian conflict has become a growth industry in the United States. According to the conventional wisdom, the Europeans have displayed cowardice and ineptitude, thereby missing an opportunity to forestall the bloodletting. The result is a major crisis that may require U.S.-led military intervention.

An unnamed high-level American official's caustic comment that the EC governments "could not organize a three-car motorcade if their lives depended on it" typifies the Bush administration's contempt. The larger lesson, many of the Eurobashers contend, is that continuing U.S. political and military leadership in post–Cold War Europe is indispensable, because the Europeans are obviously not capable of managing their own affairs.

That indictment of the European Community is, for the most part, unfair. There are two reasons the EC has not taken more decisive action in Yugoslavia, and neither reflects cowardice or ineptitude.

The first is a healthy appreciation for the deep historical roots of ethnic hatreds throughout the Balkans and the enormous potential for getting bogged down in a disastrous and debilitating military adventure.

British foreign secretary Douglas Hurd emphasized the need for caution when he reminded his EC colleagues of London's frustrating experience in Northern Ireland. He warned them that, when considering military intervention, they should be aware of two things: It is easier to put troops in than to get them out, and the scale of effort required at the start typically bears no resemblance to the scale of effort required later on.

The EC's caution is warranted. Indeed, until recently the Bush administration not only seemed to share their view, but was actually more risk averse. It was Secretary of State James A. Baker, not a European foreign minister, who made the remarks in Belgrade in June 1991 condemning secessionist movements and praising the tottering central Yugoslavian government.

Germany and other EC countries favored recognizing the independence of Slovenia and Croatia months before the United States adopted that policy. As late as December 1991, U.S. officials were still trying to dissuade Bonn from extending recognition. It is more than a little hypocritical for Washington to now criticize the Europeans for being faint-hearted.

The other reason for the EC's hesitation in Yugoslavia is simply lack of experience in taking responsibility for managing European security problems. That inexperience is largely the result of the domination the United States has exercised in security matters since the 1940s. Throughout the Cold War, Washington actively fostered Western Europe's security dependence by (among other things) insisting that NATO (an organization dominated by the United States) be the preeminent security institution.

Even the "burden sharing" complaints that surfaced periodically merely reflected a desire that the Europeans pay more of the costs of policies adopted by Washington, not a desire to accord the allies a larger role in decisionmaking. Historian Ronald Steel notes that "for all practical purposes Europe's defense and diplomacy were run from Washington."

Instead of encouraging the strengthening of independent European security institutions such as the Western European Union, the United States viewed them as threats to NATO's (and hence, Washington's) preeminence—an attitude that has carried over into the post–Cold War era. Washington's approach, which foreign policy analyst Alan Tonelson has aptly called a "smothering strategy," has had the unfortunate effect of retarding the development of European collective defense arrangements that will be increasingly needed in the coming years.

We can never know whether the Western Europeans would have been better able to adopt unified and effective policies toward the Yugoslavian conflict if Washington had not clung so tenaciously to its smothering strategy. But trying to formulate common policies and create institutional arrangements from scratch in the midst of a major foreign policy crisis is hardly the optimal situation. Unfortunately, that is what the members of the European Community have had to do.

As they have encountered difficulties, the old habit of looking to the United States for a solution has reasserted itself. Increasingly, the EC governments want the best of both worlds: decisive action in Yugoslavia without accepting more than a small portion of the costs and risks. Such an attitude is another legacy of a dependent mentality, which encourages an avoidance of responsibility.

The longer Washington insists that NATO eclipse the WEU, the Conference on Security and Cooperation in Europe and any other competing organization, the longer it will take the European states to become competent security actors. Given the number of troubles that can be anticipated throughout Eastern Europe, that is a dangerous policy and institutional vacuum.

As the Yugoslavian crisis has demonstrated, it is in neither America's nor Europe's best interest to perpetuate Western Europe's artificial security dependence on the United States.

This article originally appeared in the *Cleveland Plain Dealer*, October 2, 1992.

Treating Bosnia like Afghanistan

In recent weeks several pundits and foreign policy experts have suggested that the United States take steps to even the military odds in Bosnia. Many of them not only advocate an end to the international arms embargo, which would enable the beleaguered regime of President Alija Izetbegovic to purchase weapons on the open market; they favor an affirmative U.S. effort to arm Bosnian government forces.

A similar policy of aiding the mujahideen in Afghanistan during the 1980s worked well, they contend, and such an initiative in Bosnia might repel Serb aggression without involving U.S. troops in the conflict.

Those who favor the Afghan model for U.S. policy toward Bosnia apparently have not looked at Afghanistan recently. Washington's decision to send weapons to the mujahideen did work in the sense of causing enormous trouble for the Soviet Union by bleeding the occupying Soviet army. The operation had a definite influence on Moscow's eventual decision to withdraw its forces.

Arming the factionalized Afghan insurgents, however, has also produced some horrible side effects. Even before they ousted the Soviet-backed government from power in April 1992, feuding mujahideen units spent almost as much time battling each other as they did fighting the communists. With the fall of the Kabul regime, the infighting has sharply escalated, and thousands of Afghans have perished.

Indeed, the International Red Cross estimated that more than 2,000 fatalities occurred in just one three-week period in August 1992—nearly five times the number of deaths that resulted from the Bosnian conflict during the same period. Another round of intense fighting in late January and early February produced similar results.

The sight of Afghan forces using their U.S.-supplied weapons to wage an enthusiastic internecine slaughter should cause American officials to shrink from adopting the same strategy in Bosnia. The current situation in Afghanistan is eloquent testimony to the disastrous unintended consequences that frequently flow from U.S. interventionist initiatives. A program to arm Bosnian government forces would simply intensify and prolong the fighting and, hence, the suffering in that unhappy land; it would also make the United States the avowed enemy of the Serbs, thereby creating the possibility of terrorist reprisals.

Schemes to make the Bosnian regime a U.S. military client are based on two faulty assumptions. The first is that Washington's interest in defeating Serbian expansionism is comparable to the goal of containing Soviet aggression in Southwest Asia during the 1980s. That notion vastly exaggerates the stakes in the Balkans. Although U.S. officials may have sometimes overstated the extent of Soviet power and influence and the threat they posed to America's security, it was not unreasonable to be alarmed by Moscow's intervention in Afghanistan. Perhaps most disturbing, it was the first time during the Cold War that the Kremlin had used the Red Army outside the USSR's East European satellite empire. Aiding Afghan resistance forces seemed a relatively low-cost way of thwarting the rival superpower's expansionist ambitions.

Although Serbian territorial expansion—especially the policy of ethnic cleansing—may be morally offensive, there are no similar geopolitical stakes in the Bosnian struggle. Even alarmist scenarios of the conflict spreading beyond the boundaries of the old Yugoslavia—which are refurbished versions of the discredited domino theory from the Vietnam era—cannot transform tiny Serbia into an expansionist threat comparable to the former Soviet Union. From a strategic standpoint, there is no justification for equating Bosnia with Afghanistan.

The other faulty assumption embraced by proponents of the Afghan model is that Washington has a moral obligation to ensure the survival of Bosnia as an independent country. That attitude is irrational as well as inflexible. Bosnia is a location, not a nation; before 1992 it had not enjoyed an independent political existence since its conquest by the Ottoman Turks in the 16th century. Bosnia's current "international" boundaries were arbitrarily established by communist dictator Josip Tito as internal boundaries within the Yugoslavian federation.

The harsh reality is that Bosnia replicates in miniature the ethnic divisions and animosities that led to the disintegration of Yugoslavia. From its inception, the government in Sarajevo has lacked legitimacy with large portions of the Serbian and Croatian populations. Indeed, both Serbs and Croats seem intent on partitioning the country.

Instead of viewing the tottering Izetbegovic regime as the moral and geopolitical equivalent of the Afghan mujahideen, U.S. officials should accept the fact that Bosnia is probably not a viable political unit. Partition among its Serbian, Croatian and Muslim communities may offer the only hope for an end to the slaughter. It is highly improbable that the three factions will live together in harmony in a multiethnic state, especially after the atrocities that have been committed by all sides.

The United States should take no action that would prolong and intensify the bloodshed. It is bad enough that a policy designed to stem Soviet expansion produced that tragic side effect in Afghanistan. It would be much worse to repeat the experience in Bosnia in the absence of significant security stakes. That would be nothing more than insensitive, gratuitous meddling.

This article originally appeared in the *Indianapolis Star*, March 29, 1993.

Serbia: Analogy and Perspective

It has become a cliché among proponents of U.S. military action in the Balkans to compare Serbia to Nazi Germany, with President Slobodan Milosevic playing the role of the "new Hitler." According to that argument, the United States risks a rerun of the tragic events of the late 1930s, culminating in a larger war if it fails to stifle aggression in its early stages. Those who embrace that view adopt a simplistic, rote interpretation of history that ignores fundamental differences between the two situations.

The European crisis in the 1930s involved one of the world's great powers—one with the second largest economy and a large, well-trained military force—embarking on a frightening and highly destabilizing expansionist binge. Serbia, on the other hand, has a population of 9.8 million (about the same as Belgium's) and a gross domestic product less than one-fifth of Denmark's.

Belgrade's military, augmented by the Serb militias in Bosnia and Croatia, might be able to inflict serious casualties on an intervening force, but it could not mount credible offensive operations against neighboring states, much less against the major industrial powers of Europe. We are not going to see Serb Panzer divisions advancing on Paris or Serb invaders conquering Ukraine as part of a quest for lebensraum.

Nazi Germany was capable of creating a massive disruption of the international system; Serbia is capable only of modestly strengthening its position at the expense of its ethnic rivals within the boundaries of the former Yugoslavia. Not only does Belgrade not have territorial ambitions outside those borders, it lacks the economic and military power to pursue broader ambitions.

The other comparison to the 1930s made by proponents of intervention is also flawed. The rabid nationalism and ethnic hatred exhibited by the Milosevic regime and its followers, interventionists contend, is reminiscent of the Nazis. Therefore, America and its allies cannot stand by while "ethnic cleansing" continues in Bosnia, or the West will again be passive accomplices to genocide.

Although that argument is more plausible than the notion of the Serbs as a serious strategic threat, it hardly justifies a costly and risky NATO military response. Both the Belgrade government and Serb forces in Croatia and Bosnia have undoubtedly practiced vicious chauvinism. Nevertheless, the extent of ethnic cleansing and other deplorable actions must be viewed in context.

As columnist Charles Krauthammer and other skeptics point out, what is going on in Bosnia cannot accurately be termed genocide. Instead of exterminating members of other ethnic groups, the Serbs have generally expelled them from specific territories as part of an effort to create a "greater Serbia." Although that is certainly a loathsome practice—and has been accompanied by sporadic acts of murder—it hardly constitutes genocide.

Events in such places as Sudan and Rwanda more closely fit the definition of genocide. Nearly 1 million black Sudanese have perished at the hands of the Arab government in Khartoum during the past decade. Recent strife between Hutus and Tutsis has claimed the lives of 100,000 people, almost all of them civilians who belonged to the "wrong" ethnic faction, over a period of two weeks. Estimates of fatalities—including those of military personnel—in Bosnia range from 115,000 to 200,000 in more than two years of warfare. Yet there are few voices insisting that the Western powers have a moral obligation to intervene in Sudan or Rwanda.

Ethnic cleansing itself is hardly a unique practice in this century. When the British colony of India was partitioned and granted independence in 1947, millions of Hindus were expelled from the new Islamic nation of Pakistan while millions of Muslims had to flee predominantly Hindu India. Nearly 250,000 people perished in the attendant bloodshed.

From the standpoint of U.S. culpability, an even more odious episode took place at the end of World War II when nearly 16 million ethnic Germans were expelled from Poland, Czechoslovakia, and other East European countries solely because of their ethnicity. Not only did the United States fail to prevent that forced exodus, President Harry Truman endorsed the step at the Potsdam Conference, with the absurd proviso that the process be "humane."

More recently, Greek Cypriots were driven from the northern portion of Cyprus when Turkish forces invaded and occupied nearly half of the island in 1974. It is instructive to compare the passive U.S. response to Ankara's actions with Washington's vehement condemnation of Serb policy in Bosnia and NATO's periodic bouts of saber rattling about ethnic cleansing. There has never been the slightest consideration given to using military action against Turkey to restore the Greek Cypriots to their homes. The Serbs have a point when they contend that the United States and its allies employ a blatant double standard.

The fighting in Bosnia is an ugly but parochial conflict with little importance outside the immediate region. It is a mundane struggle over the territorial spoils resulting from the breakup of the Yugoslav federation. Although it may be an especially acrimonious political divorce, it need not and should not have wider strategic or moral significance.

Events in Bosnia certainly are not a repetition of the calamitous developments in the late 1930s, which had major global consequences. Advocates of Western intervention who contend that the Bosnian conflict fits the 1930s model must use a crowbar to make it fit.

This article originally appeared in the *Washington Times*, June 12, 1994.

Bosnia: The Moral Imperative

There is no question that the suffering in Bosnia tugs at the emotions of all decent people. The desire to help end the carnage is an entirely normal and understandable reaction. But a crusading moralism is a dangerous and ill-advised rationale for putting U.S. military forces in harm's way. It inevitably leads to either hypocritical policies or an endless succession of foolish and unsustainable interventions.

To send troops to enforce the U.S.-brokered peace agreement is, in the broadest and most fundamental sense, a violation of the U.S. government's moral obligation to its own citizens.

The United States is a constitutional republic based on the principle of limited government. The lives, freedoms and financial resources of the American people are not rightfully available for whatever missions suit the whims of political leaders.

The federal government has a constitutional and moral responsibility to protect the security and liberty of the Republic. That government has neither a constitutional nor a moral writ to risk lives and resources to police the planet, promote democracy or enforce peace accords to end murky civil wars.

It is hard enough to see American soldiers brought home in body bags when the mission is necessary to defend the country's vital security interests. Such a terrible sacrifice should never be called for when the United States has no security interests at stake—which is the case in Bosnia.

There is no provision of the Constitution that empowers the government to commit blood and treasure for the purpose of doing good deeds in the world. However worthy the Bosnian peace agreement may be—and it appears to be hopelessly flawed—President Clinton does not have the right to risk the lives of U.S. military personnel to enforce it.

In addition to that fundamental flaw in the president's plans, much about Washington's specific role in the conflict argues against a moral imperative for troop involvement.

U.S. policy toward Bosnia has been characterized by hypocrisy on several levels. American officials, pundits and human rights activists who repeatedly decry the atrocities there and demand U.S. military action seem noticeably less agitated about similar (and in some cases, far worse) events elsewhere.

More than 1 million black Sudanese have perished at the hands of the Arab government in Khartoum in the last decade. Strife between Hutus and Tutsis in Rwanda in spring 1994 claimed the lives of at least 500,000 people—and perhaps as many as 800,000—almost all of them Tutsi civilians, over a period of three months. Even the highest estimates of fatalities—including those of military personnel—in Bosnia range from 200,000 to 250,000 in nearly four years of warfare. (Both the International Red Cross and the Stockholm Peace Research Institute, organizations without political agendas in Bosnia, put the figure at a much more modest 50,000.) Yet few of the individuals who demand that the Western powers stop the "genocide" in Bosnia called for military intervention in Rwanda, and virtually none of them contends there is any moral obligation to intervene militarily in Sudan.

A similar indifference is evident regarding the bloody struggles in such places as Tajikistan, Liberia and Afghanistan. Far more civilians have been killed in Kabul than in Sarajevo this year.

Yet there is a dearth of calls for the United States to use its military power to end that terrible conflict even though U.S. support for Islamic extremists fighting the Soviets in Afghanistan in the 1980s helped create the tragedy.

The response is partly the result of the difference in media coverage. Put bluntly, the Bosnian conflict has been the media's pet war. But there also appears to be a dollop of Eurocentrism, if not outright racism, at work.

President Clinton and other advocates of action in the Balkans contend that the United States cannot intervene everywhere, and that is undoubtedly true. But what, then, are the criteria for selective intervention on humanitarian grounds?

It is at least curious that the only place most members of the U.S. political and foreign political elites advocate a large-scale military mission for moral reasons is Bosnia. Third World peoples might well suspect that it is because those elites regard mass killings as inevitable in Africa and Asia but intolerable in Europe.

Even within the context of the former Yugoslavia, U.S. policy has been characterized by a double standard. The administration and its political allies have repeatedly (and justifiably) excoriated the Serbs for their campaign of ethnic cleansing. But the condemnations of similar actions by the Muslims and Croats have been muted by comparison. When the Croatian army last summer expelled 150,000 Serbs from the Krajina, a region where Serbs had lived for centuries, Washington's criticism was brief and perfunctory. Indeed, administration officials privately expressed support for the offensive, contending that it restored the military balance, "cleaned up the map" and improved prospects for a peace settlement.

So much for righteous indignation about ethnic cleansing.

The double standard has been apparent in other ways. Proponents of U.S. intervention implicitly, and sometimes explicitly, assume that every ethnic group in the former Yugoslavia, save one, has an inherent right of secession. Thus, the Slovenes, Croats, Bosnian Muslims, and Macedonians all had the right to withdraw from Yugoslavia. Apparently the Albanian residents of the Serbian province of Kosovo even have the right to secede from Serbia. But the Serb population of Bosnia has no similar right to secede from that newly minted country.

Indeed, that is the underlying logic of the Dayton peace accord that the United States pressured the parties to sign and is now committed to enforce.

The creation of two powerful "self-governing entities" within the territory of the Bosnian state increases the likelihood of a de facto ethnic partition, but the provisions of the agreement stress that Bosnia must remain intact and is entitled to the international boundaries it claimed when it declared independence. President Clinton, Secretary of State Warren Christopher and other U.S. officials have gone out of their way to emphasize that the Bosnian Serbs will not be allowed to secede.

That double standard reflects the flawed thinking that characterizes the U.S. model in Bosnia, and further calls into question the president's assertion in his address to the nation Monday that sending troops into Bosnia is "the right thing to do."

This article originally appeared in the *Boston Sunday Globe*, December 3, 1995.

Bizarre Peace Plan for Bosnia

Despite the tragic deaths of three high-ranking negotiators, the Clinton administration remains determined to be the architect of peace in the Balkans. Most public and media attention has focused on Washington's proposed formula for allocating territory among

Bosnia's feuding factions. But the political provisions of the latest U.S. peace plan deserve a withering appraisal, for they involve some bizarre (and potentially dangerous) ideas. Indeed, the enterprise is so strange that it could only have come from the precincts of Foggy Bottom.

The root problem is Washington's insistence that Bosnia continue to exist as a country after a peace settlement. That objective is largely an exercise in diplomatic fiction. Bosnia has been divided among its three factions—Muslim, Croatian and Serbian—since the earliest weeks of the civil war, and any feasible peace accord will solidify that de facto partition.

The logical solution would be to recognize reality and allow the predominantly Croatian territories to merge with Croatia, the predominantly Serbian lands to merge with Serbia, and the predominantly Muslim lands to form a new, much smaller country. But Washington refuses to take that path, contending that official ratification of Bosnia's partition would reward Serbian aggression and allow a member state of the international system to be expunged from the map by military force. Yet few U.S. officials are prepared to advocate the massive military intervention and lengthy occupation that would be required to make Bosnia a functioning political entity.

Such conflicting pressures have produced an elaborate diplomatic charade—a game of "let's pretend there is a real Bosnia." How fanciful U.S. schemes are for preserving the fiction of a Bosnian state can be gauged by the remarks of a "senior official" shortly after Washington helped orchestrate the creation of Bosnia's Muslim-Croatian federation in 1994. "What we have in mind is that the central government of [Bosnia] would be weak, but the Muslim-Croat part would be stronger. The links to Croatia on the outside could be stronger than those to the Serbs within the country of Bosnia. You'd end up with an asymmetrical federation in Bosnia."

It is more likely that one would end up with a colossal mess. The notion of a country in which the constituent population groups have stronger political ties to an outside power than they do to each other is, to put it charitably, peculiar. At the time, it was uncertain whether U.S. policymakers envisioned that the Bosnian Serbs would have stronger ties to Serbia than they would to the Muslim and Croatian communities in Bosnia—although that was the implication of the official's remarks. Recent reports make it clear that Washington's peace plan does indeed embrace that objective. Such a hopelessly convoluted political entity may be called many things, but "viable country" is not one of them.

Americans have reason to be concerned about these strange diplomatic machinations. The Clinton administration has repeatedly stated that the United States will provide troops as part of a North Atlantic Treaty Organization peacekeeping force to implement a Bosnian peace agreement. That would be an unwise commitment in any case, since the United States has no interests at stake in the Balkans that warrant risking the lives of U.S. military personnel.

It would be especially unwise, however, to put U.S. troops in harm's way to enforce a peace accord that has no realistic chance of success in the long term. Sooner or later, the Bosnian Serbs (and probably the Bosnian Croats, as well) will attempt to politically meld with their ethnic brethren across the border. American leaders will then face an unpalatable choice. They can either watch their Potemkin Bosnian state disintegrate, or they can use military force to try to preserve a diplomatic fiction.

A more realistic policy now would avoid such a choice between humiliation and disaster in the future. The notion of a united Bosnia was a utopian fantasy from the outset. There is no Bosnian nation; Bosnia is merely a battleground for contending ethno-religious factions. An official partition, negotiated by the belligerents and reflecting their respective fortunes on the battlefield, would merely recognize a reality that has long been obvious.

Washington's insistence on preventing an official partition will only prolong the suffering in the former Yugoslavia. The administration's overly creative peace architects should cease their labors. They threaten to make an already bad situation even worse.

This article originally appeared in the *Washington Times*, August 27, 1995.

Clinton Trying "Bait-and-Switch" Tactic in Bosnia

"Bait and switch" has long been a favorite tactic of unethical merchants. The scheme involves luring customers into the store with an exceptionally low price on a product (the bait). When the unwary customers arrive, they are told that the product has been sold out but that another, higher priced, version would be an even better choice (the switch). Having already invested a good deal of time and gasoline, some customers fall for the ploy, even though in most jurisdictions bait and switch is considered fraud.

The Clinton administration's Bosnia policy is the foreign policy equivalent of bait and switch. In December 1995 the president sent more than 16,000 U.S. troops to Bosnia as part of the NATO Implementation Force, or IFOR.

Presented with a fait accompli, a reluctant Congress endorsed the move—but only after the administration gave assurances that the troops would be back home in one year.

That promise has now disappeared down the memory hole.

Secretary of Defense William Perry informed the Senate Armed Services Committee last week that the United States would keep 7,500 troops in Bosnia through mid-March 1997. Moreover, a 5,000-strong "cover force" would be sent to assist in the (now partial) withdrawal between December and March. In other words, the number of U.S. military personnel in Bosnia will actually rise in the next few months.

There is, in fact, no guarantee that American troops will not be stuck in Bosnia long after March 1997. The West European powers have been pressuring Washington for months to authorize U.S. participation in a "follow-on" force to IFOR, and administration officials seem increasingly receptive to their arguments. The Clinton administration, having secured grudging endorsements from a skeptical Congress and public for a limited, one-year mission to separate the belligerents in Bosnia, is apparently embarking on a nation-building crusade with no termination date. One would be hard-pressed to find a more cynical application of bait and switch.

Unfortunately that ploy has been an all too common feature of American foreign policy in recent decades. Foreign policy officials, regardless of party affiliation, typically hold the elitist view that Congress and the American people are nothing more than annoying obstacles to be overcome. If deception must be practiced to prevent ignorant citizens and their elected representatives from obstructing the implementation of enlightened policies, so be it.

Indeed, bait and switch has been used on numerous occasions. The Somalia mission began as a humanitarian effort to distribute food and medicine to starving civilians. Not only did the Bush administration, which initiated the troop deployment just weeks before leaving office, stress the mission's limited scope, but the Clinton administration initially did the same.

By the summer of 1993, however, U.S. troops were assigned to hunt down the leader of one Somali political faction and Washington had signed on to the United Nations' ambitious nation-building agenda.

Even the creation of Washington's principal alliance, NATO, was sullied by the use of bait and switch. Secretary of State Dean Acheson and other officials assured the Senate and the American people that there was no intention to station U.S. troops in Europe to implement the North Atlantic Treaty. Barely a year after the Senate ratification, which occurred in part because of those assurances, the administration announced plans to send four U.S. divisions to Europe and to place an American general in command of an integrated NATO force.

The Truman administration then exercised a second bait and switch, promising that both the troop deployment and the assumption of command responsibilities would be temporary. They were to last only until the West European countries had recovered economically and could take primary responsibility for their defense. Forty-six years later, the U.S. troops are still in Europe.

Congress and the public should remember that two-stage bait and switch when the debate takes place about whether to enlarge NATO. The Clinton administration is already indicating that the enlargement would not involve stationing U.S. troops or nuclear weapons on the territory of the new members—since such a step could lead to a nasty confrontation with Russia.

Given the history of bait and switch regarding NATO, and the current administration's fondness for the tactic in Somalia and Bosnia, such assurances should be taken not only with a grain of salt but with the entire salt shaker at hand.

The political use of bait and switch should be offensive to anyone who believes in democratic accountability. Congress and the American people are not merely inconvenient obstacles to be circumvented in the conduct of the nation's foreign policy.

Officials should be held to their word when they make a commitment, and if the substance of that commitment is about to change, both Congress and the public ought to be brought back into the debate.

The incoming 105th Congress would do the nation a great service by insisting on that point in connection with the Clinton administration's rapidly expanding mission in Bosnia.

This article originally appeared in the *Houston Chronicle*, October 9, 1996.

Bringing PC "Democracy" Back to Bosnia

The Clinton administration insists that the goal of the U.S.-led mission in Bosnia is to bring democracy as well as peace to that unhappy country. Indeed, the 1995 Dayton Accords go far beyond such mundane matters as establishing a cease-fire between the belligerents and recognizing the respective territorial jurisdictions of the Bosnian Serb Republic and the Muslim-Croat federation. Numerous provisions deal with the political structures of a rebuilt Bosnia and its subnational units.

Critics of the Bosnia intervention warned from the outset that those provisions would entangle the United States and the other NATO powers in the country's complex political rivalries. Such fears are being borne out with a vengeance. Not only is the NATO Stabilization Force (SFOR) caught up in the quarrels between the Serbs and their Muslim and Croat adversaries, it is now deeply involved in an intramural struggle among rival Bosnian Serb factions.

Even worse, U.S. and NATO meddling in the internal politics of the Bosnian Serb Republic has taken the form of actions that make a mockery of any meaningful concept of democracy. Those actions reflect the vision of democracy that advocates of speech codes and other forms of political correctness would love to impose in the United States—if only they had unchallenged power. The Bosnian Serb Republic has become a laboratory for their experiments in Frankensteinian democracy.

U.S. and West European policymakers have thrown their support to Bosnian Serb president Biljana Plavsic in her power struggle with her one-time mentor, former president (and accused war criminal) Radovan Karadzic. There are few ideological differences between the two politicians on such matters as ethnic cleansing, but the

United States and its allies concluded that Mrs. Plavsic would be a more pliable client.

Consequently, SFOR has become her combination palace guard and political sponsor. The extent of Western meddling is breathtaking. When the Bosnian Serb Republic's constitutional court ruled in August that Mrs. Plavsic's dissolution of parliament and call for new elections was illegal, the Organization for Security and Cooperation in Europe (OSCE)—the civilian arm of the Bosnia mission—summarily dismissed the court's decision and proceeded to organize the disputed elections. That is a curious way to give lessons in democracy.

SFOR and OSCE have taken it upon themselves to decide which faction was entitled to control police stations in several cities. (Invariably, it was the Plavsic faction.) They also sought to impose political purity tests on candidates for office. In September, an OSCE functionary disqualified a slate of candidates because of their "continuing ties" to Mr. Karadzic. Former State Department official Robert Frowick, who now heads the OSCE operation in Bosnia, overruled that decision—but he did so not because it was anti-democratic but because he feared that Karadzic supporters might violently retaliate against American and West European election observers.

The exercise in U.S.-sponsored politically correct micromanagement reached new heights in early October when SFOR troops seized four television stations operated by Karadzic supporters. Gen. Wesley Clark, NATO's new supreme commander, informed reporters that the stations would quickly reopen under "new management." The "new management" turned out to be supporters of Mrs. Plavsic.

Even more disturbing than the high-handed action of shutting down the stations were the justifications given. Anonymous "senior Western officials" emphasized that the purpose was to force a "more balanced presentation" of views. Walter Slocombe, U.S. under secretary of defense, stated that the raids would end "the poisonous stream of material" coming from those stations. Another Western official boasted, "We are in a position to do whatever we want with transmitter sites" and that the goal was to ensure "responsible broadcasts."

The Action Council for Peace in the Balkans, a prominent American cheerleader for the Bosnia intervention, praised the crackdown, noting that Mr. Karadzic's supporters "will no longer be able to use the transmitters to disseminate anti-NATO commentaries" or other odious messages.

Among other things, pro-Karadzic broadcasters had dared to argue that both SFOR and the special United Nations war crimes tribunal exhibited an anti-Serb bias. One might think that freedom of expression, even when the views expressed are strident and one-sided, is an important feature of democracy. But that is not the attitude of the nation builders in charge of the Bosnia operation.

The U.S.-led democracy mission in Bosnia has become a grotesque parody of democratic principles. We are propping up an authoritarian Serb chauvinist whose primary appeal is that she is willing to be Washington's quisling—at least for the time being. American troops are entangled not only in the petty politics of Bosnia as a whole but also in the even more petty politics of the country's Bosnian Serb subunit. Moreover, we are teaching the Serbs the virtues of democracy by showing them that an outside power, if it possesses enough military clout, has the right to overrule court decisions, establish political purity tests for candidates for public office and suppress media outlets that transmit politically incorrect views.

It would be a tragedy if the life of even a single American soldier were lost to implement such an ugly, hypocritical mission.

This article originally appeared in the *Washington Times,* October 24, 1997.

Involvement Not Worth the Cost

As NATO warplanes maneuver over Albania and Macedonia to overawe Serbian president Slobodan Milosevic, the American people ought to worry about the alliance's steady descent into the quicksand of Balkan quarrels.

The transformation of NATO has been both breathtaking and alarming. It was once an alliance to keep Western Europe, a major strategic and economic prize, out of the orbit of an aggressively expansionist superpower, the Soviet Union. It now has become the babysitter of the Balkans. Not content with the futile and seemingly endless nation-building mission in Bosnia, NATO is meddling in the conflict between Serbia and its restive, predominantly Albanian region of Kosovo.

As NATO's leader, the USA is being saddled with expensive and thankless responsibilities. The Bosnia mission already has cost U.S. taxpayers nearly $10 billion, and the meter still is running. If the USA is foolish enough to lead a NATO intervention in Kosovo, the financial costs will mount and the lives of U.S. military personnel will be at risk.

The USA is the most strategically and economically secure great power in history. For a country with our multiple advantages to obsess about the status of a Serbian province (or to risk lives and treasure anywhere in the Balkans) is a manifestation of foreign policy hypochondria.

The conventional wisdom is that if the USA and NATO don't stop the rising violence in Kosovo, the fighting will spread throughout the Balkans and eventually cause another massive European war. But that argument is merely a rehash of the domino theory, which was thoroughly discredited in Southeast Asia in the 1970s and Central America in the 1980s.

As long as Europe's major powers remain at peace, legitimate U.S. interests in Europe are secure. We do not need to worry about every petty conflict that might erupt somewhere on the Continent.

Washington should concentrate on anticipating and preventing large-scale adverse changes in the international system. Put bluntly, the behavior of a country like China in an economically and strategically important region like East Asia matters to the United States. The political status of a Serbian province does not.

This article originally appeared in *USA Today*, June 17, 1998.

Repeating Bosnia Mistake

Whether the tentative agreement between NATO and Slobodan Milosevic holds together or the alliance resumes its plan to launch air strikes on Serbia matters little in the long run. Either way, the United States is on the brink of another messy intervention in the Balkans. That policy should appeal only to masochists.

Western meddling in Kosovo would be hypocritical, dangerous and futile.

The hypocrisy of the United States and its allies is breathtaking. There have been approximately 500 fatalities in Kosovo since fighting erupted in February. That total—a tragic but hardly unusual number of victims in a civil war—has led to cries of genocide and demands from armchair war hawks for NATO intervention.

Yet more than 1,200 people perished in three days of fighting last week in Sri Lanka—in another struggle for secession. Turkey's brutal suppression of its secessionist-minded Kurdish minority has led to the deaths of about 30,000 people and the razing of nearly 1,000 Kurdish villages over the past decade. Proponents of Western action in Kosovo practice a curious double standard.

Even if an attack on Serbia were morally justified, it would likely make matters worse in the Balkans. NATO's meddling will encourage the Albanian Kosovars to press their campaign for independence from Serbia and unification with neighboring Albania.

All NATO countries officially oppose an independent Kosovo, realizing that it would intensify efforts to create a "Greater Albania" and threaten the territorial integrity of Macedonia and Greece. Is NATO prepared to suppress the Kosovo Liberation Army to keep Kosovo part of Serbia?

If so, the United States and its allies may find themselves in the unenviable position of fighting both the Serbs and the Albanians.

The interminable Bosnia mission should have taught U.S. policymakers the futility of making the United States the babysitter of the Balkans. That mission was supposed to last one year and cost U.S. taxpayers $1.5 billion. The cost has already reached $10 billion, and President Clinton has extended the mission indefinitely.

Bosnia is no closer to being a viable country now than it was when NATO intervened. Yet the United States is flirting with an even more difficult and futile crusade in Kosovo. Some policymakers never learn.

This article originally appeared in *USA Today*, October 14, 1998.

Perverted Democracy in Bosnia

The U.S.-led nation-building effort in Bosnia has moved from the impractical to the repulsive. It was always a dubious assumption that NATO troops and an army of international bureaucrats could transform Bosnia into a viable, democratic country.

The three feuding ethnic groups—Serbs, Muslims and Croats—had made it clear on numerous occasions that they did not want to live together in a multiethnic state. The much-touted Dayton peace accord merely facilitated a cease-fire. It has not, and almost certainly will not, effect a reconciliation.

Rather than admit failure, the would-be nation builders, led by "High Representative" Carlos Westendorp, are now resorting to tactics that make a mockery of any reasonable concept of democracy. The latest outrage was Mr. Westendorp's removal of Nikola Poplasen as president of the Bosnian Serb Republic—one of the two subnational political entities that make up the convoluted Bosnian state. Last September, voters dared to elect the radical nationalist Mr. Poplasen over the candidate preferred by the Western powers, even though it meant spurning offers of lucrative financial aid for the hard-pressed Serb Republic. The offense that led to Mr. Poplasen's dismissal was his refusal to reappoint the incumbent prime minister, Milorad Dodik, favored by Mr. Westendorp and the Western governments.

The form of democracy Mr. Westendorp and his cohorts are bringing to Bosnia is a version Leonid Brezhnev would have loved. Indeed, the ouster of a duly elected president was hardly the first authoritarian step taken by the high representative or his NATO backers. Mr. Westendorp had previously removed lower-level officials in both the Serb Republic and the Muslim-Croat federation when they tried to criticize or otherwise resist the enlightened nation-building crusade. More than a year ago, NATO forces shut down radio stations that opposed the peacekeeping mission, and international authorities have routinely struck hard-line nationalist candidates from ballots, often on utterly flimsy grounds. Merely displaying the image of former Bosnian Serb president Radovan Karadzic can earn a candidate a ban. So can giving a media interview or making a campaign appearance during the "news blackout" period that the international authorities impose prior to elections.

Even the voter registration lists have been manipulated to increase the likelihood of the results desired by the intervening powers. Many of the voters who cast ballots for candidates in the Bosnian Serb Republic, for example, are Muslim refugees who fled during the civil war, do not now live in the Serb Republic and have little prospect of ever doing so again. More than 20 percent of the representatives in the parliament owe their seats to the existence of such "rotten borough" electoral precincts. That system would be akin to having Palestinian exiles, who left during the 1948 war, vote in Israel's elections.

One ought to ponder what unintended lessons such arbitrary actions are teaching the people of Bosnia about democratic principles. After their experiences at the hands of Mr. Westendorp and his associates, they might be excused for regarding Western rhetoric about the virtues of democracy as nothing more than hypocritical blather.

Mr. Westendorp's trampling of democratic electoral norms is merely one manifestation of how far the international nation builders are willing to go in their frantic effort to preserve the fantasy of a viable Bosnian state. The high representative has imposed his choice for Bosnia's currency, flag, national anthem and auto license plates. Even the most ardent nation builders ought to ask: What kind of a country is it when the people living there cannot even decide on such things as a national anthem or the design of the national currency or flag? Nations are built from within; they cannot be imposed by foreign officials, however well-meaning.

The pseudo-democratic nation-building enterprise in Bosnia is international social engineering run amok. It reflects the congenital arrogance of the Clinton administration and the (mostly Left-leaning) governments of Western Europe: All that is required for constructive political, social and economic change in any society is to develop a plan; hire smart, energetic officials to carry it out; and fund the scheme generously. Bosnia has been their real-world laboratory for testing those theories, and test them they have.

The evidence is mounting that the experiment is a flop. Bosnia is more ethnically segregated today than it was when the Dayton Accords were signed. (Most of the refugees who have "returned home"—and it is a depressingly modest number—have gone from postwar areas in which they were in the minority to areas in which they would be in the majority.) Economically, the country is a basket case. A recent assessment of global economic freedom by a prominent Washington think tank put Bosnia 155th—right between Iran and Somalia. Nearly three-quarters of Bosnian respondents in public opinion surveys state they will not consider voting for a candidate from another ethnic group.

Bosnia is not a viable country and in all likelihood it never will be. Resorting to ever more desperate, undemocratic and sleazy tactics in the name of democratic nation building will not change that reality. It is a disgrace for U.S. troops to be put at risk to carry out such a futile and shameful mission. This misguided experiment should be terminated.

This article originally appeared in the *Washington Times*, March 15, 1999.

Clinton Strikes Out on All Three Justifications for Bombing

President Clinton asserts that there are strategic and moral imperatives for launching air strikes against Serbia.

Yet his three major justifications—the fear of a wider conflict, the horror of ethnic cleansing and the credibility of NATO—are all deeply flawed.

The Fear of a Wider War

The president contends that, without NATO's intervention, the conflict in Kosovo could lead to a much wider European war, as in 1914 and 1939. That argument is a grotesque oversimplification of history. Europe's strategic environment is vastly different today than it was prior to either world war.

In 1914 the Continent was cleaved by two rival military alliances, and all of Europe's major powers were members of one alliance or the other. Even worse, several of those powers foolishly tied their fortunes to the actions and agendas of Balkan clients.

The alliances then became transmission belts for war, converting a parochial Balkan spat into a continental conflagration.

Today, there is no bitter animosity among the European great powers. (Indeed, most of them are members of the same multilateral association, the European Union.) Nor are there rigid rival alliances enabling Balkan disputes to produce a rerun of World War I. The broader strategic context is a crucial factor.

Worrying about a Balkan conflict leading to a massive European war in 1999 makes as much sense as Americans worrying about a new war against the British because we fought them in the War of 1812.

The World War II model is even less applicable. In the late 1930s Germany was one of the world's great powers with a first-class military force. It had the ability not merely to destroy the European balance of power but to disrupt the entire international system and even make a bid for global domination.

Serbia is a small, weak country that could not begin to pose a serious expansionist threat.

Even the administration's argument that the war in Kosovo might spread southward, eventually drawing in NATO members Greece and Turkey, is little more than a refurbished version of the discredited domino theory.

If Greece and Turkey ever come to blows, it is far more likely to be because of the festering situation in Cyprus or territorial disputes in the Aegean Sea.

Neither Ankara nor Athens shows any desire to become involved in the quarrels of the former Yugoslavia.

Ethnic Cleansing

Clinton's assertion that NATO has a moral imperative to prevent "ethnic cleansing" and "genocide" in Kosovo exaggerates the suffering there to the point of absurdity. Approximately 2,000 people had perished in more than 13 months of fighting before NATO's bombing campaign began. That is hardly comparable to the millions slaughtered by Hitler, Stalin and Mao. While the loss of life in Kosovo is certainly tragic, the level of casualties would not put the Kosovo struggle even in the top dozen conflicts that have taken place around the world in this decade alone.

More than a million people have died in the war in Sudan, tens of thousands in Afghanistan and Algeria, and many thousands in such places as Sri Lanka, Liberia and Sierra Leone. The war between the government of NATO member Turkey and Kurdish insurgents has claimed 37,000 lives. Yet the alliance does not issue ultimatums in those wars much less launch attacks on one of the parties.

NATO Credibility

Finally, the administration insists that the credibility of the United States and NATO is on the line and, therefore, the alliance had to act. Of all the arguments for striking Serbia, this one is the weakest and most infuriating. The only reason U.S. credibility is at stake is that Washington foolishly put it on the line in connection with a petty, third-rate civil war in the Balkans. Smart great powers do not make such blunders.

As far as NATO's credibility is concerned, if the United States as the leader of NATO must become the babysitter of the Balkans,

Americans ought to seriously reconsider the wisdom of continued U.S. membership in the alliance. Alliances are supposed to be a means to enhance America's security; the preservation of an alliance and its credibility should not become an end in itself—especially if it requires the United States to undertake unnecessary, futile and dangerous missions.

Worst of all, the U.S.-led crusade in the Balkans is having ominous ripple effects far beyond the region. Russia has reacted angrily to NATO's brazen disregard of long-standing Russian interests in the Balkans and Moscow's opposition to the use of force against Serbia. The Russian government has responded by suspending its participation in the Partnership for Peace program as well as the liaison with NATO. Already smarting from NATO's enlargement eastward to Russia's border by the admission of Poland, Hungary and the Czech Republic, Moscow may now intensify military ties with Iran, China and other countries seeking to neutralize America's dominant global status.

Russia is not the only country to react angrily to the NATO attack. Ukraine's parliament has condemned the action and voted 231 to 43 to reconsider the country's renunciation of nuclear weapons. Such a decision would be hugely damaging to Washington's goal of preventing nuclear weapons proliferation.

The U.S.-led NATO attack on Serbia is foolish and unnecessary. Most worrisome of all, if the air strikes fail to impel Slobodan Milosevic to capitulate, NATO may decide to escalate and send in ground forces. That could easily entangle the United States in a larger version of Washington's earlier misadventures in Lebanon and Somalia. No American president should risk the lives of American military personnel in a strategically and economically irrelevant snake pit like the Balkans.

This article originally appeared in the *Orange County Register*, April 4, 1999.

International Mission Is Now a Mockery of Democratic Principles

With the signing of the Dayton peace accords in 1995, the United States and its NATO allies committed themselves not only to helping bring peace to Bosnia-Herzegovina but also to helping build a democratic political system after the breakup of Yugoslavia. That effort has failed. Despite systematic attempts by Western powers to undermine them, nationalist parties fared well in the November elections, as they have in every election since 1995. Bosnia is a Potemkin democracy: a colony of the West run by increasingly arrogant and autocratic international bureaucrats. Equally troubling, the North Atlantic Treaty Organization has adopted similar tactics in Kosovo, and that pattern threatens to become the norm wherever nation-building missions are undertaken.

One glaring abuse has been the lack of respect for freedom of expression. Officials from NATO, the Organization for Security and Cooperation in Europe (OSCE) and the United Nations harass or suppress media outlets that dare to criticize the Dayton Accords, the conduct of the NATO peacekeeping force, or the decisions of the special war crimes tribunal. How far such powers can go became apparent in April 1999, when the OSCE's puppet media commission ordered a Bosnian Serb television station to carry an address by U.S. Secretary of State Madeleine K. Albright on the Kosovo crisis. Apparently freedom of the press in Bosnia means that media outlets can be required to transmit statements by a foreign official dealing with events in a neighboring country.

The international authorities also have used questionable tactics with regard to a core component of any democratic political system: the holding of elections. Candidates for public office have been barred from the ballot by the Office of the High Representative (the top international civilian body in Bosnia)—often for transparently cynical reasons. In the 1998 national elections, for example, commissioners disqualified four Bosnian Croat candidates because of alleged biased coverage in their favor by television stations *in Croatia*.

The authorities also toyed with the idea of disqualifying the Bosnian Serb Radical Party's Nikola Poplasen, who ultimately won the presidential election, for making a television appearance in neighboring Serbia on the eve of the election. Such an appearance, some election watchdogs argued, violated the 24-hour "media blackout period" imposed in Bosnia.

Matters escalated before the spring 2000 municipal elections, when the commission in charge banned the entire slate of the Radical Party (which had won the presidency in the previous national elections).

That action would be akin to the Federal Election Commission in the United States disqualifying the Republican or the Democratic Party.

Banning candidates they dislike is not the only method international authorities have used to manipulate election results. Manipulating voter registration lists has been a more pervasive tactic. Instead of requiring a voter to cast a ballot in the district in which he or she currently resides, election rules allow the voter to cast a ballot for candidates in the place where he or she resided in 1991, before the Bosnian civil war erupted.

But most of the refugees have little prospect of returning to their prewar homes. In the 1997 elections, six municipalities elected exile governments. About one-fifth of the parliament in the Bosnian Serb Republic (one of the two political entities that make up Bosnia-Herzegovina) consists of delegates of Muslim parties "elected" by voters who are unlikely ever to set foot in the Serb Republic. Indeed, the 1998 victory of the West's favored candidate for the Serb seat on Bosnia's three-member presidency was due almost entirely to the votes cast by about 200,000 displaced (primarily Muslim) voters. Allowing massive numbers of nonresidents to cast ballots delegitimizes the democratic process.

When all else fails, international authorities simply remove elected officials they dislike. The most prominent official purged to date was Poplasen, but he is hardly the only one. Literally dozens of Serb, Croat and Muslim officials have been ousted—and often prohibited from running for office again.

The international authorities are running Bosnia as a protectorate with an increasingly tattered democratic facade. The high representative's dictatorial tendencies include matters large and small. He has imposed his own choices for the country's currency and the design of new coins. His office even directed the selection of a new national anthem.

What is occurring in Bosnia today is not the evolution of a democratic system but the ugly face of new-style colonialism. Worst of all, ambitious would-be nation builders apparently see the Bosnia intervention as a template for similar missions in the Balkans and beyond.

The same pattern of media control, for example, is already emerging in Kosovo. NATO forces shut down one Albanian-language newspaper in Pristina, the capital of Kosovo, for publishing a story contending that the peacekeeping force was biased in favor of the Serbs. Another was threatened with a fine and closure for having the temerity to describe KFOR, the NATO-led peacekeeping force, as an occupying army. Political correctness reigns supreme in Kosovo, with international officials decreeing that one-third of the candidates for the recent municipal elections must be women.

The nation-building effort in the Balkans may have begun as a well-meaning attempt by Western leaders to help construct pluralistic, democratic societies from the ruins of civil war. The results, however, confirm Lord Acton's observation that absolute power corrupts absolutely. Regardless of the initial motives, the international missions in Bosnia and in Kosovo have turned into a mockery of democratic principles.

This article originally appeared in the *Los Angeles Times*, December 31, 2000.

Exit the Balkans Pronto

One of the first foreign policy decisions President Bush must make is whether to keep U.S. troops in the Balkans or withdraw them and transfer peacekeeping duties exclusively to the Europeans.

He would be wise to seek a speedy exit. Otherwise, the Balkans are likely to become an albatross around the neck of the new administration.

Despite a barrage of upbeat propaganda, the missions in Bosnia and Kosovo are not going well. Bosnia is no closer to being a viable country than it was when the Dayton peace accords were signed in 1995.

It is an ethnically segregated international colony with NATO troops policing a delicate cease-fire. In election after election, Serb, Croat, and Muslim voters reject moderate, multiethnic parties in favor of hard-line nationalist forces.

The elections are not meaningful in any case, because most real political power is exercised by an army of arbitrary and arrogant international bureaucrats, namely the high representative and assorted other officials.

The economy is a shambles. A recent index of economic freedom published by the *Wall Street Journal* and the Heritage Foundation ranked Bosnia 141st out of 156 countries surveyed—right between Syria and Yemen.

The situation in Kosovo is even worse. Since NATO took control in June 1999, there has been massive "reverse ethnic cleansing." More than 220,000 Serbs and other ethnic minorities—nearly 75 percent of the prewar non-Albanian population—have been driven from the province by the Kosovo Liberation Army. The ethnic cleansing has been accompanied by hundreds of murders and kidnappings.

More ominous, the KLA and its front groups are now fomenting violence in the Presevo Valley—the portion of Serbia next to Kosovo—and in western Macedonia. Greater Albanian nationalism is now the main disruptive element in the Balkans, and NATO forces—including U.S. troops—may soon be called on to combat such expansionism. That would be profoundly dangerous.

Mr. Bush has two possible models for dealing with the Balkan problem:

1. The strategy Dwight Eisenhower employed with the Korean War he inherited from the Truman administration.
2. The strategy Richard Nixon followed with the Vietnam War he inherited from the Johnson administration.

General Eisenhower worked to end the Korean War as soon as possible. He succeeded within months of entering office and enjoyed great public acclaim for ending what had become a frustrating and unpopular venture.

Mr. Nixon, on the other hand, sought to end U.S. involvement in the Vietnam War gradually. That approach proved far less successful. By the spring of 1970—barely a year after he took office—Nixon was already receiving much of the blame for the war and its failures.

The incoming Bush administration should absorb the lesson of those contrasting experiences. The new president is likely to have only a brief window of opportunity to extricate the United States from the Balkan morass before the American people begin to hold him responsible for anything that goes wrong.

If the Bosnia and Kosovo missions turn sour—as they show every sign of doing—a restless public will blame the person occupying the White House at the time. It may not be fair, but it will do President

Bush little good to proclaim in 2002 or 2003 that he inherited a mess from Bill Clinton.

The crusading ventures in the Balkans are the kind of futile diversions of foreign policy resources that the new administration should repudiate. It is in the nation's best interest that Bush make that repudiation quickly and clearly. It is also in his political self-interest.

This article originally appeared in the *Christian Science Monitor*, January 29, 2001.

3. NATO Policy

Introduction

As the Soviet empire disintegrated, the conventional wisdom in the United States and Western Europe was that NATO, which had been formed to contain the USSR, would soon follow its Cold War rival into oblivion. I was less confident of that outcome. Although it was clear that NATO *should* be given a well-earned retirement party, since its mission had been accomplished, it is always hazardous to underestimate the ability of powerful constituencies to preserve an institution that has benefited them. And an assortment of very powerful constituencies had grown up around NATO during its four decades of existence. It was an ominous development that, as early as the autumn of 1989, NATO partisans were already advancing a wide array of (sometimes far-fetched) "alternative missions" for the alliance.

By late 1993, it had become clear to me that not only were the United States and its European allies determined to preserve NATO, they were charting a course to both expand the membership of the alliance and transform its mission from territorial defense to "out-of-area" crisis management. Less than two years later, NATO intervened militarily in Bosnia's civil war. Barely two years after that episode, alliance leaders extended membership invitations to Poland, Hungary, and the Czech Republic.

Those were watershed developments. The Bosnia intervention signaled that NATO was no longer a purely defensive association; it was now a proactive, offensive alliance. That change carried with it an enormous potential to entangle the United States in an assortment of parochial conflicts. The only remaining question was how far out of area the alliance would be willing to venture. That the entire Balkan region had become an arena for NATO military operations became clear in 1999 when the alliance attacked Serbia for that country's behavior in one of its own provinces. Some officials of the Clinton administration wanted to erase all geographic limitations on

NATO's activities and have the alliance defend "Western interests" wherever in the world they might be imperiled. The European members balked at that suggestion, however, and their opposition meant that NATO would remain a Eurocentric body—at least for the time being.

The enlargement of NATO's membership also had important implications for the United States. As the alliance expanded eastward, Washington was undertaking obligations to defend nations in a region that had never before been considered a vital American interest. Given the volatile history of that region, and its proximity to a prickly Russia, it was an obligation that should not be undertaken lightly. That point was especially true since it was clear that the first round of enlargement was not going to be the last. And, indeed, as 2002 draws to a close, NATO leaders show every intention of inviting other nations, including the three Baltic republics, into the fold.

Early on, I cautioned against the promiscuous extension of security guarantees to Central and East European client states—security guarantees that, if ever challenged, could prove to be a disastrous U.S. liability. Unless NATO expansion were simply an exercise in empty symbolism (which is a possibility), the expansion of the alliance's membership was both potentially expensive and potentially dangerous.

I also noted the effect that NATO's decision to expand eastward and become an out-of-area crisis intervention organization was having on Russia's policy. It was revealing that Moscow's growing security ties with such countries as Iran and China coincided almost precisely with the upsurge of NATO's activism. Although the danger of an open breach between Russia and the West has receded somewhat, given Russian president Vladimir Putin's surprisingly accommodationist policies, the long-term danger remains. NATO's (and America's) security obligations to the alliance's new members go on indefinitely. All that would be needed for a major crisis is for one of Putin's successors to decide that a NATO presence on Russia's doorstep is intolerable. It ought to be a firm rule of American foreign policy not to extend security commitments that would be disastrous for the United States to honor. In their dealings with the "new, improved NATO," American officials are violating that cardinal rule.

Bush's NATO Plan Is Timid and Wasteful

President Bush's proposal to withdraw approximately 10 percent of the USA's troops stationed in Europe as part of an overall reduction in NATO and Warsaw Pact conventional forces is little more than timid tokenism.

It may temporarily wrest the diplomatic initiative from Mikhail Gorbachev, but it does not alter the burdensome nature of the USA's NATO obligations.

Equally important, it does not take into account fundamental changes in the international system that are making NATO obsolete.

The Bush withdrawal offer would leave nearly 300,000 U.S. troops in Europe for an indefinite period. That total is approximately the same number as the USA maintained during the years following the Soviet invasion of Czechoslovakia in 1968.

Yet even Bush acknowledges that the Soviet Union is less of an expansionist threat today than it was two decades ago.

If that is true, there is no justification for continuing a large and expensive U.S. military presence on the European continent.

The USA's commitment to NATO imposes an unacceptable burden on American taxpayers. Approximately $160 billion of the USA's current $300 billion military budget is used to defend Western Europe.

The USA spends $1,164 per person on the military while West Germany, the NATO member with the most to lose from a Soviet invasion, spends $454. At the dawn of the Cold War, such a disparity might have been understandable, given the weakness of the USA's European allies and the serious danger of Soviet aggression. But neither condition applies today.

Not only has the Soviet threat receded, but NATO's European members have the economic strength to build defenses adequate to meet any future challenge.

NATO is showing signs of accelerating obsolescence on its 40th anniversary. As the recent acrimonious dispute over the modernization of short-range nuclear weapons demonstrated, the security interests of the USA and its alliance partners are rapidly diverging.

Instead of offering cosmetic changes in a vain effort to preserve NATO, the Bush administration should move boldly to create a post-NATO security strategy for the USA.

The heart of that new strategy should be a proposal for the mutual withdrawal and demobilization of all superpower military forces now stationed in Central Europe (Poland, Czechoslovakia, Hungary and the two Germanys). Such an agreement would eliminate even the vestige of a Soviet threat to Western Europe and would enable the USA to decrease its burdensome NATO commitments.

The new international political environment both permits and justifies a new, more cost-effective strategy for the USA.

It is time to move beyond the Bush administration's troop reduction tokenism at Brussels.

This article originally appeared in *USA Today*, May 31, 1989.

Preserving an Obsolete NATO

The stunning events of the past year have transformed the political landscape of Europe, but they have had little discernible impact on proponents of the NATO alliance and America's military presence on the Continent. Many NATO partisans are so determined to preserve the Cold War status quo that they now embrace an assortment of obsolete, implausible, and frequently contradictory policies. If they succeed, they will continue to saddle American taxpayers with an expensive military commitment despite the waning Soviet threat and the rush by Washington's West European allies to cut their own defense forces and cash in on the "peace dividend." Why NATO partisans seem willing to sacrifice America's well-being in that fashion is a study in the politics of institutional self-preservation.

Die-hard Atlanticists believe that, despite the political transformation of Eastern Europe, NATO and the U.S. military presence on the Continent should be permanent geopolitical fixtures. That is a curious assumption. Why should such arrangements be perpetuated if the Soviets relinquish their political grip on Eastern Europe—and especially if Moscow demonstrates a willingness to end its military occupation of the region? After all, the purpose of an alliance is not simply to have an alliance. Nor should the United States retain its troop presence out of a sense of tradition—especially when that commitment costs American taxpayers $130 billion a year.

NATO advocates, including President Bush, either do not realize or do not care that the alliance's original reason for existence is rapidly becoming irrelevant. NATO was created four decades ago to protect a weak, war-devastated Western Europe from a rapacious Soviet Union that had already extinguished liberty in Eastern Europe. The subsequent U.S. troop commitment that began in 1950 has continued to the present day, even though Western Europe long ago ceased to be a war-ravaged waif incapable of providing for its own defense. As long as the Soviet threat remained, however, enabling the Pentagon to periodically trot out its tables and charts showing overwhelming Warsaw Pact military superiority, American participation in NATO's security arrangements was viewed as indispensable.

But the Soviet threat is hardly what it was in Stalin's—or even Brezhnev's—day. Moscow's new tolerance of political pluralism in Eastern Europe, the de facto dismantling of the Warsaw Pact, means that NATO should be given a well-earned retirement. That cannot be done in the next six months, perhaps, but it should be easily attainable before the end of the century.

Yet retiring the alliance, or even seriously reducing the scope of the U.S. military role, is certainly not on the mind of President Bush, who, for instance, told the nation before the Malta summit that "the American role may change in form but not in fundamentals." The "utopian day when there might not be" a need for NATO "hasn't arrived," he later added, "so the United States must stay involved." Bush's determination to preserve the U.S. military presence was also evident following his proposal in the January 1990 State of the Union address to reduce superpower forces in Central Europe to 195,000 on each side. National Security Advisor Brent Scowcroft quickly squelched speculation that even larger cuts might be forthcoming. The 195,000 figure was a ceiling for the Soviet Union but a floor for the United States, Scowcroft emphasized.

A Public Choice View

NATO partisans, in a practical demonstration of the public choice economic theories that won James Buchanan the Nobel Prize in 1986, have circled the wagons in a desperate attempt to preserve their beleaguered institution. They have also been astonishingly creative in coming up with new reasons not only to maintain NATO but to keep U.S. troops in Europe.

The first rationale is based on outright denial of changes in the Eastern bloc. Gorbachev's internal reforms and Moscow's repeal of the Brezhnev Doctrine are said to be simply a sophisticated Leninist ruse to lull the West into a false sense of security. Soviet expansionist objectives remain fundamentally unaltered, so naturally NATO must be maintained or even strengthened. That school of thought was more prominent before the breathtaking developments in the last half of 1989. Now it seems confined to the political fringe and a few unreconstructed cold warriors, primarily in the armed services leadership.

One must give such defenders of the status quo credit for tenacity. It is difficult for them to keep the faith in the face of mounting evidence that threatens to make them look as quaint as their ideological forbears who still argued in the late 1960s that the Sino-Soviet split was a sham. Probably for that reason, most NATO defenders have moved on to a more sophisticated and plausible response: "nothing's permanent."

Members of the "nothing's permanent" faction concede that the changes in Soviet foreign and domestic policies are genuine and significant, but they doubt their durability. Gorbachev might be overwhelmed by the ethnic turmoil and economic problems in his country and revert to Stalinist tactics to restore order, or his conservative adversaries might stage a palace coup. Consequently, the West must keep up its guard, which naturally requires maintaining NATO with only minor alterations, until it is certain that the changes in the Eastern bloc are permanent.

That view has a number of advocates, including former secretary of defense Caspar Weinberger, who contends that "even if Mr. Gorbachev should be completely honest and sincere in all that he has said, we have no indications whatever of how long he may remain in office, and we do not know who or what his successor would be. Under those circumstances, it would be folly for us to reduce the strength of our military." Within the administration, National Security Council deputy director Robert Gates—a reluctant convert from the "nothing's changed" camp—and, until recently, Secretary of Defense Richard Cheney have been prominent adherents.

Their argument is more plausible because it does contain an element of truth: a reversal of trends in the Soviet Union and Eastern Europe could take place. But even Central Intelligence Agency director William Webster does not believe that such a reversal is likely. Even if it did occur, it would not mean a complete resurgence of the Soviet military threat. Objective economic and political conditions in the Soviet Union will create serious constraints on external adventurism for the foreseeable future. And even an expansionist Soviet regime would find it exceedingly difficult to put the fragmented Warsaw Pact back together as a military organization capable of offensive operations.

Furthermore, the whole argument is insidiously deceptive. Proponents never bother to answer the question of how the permanence of Eastern bloc reforms is to be measured. Will five years of uninterrupted progress be enough? Ten? Twenty? Nor do they acknowledge the ability of the prosperous and populous West European nations to defend themselves should a Soviet military threat reemerge.

The most revealing aspect of the "we can't be sure the reforms are permanent" argument, though, is the marked unwillingness of most Atlanticists to consider phasing out NATO even if the Eastern bloc changes *do* prove enduring. President Bush, for one, posited approximately a century before "the utopian day" might arrive when NATO would not be needed. That assumption raises doubts about whether the professed apprehension concerning the permanence of Soviet bloc reforms is genuine or merely a more sophisticated excuse for maintaining the status quo.

Alternative Missions for NATO

As the magnitude of the changes in Eastern Europe and the Soviet Union has undermined the lack-of-permanence ploy, NATO supporters have fallen back to the final Atlanticist redoubt—finding an "alternative mission" for the alliance. Robert Zoellick, Secretary of State James Baker's counselor, cheerfully acknowledges that the department's policy planning staff is working with the European Affairs Bureau "to look at how you transform established institutions, such as NATO, to serve new missions that will fit the new era." That is not an easy task, however, for NATO has been the quintessential anti-Soviet security arrangement. NATO was established to defend Western Europe against either Soviet blackmail or an all-out Warsaw Pact invasion. The latter danger has now receded into the realm of paranoid fantasy; even such Cold War hard-liners as Richard Perle and James Schlesinger concede that the Warsaw Pact is an empty shell with no military significance. And the prospect of Soviet blackmail seems increasingly improbable as Moscow gropes toward a market economy and a multiparty political system. If NATO is no longer needed to counter such threats, one must ask what on earth its purpose should be.

The creativity of Atlanticists in formulating alternative missions is boundless. Robert Hormats, vice chairman of Goldman Sachs International, writes in *Foreign Affairs* that Western leaders must "expand the range of issues on which NATO engages the common efforts of the European and North American democracies—from student exchanges, to fighting the drug trade, to resisting terrorism, to countering threats to the environment." Hormats is not alone in believing that a military alliance can be transformed into a combination student exchange placement agency and public-sector version of Greenpeace. Former U.S. ambassador to NATO David Abshire also insists that NATO "could coordinate the transfer of environmental-control and energy-conservation technology to the East, thereby benefiting the global ecology."

In the frantic search for new tasks, however, three have emerged as the most prominent candidates. The first, propounds *The Economist*, is to respond to security threats in other regions. But NATO has never been an effective instrument for power projection outside Europe; in fact, the United States has consistently met resistance from its NATO allies to its policies toward Central America, Libya, and the Mideast. The lack of a looming Soviet threat will undoubtedly make such cooperation more rather than less difficult.

That difficulty has become evident in the Persian Gulf crisis. Although the European members of NATO followed Washington's lead in securing a United Nations' condemnation of Iraq's takeover of Kuwait and agreed to support international economic sanctions against Baghdad, the reaction was far different when it came to providing more tangible assistance. For example, the Europeans politely but firmly rebuffed Secretary of State Baker's bid to enlarge NATO's scope of geographic responsibility to include portions of the Middle East. Baker contended that because a NATO member (Turkey) borders on Iraq, the alliance should formulate a collective response to Baghdad's breach of the peace. The European governments responded that it was inappropriate for NATO to take such action.

NATO's general uselessness for out-of-area missions was made even clearer by the paltry European contribution to the U.S.-led "multinational" force in the Persian Gulf. Britain and France initially provided small contingents of air and naval forces but pointedly declined to send in ground units to join the tens of thousands of

U.S. troops pouring into Saudi Arabia. Even their token deployments vastly exceeded those of the other NATO powers. Germany, in particular, insisted that its constitution prohibits sending forces outside the NATO region, despite the arguments of many German constitutional scholars to the contrary. The Persian Gulf operation increasingly looks like a repeat of the multilateral intervention in Korea during the early 1950s in which the United States provided more than 90 percent of the troops and absorbed more than 90 percent of the casualties.

The second alternative role, mentioned prominently by high-level NATO officials, is to "manage" the political transition in Eastern Europe. How a predominantly military association would be able to make a productive contribution to what is a political and economic process has been left, shall we say, a trifle vague. The notion of NATO as an effective political vehicle is especially dubious when one considers the debilitating disagreements that have plagued the alliance over the years. In recent years the members have not even agreed on the seriousness of the Soviet threat, let alone the proper response. The acrimonious U.S.–West German controversy over nuclear modernization in the spring of 1989 was only the most visible manifestation of such discord.

Policing Europe

A third possible task for a "new NATO" is to promote stability in Europe. Put bluntly, Europeans have spent centuries killing each other. Only when the United States (and some would argue the USSR as well, though that point is disputed) deigned to occupy the Continent did peace reign. Therefore our troops should stay. (A more subtle version was the *New Republic's* formulation: "There simply is enough change going on in Europe now without introducing new and unpredictable forces.") President Bush has stressed that theme, asserting that NATO and the U.S. military presence will be needed in the future not to deter a Warsaw Pact invasion (which he concedes is now highly improbable) but to guard against "instability and unpredictability."

But the prospect of greater instability, especially in Eastern Europe, is an argument for a lower U.S. military profile on the Continent. It is difficult to argue that the United States should be unduly concerned about disputes between small European states, since such quarrels would rarely impinge on vital American interests. Indeed, it would be better to insulate the United States from a conflict between, say, Hungary and Romania over the status of Transylvania than to preserve security arrangements that might entangle American troops in it.

Many Americans as well as Europeans have narrowed the stability argument to apply to just one country: Germany.

The United States, it is argued, must maintain troops in Europe (namely West Germany) to contain German power. The *New York Times* reports that members of the State Department's policy planning staff assume that NATO will be needed "more than ever as a mechanism for alleviating friction among the allies, and, in its bluntest form, to help constrain German influence and keep Germany under a Western umbrella." Far blunter was former U.S. Army chief of staff E. C. Meyer who propounded a new version of moral equivalence: a reunified Germany (along with a more assertive Japan) will replace Soviet aggression as the major threat to Western security. (That was not the first time NATO was viewed as anti-German; Lord Ismay, NATO's first secretary general, once remarked that the alliance existed to "keep the Russians out, the Americans in, and the Germans down.")

The cynicism of the convenient reemergence of a "German threat" is astonishing. Not long ago the Federal Republic was being hailed as NATO's brave front-line state and the West Germans as dedicated allies in the struggle to contain the Soviet menace. Now those prosperous, freedom-loving burghers have apparently reverted to being the rapacious Hun; avuncular Helmut Kohl is projected to become the new Kaiser Wilhelm; and the 495,000-member Bundeswehr, facing cuts of one-fifth by the mid-1990s, is deemed capable of threatening a Soviet military nearly 10 times its size backed by thousands of nuclear warheads.

Atlanticists have really entered the conceptual Twilight Zone when they think it reasonable for NATO's primary mission in the 1990s to be the containment of the alliance's most vibrant European member. While history can never be forgotten, it also cannot justify obsolete alliances. (Else we would need a mechanism to constrain a potential Napoleonic revival in France.) The German containment thesis seems more the product of a desperate search for a "necessary enemy" to justify NATO's continued existence than of any reasonable geopolitical analysis. Ironically, some East European leaders,

who would supposedly be the most uneasy about German reunification, have been the first to denounce the hypocrisy. Czech foreign
minister Jiri Dientsbier dismissed the containment of German power
rationale as "a new argument developed just for the occasion" to
justify a continued U.S. troop presence.

NATO's Vested Interests

But then, necessity is the proverbial mother of invention. There are
innumerable vested interests that are jeopardized by any significant
change in NATO. The American military, and especially the U.S.
Army with its 764,000 personnel, faces the prospect of deep cuts—
and the resulting loss of institutional prestige and power. Before
the formation of NATO the United States had never fielded a peacetime army of more than 200,000 men. Even the Army's most imagina-
tive defenders would be hard-pressed to find a plausible mission
for large numbers of armored and infantry divisions if the European
commitment comes to an end. The defense-industrial establishment
is also at risk whenever military spending slows. And so is much
of the intellectual establishment, the think tank scholars, academics,
and government consultants who have built their careers around
the issues associated with the continued division of Europe. Someone
who has spent his career counting NATO and Warsaw Pact tanks
and artillery pieces will probably feel like the East German border
guard who, after his government opened the Berlin Wall, complained: "It's not good. We will lose our jobs."

If NATO's original mission of protecting Western Europe from the
USSR has been fulfilled, then the alliance—in contrast to American
political, economic, and cultural engagement in Europe—is no
longer needed. We should celebrate its success and enjoy the financial benefits of reduced military obligations. But the tenacious efforts
of NATO partisans to preserve the alliance suggest that obsolete
institutions are even more durable than old soldiers, who, intoned
Gen. Douglas MacArthur, "never die, they just fade away." NATO
is not fading away; it is trying to achieve organizational immortality.

This article, coauthored with Doug Bandow, originally appeared in *Cato Policy Report*,
September/October 1990.

United States Must Shake Its NATO Habit

Ever since NATO was established, U.S. political leaders have been
urging the European nations to assume more responsibility for their

own defense and to pay a larger portion of the cost. Washington has also consistently expressed its support for greater European unity on both economic and security matters.

Despite such official enthusiasm for a strong "European pillar" to support NATO, U.S. policymakers have, in reality, always been profoundly ambivalent about their European allies' taking greater initiative. Secretary of Defense Dick Cheney's opposition to the creation of a "rapid response force" under the auspices of the European Community is merely the latest manifestation of that ambivalence.

Even during the Cold War, Washington viewed with suspicion any signs that European powers were pursuing independent policies, such as Bonn's Ostpolitik strategy in the 1970s or Chancellor Helmut Kohl's reunification overtures to Moscow in the weeks following the opening of the Berlin Wall. U.S. officials were even more upset when the NATO allies dared to oppose American policy preferences on such issues as the Arab-Israeli dispute and the Soviet gas-pipeline project.

Washington's uneasiness about a meaningful European security role has become even more apparent now that the Soviet threat has receded and the maintenance of alliance unity at all costs seems less imperative. National Security Advisor Brent Scowcroft epitomized that attitude when he complained recently that the Western European nations were acting increasingly through the European Community on security issues and tending to "present the United States with previously developed positions."

What the United States has always wanted is the best of both worlds: a democratic Europe strong enough to relieve the United States of some of its security burdens but not so strong as to challenge U.S. primacy. Sharing alliance costs is one thing; sharing decision-making authority is quite another.

Washington's frantic efforts to find alternative missions for NATO after the collapse of the Warsaw Pact and U.S. officials' repeated assertions that NATO must remain the mechanism for ensuring European security in the post–Cold War era are recent expressions of the desire to preserve U.S. primacy.

Such efforts are doomed to fail. It is becoming evident even to NATO's most ardent supporters that a Cold War military alliance is ill suited to deal with the more subtle and complex security problems of post–Cold War Europe. And it is unrealistic to expect the populous and economically vibrant European nations to continue to defer to Washington on political or military issues. Indeed, if U.S. leaders insist on preserving their virtual monopoly on decisionmaking, the long smoldering European resentment may explode into open rebellion.

Theoretically, Washington might move to resolve the problem by accepting full European equality in determining alliance policy. But that change is unlikely. Despite their professed enthusiasm for multilateral security arrangements, U.S. leaders have always sought to preserve decisionmaking autonomy for the United States. There has never been any enthusiasm for subjecting American policy on important security matters to vetoes by foreign governments, even friendly ones.

Given the growing perception in the U.S. policy community that America is "the sole remaining superpower," the desire to avoid external constraints on U.S. actions will increase, not diminish.

More important, the post–Cold War international system does not lend itself to a true transatlantic security partnership. Although U.S. and European security interests overlap, they are by no means congruent. Even during the Cold War, there were significant areas of divergence (e.g., Middle East policy and East-West trade). That divergence is likely to become more pronounced in a post–Cold War setting in which the common Soviet threat no longer provides the glue to ensure alliance cohesion.

U.S. leaders are reluctant to accept the reality that a strong, prosperous Western Europe will adopt security strategies tailored to its own distinct interests. Those strategies will be increasingly independent of the United States and may sometimes run directly counter to U.S. wishes, but it is unrealistic to expect the European nations to remain pliant junior partners in a security system run by Washington. That may have been an acceptable arrangement in the early stages of the Cold War when Western Europe was still traumatized by the devastating effects of World War II, but it is no longer viable.

Instead of vainly striving to preserve U.S. preeminence in an obsolescent alliance and getting mired in rancorous disputes about burden sharing, American leaders should learn to accept European security independence with a maximum of grace.

This article originally appeared in the *Christian Science Monitor*, June 19, 1991.

Admit Poland as a NATO Member?

Proposals to expand NATO have recently become a growth industry on both sides of the Atlantic.

Poland, the Czech Republic, and Hungary are the most frequently mentioned candidates for membership, but advocates of expansion also seek to extend NATO's security benefits to other countries in Central and Eastern Europe.

Proponents were encouraged in late August when Russian president Boris Yeltsin indicated that his government would not object to Poland's joining the alliance. The fear that Moscow might regard NATO's incorporation of Poland as a provocative act had inhibited members of the "expand NATO" crowd from pushing their agenda. With that obstacle apparently removed, the campaign to transform the alliance has gained new momentum.

Such proposals are ill-advised. Even many NATO diplomats concede that Mr. Yeltsin's accommodating attitude is not necessarily shared by Russia's political and military hierarchy. A future Russian regime might well adopt a more confrontational position.

The possibility of renewed Russian opposition is only one reason membership invitations should not be extended to Poland or other Central and East European states.

That step would convert an alliance designed to achieve clear and limited security objectives in a relatively stable Cold War setting into a nebulous crisis-management organization in a highly unstable post–Cold War setting.

Even if the formal membership of the alliance is not expanded, the de facto extension of NATO's security jurisdiction eastward would be fraught with danger.

During the Cold War, NATO's purpose was straightforward: to deter Soviet aggression against Western Europe. Most Americans accepted the risks entailed in the obligation, fearing that otherwise the Soviet Union—which already posed a serious threat to America's security—would gain control of the population and technology of Western Europe and become an even greater menace.

NATO's proposed new mission to prevent "instability" in Eastern Europe has no comparable relevance to America's security interests. With the demise of the Soviet Union, the United States faces no serious great power threat to its well-being, nor is it likely to do so in the foreseeable future. The conflicts in the Balkans and along the perimeter of the former Soviet empire may be important to the parties involved, but they are parochial.

Extending NATO's security jurisdiction would entangle the United States in the myriad ethnic, religious and territorial disputes of Central and Eastern Europe without any compelling need or prospective benefit. There already has been some friction between Poland and Lithuania over the treatment of Lithuania's Polish minority. Yet that problem is minor compared with the festering disputes that exist elsewhere in the region.

For the United States to involve itself in such conflicts through an expanded NATO would be foreign policy masochism.

The authors of one celebrated article state candidly that "NATO must go out of area or it will go out of business." But if NATO has accomplished the mission for which it was designed, then perhaps it *should* go out of business.

Today, NATO is an alliance in search of a purpose. American leaders should firmly reject suggestions to enlarge NATO's security jurisdiction. Indeed, they should begin to give the alliance a well-earned retirement.

As part of that process, Washington must urge the European states to form new security structures—"Europeans-only organizations"—appropriate for dealing with the purely regional problems and quarrels of the post–Cold War era.

This article originally appeared in the *Washington Times*, September 19, 1993.

NATO Expansion: Unsafe at Any Speed

As President Clinton prepares for this week's NATO summit, he faces criticism from European leaders, Capitol Hill, and an assortment of pundits who feel that the administration is proceeding too slowly in its plans to extend alliance membership to members of the former Warsaw Pact. Yet the very idea of NATO expansion makes no sense for America strategically, economically or in terms of domestic politics. Neither the American public nor the alliance itself is prepared for the extension of defense commitments to cover one of the world's most dangerous and turbulent regions.

Here at home, our budget deficits are still astronomical. The Pentagon is struggling to field the forces needed to fight two near-simultaneous Persian Gulf–size wars. The U.S. military has been humbled in Somalia and scared away from Haiti and Bosnia. And the American people indicate by word and deed that they want a cost-effective, risk-averse foreign policy.

True, the president's Partnership for Peace plan is the tamest of several NATO expansion proposals in the air. Sen. Richard Lugar (R-Ind.), for example, suggests that the alliance extend membership invitations immediately to several of the former Warsaw Pact countries.

Former secretary of state James A. Baker III and former UN ambassador Jeane Kirkpatrick go even further, urging the expansion of NATO to embrace most of the former Soviet republics, including Ukraine and Russia, creating an utterly unwieldy military association spanning every time zone on the planet.

By contrast, Clinton's Partnership for Peace seeks to reassure the countries of the former Soviet bloc of Western support while postponing the issue of formal NATO membership even for such prime candidates as Poland and the Czech Republic. To these countries, the Clinton plan would offer joint military exercises and establish other forms of security cooperation. Nevertheless, like its more ambitious counterparts, the Clinton plan assumes that a higher Western— and particularly American—military profile in Central and Eastern Europe can stabilize the region and keep the increasingly surly Russians at bay.

Given the rise of Russian reactionaries, the U.S. desire to "do something" about the region is understandable. But expanding NATO in any form and at any speed is a fatally flawed idea. It lacks meaningful public support and it overestimates America's power, resources and influence. It also misreads the nature of real U.S. interests in Europe. In fact, with the Cold War over, the arguments for NATO's future in any form have become so arcane and ethereal that they cast doubt on the value to America of continuing its dominant role in European security.

That any NATO expansion plan is a nonstarter with the American people is clearest from the administration's handling of the issue. This potential watershed in post–Cold War American foreign policy has been largely planned behind closed doors. Before Vice President Gore's 11th-hour address on Jan. 6, no administration official had discussed the Partnership for Peace—much less the possible costs and risks—in a high-profile speech.

84

Yet as Clinton and the rest of the foreign policy establishment should know by now, significant security initiatives are not sustainable without explicit public endorsement. Mission creep led to disaster in Somalia. Will mission leap in vastly more challenging Eastern and Central Europe really produce happier results? At the very least, a wide-ranging public and congressional debate similar to the one that accompanied the creation of NATO 45 years ago is needed. Public skepticism about an expanded NATO, moreover, would be amply justified. As revealed in mid-December, the administration's existing national security strategy will be tens of billions of dollars short of funds over the next five years. Departing Secretary of Defense Les Aspin has acknowledged that the latest proposed defense spending levels would prevent the United States from tackling a major peacekeeping mission on top of its other security obligations.

More peacekeeping, however, would be the least of the new missions facing the U.S. military if NATO expands. The Russians clearly regard NATO expansion as a threat. When Lithuania requested NATO membership last week, Russian president Boris Yeltsin objected, saying it would "prompt a negative public opinion reaction in Russia" and could destabilize the region. Should our worst nightmares about Yeltsin's authoritarian rivals come true, U.S. troops could be confronting Russian forces on the border of the Russian Federation itself—as part of an obligation to defend new NATO members.

Moreover, the amount of help that could be expected from the West European members of NATO for missions in Eastern Europe would be problematical at best. Whatever their theoretical obligations to fellow treaty signatories, their military budgets and forces are shrinking faster than America's. The gap between NATO's pretensions and its military resources would widen.

Even more important, advocates of expansion confuse our fundamental stakes in Europe with lesser matters, imagining vulnerabilities that no longer exist and embracing policies that cannot meet their own grandiose objectives, much less serve America's needs. Despite several generations of misleading boilerplate, America's core interest in Europe has always been relatively narrow—to prevent any power or combination of hostile powers from controlling the major industrial states of Western Europe.

A major motive for U.S. entry into both world wars as well as Washington's willingness to join NATO was to ensure that this vast reservoir of economic and military strength was not mobilized against America. Another less openly discussed interest has been to help Western Europe become stable enough to stay at peace and remain a profitable economic partner. America's NATO defense umbrella, in particular, aimed not only at protecting Western Europe from the Soviets but at smothering that area's historically bloody politics. Given the specific, limited nature of America's European interests—especially the focus on Western rather than Eastern Europe—the lessons for the present are clear, but they are not what the NATO expansionists believe. Leading NATO on a mission to impose stability on a fractious Eastern Europe would be a utopian attempt to micromanage the Continent's security. That is a pipe dream, not a policy.

Precisely because Eastern Europe is so conflict ridden, the United States cannot escape identifying priorities. Contrary to alarmist scenarios—replete with images of a second cold war, a Fourth Reich or toppling geopolitical dominoes—Eastern Europe's current conflicts, however numerous, are parochial. American leaders must learn to distinguish between those few troubles and conflicts truly capable of engulfing all of Europe or of being exploited significantly by a powerful aggressor and those likely to stay local. An expanded NATO would be a blunt policy instrument that would make such discrimination difficult, if not impossible.

Proponents of NATO's expansion insist that a U.S.-led effort to stabilize the East would calm the entire Continent and thereby protect U.S. interests by benefiting Western Europe as well. But that argument fails on two counts.

First, many of Western Europe's most pressing troubles are only marginally related to Eastern European security issues. The most severe tensions center around uncompetitive industries, sluggish rates of economic growth and social strains associated with immigration not only from Eastern Europe but the Third World. Neither NATO in its current incarnation nor an expanded version can have a meaningful impact on such nonmilitary problems.

Second, in the unlikely event that the East could be pacified, it would entail more than merely offering a "partnership" or even NATO membership to the nations in that region. To be credible, such a mission would require NATO—including American—trip-wire forces on the ground throughout Eastern Europe and the former Soviet republics.

Yet think of the frightful military planning issues raised by such deployments. The Central and East European countries are threatened not only by the possibility of Russian expansionism in the long term but more immediately by their own myriad ethnic, religious and territorial disputes. The United States could easily find itself in the middle of an armed conflict between two NATO members or between a new NATO member and an obscure regional or internal adversary.

To make matters worse, the embryonic democracies in Eastern Europe are noticeably fragile and unstable. Russia is not the only Eastern country vulnerable to a takeover by authoritarian political elements. Therefore, throughout Eastern Europe, the same military forces eligible to receive weapons, intelligence and training as a benefit of a NATO partnership today could become enemies tomorrow.

The proliferation of NATO expansion schemes has more to do with the politics of institutional self-preservation than with bona fide U.S. security interests. Today NATO is an alliance in search of purpose. Lugar states candidly that NATO must "go out of area" or "it will go out of business." But the responsibility of U.S. policymakers is to protect the interests of the American people, not to preserve an alliance for its own sake.

American leaders should not only reject suggestions to enlarge NATO's membership or security jurisdiction, they should start moving in precisely the opposite direction—toward facilitating greater European military self-reliance. The West Europeans certainly have the capability to build whatever forces are needed to protect their own security and to resolve quarrels among themselves. The member-states of the European Union collectively have more than 350 million people and a $6 trillion a year economy. Consistent with America's limited, tightly focused interests on the Continent, Washington must encourage the European states to form new security structures or to strengthen such existing bodies as the Western European Union and the Franco-German Europcorps as eventual replacements for NATO.

Given our inevitably limited financial and military resources, America's future foreign policy success will hinge on defining our own interests much more soberly and precisely than during the "anything goes" days of the Cold War. We need to understand that "turmoil" does not always equal "threat," and that noble intentions do not automatically create good policies. Dropping the foolish plans to expand NATO is an excellent place to start.

This article, coauthored with Alan Tonelson, originally appeared in the *Washington Post*, January 9, 1994.

NATO Solidarity and Bosnia

The Clinton administration seems determined to deploy approximately 20,000 troops as part of a NATO force to implement a peace agreement in Bosnia. Why should America undertake a mission that entails a multitude of obvious risks? An increasingly prominent rationale is that the United States has an obligation to assist its NATO allies, whose troops are already on the ground. Reneging on promises to lead a Bosnian peacekeeping enterprise, it is said, would irreparably damage Washington's credibility and shatter NATO. Although administration officials generally concede that Bosnia itself is not a vital U.S. interest, they insist that the preservation of the alliance is crucial to America's security.

The "NATO solidarity" justification is extremely dubious. Even during the Cold War, the European members of NATO did not exhibit an abundance of loyalty to the United States. They certainly were never willing to make blood sacrifices when their own vital interests were not at stake—which is what the United States is being asked to do in Bosnia.

Risking a Vietnam-style entanglement simply to help the European allies would be ironic, to say the least. During the 1960s, those same allies refused to assist the U.S. war effort in Southeast Asia despite pleas from Secretary of State Dean Rusk and other officials in Lyndon Johnson's administration. Indeed, most NATO countries traded extensively with Hanoi throughout the Vietnam War. Later, they supported other pro-Soviet regimes, such as Nicaragua's Sandinista government, economically and politically. Several NATO governments refused to allow U.S. transports to resupply Israel from European airports in the 1973 Middle East War and, in 1986, denied American bombers overflight rights for the attack on Libya.

There is little evidence of greater alliance solidarity since the end of the Cold War. Even as they seek Washington's help in Bosnia, the Europeans have spurned U.S. attempts to economically isolate Iran, despite the Tehran regime's lengthy record of sponsoring terrorism.

The point is not that the NATO allies have always been wrong. In fact, their policy positions are sometimes more sensible than those embraced by the United States. But the record demonstrates that the European powers regularly put their narrow national interests ahead of any notion of obligations to their U.S. ally—even when American lives are endangered. They have never been inclined to sacrifice national interests for the abstraction of NATO unity.

America should adopt the same attitude when asked to risk its troops to police a fragile Bosnia peace accord. Gen. John Shalikashvili, chairman of the Joint Chiefs of Staff, concedes that "from a purely military standpoint" the West European nations could undertake the Bosnia mission on their own. They should be told to decide for themselves whether to incur the costs and risks of doing so.

An uncompromising refusal to squander American lives in Bosnia would undoubtedly have an impact on NATO. At the very least, it would require U.S. and West European leaders to ponder whether the alliance has a meaningful purpose in the post–Cold War era. Such a reappraisal is long overdue in any case.

The attempt by Atlanticists to make Bosnia a litmus test of NATO's continued relevance shows how dramatically the alliance's mandate has expanded since the end of the Cold War to include missions never even remotely contemplated by NATO's founders and wisely avoided by subsequent policymakers. NATO was conceived as a relatively straightforward military alliance to deter a Soviet attack on Western Europe. The underlying objective was consistent with a goal of U.S. foreign policy since the days of Thomas Jefferson— preventing a potential aggressor from controlling the Continent's resources and turning them on the New World. Bosnia is unlikely to save NATO from epochal change. The alliance cannot easily be transformed from an organization to guard the territory of member-states against attack by a powerful enemy into an organization to conduct out-of-area interventions in murky, parochial conflicts. Those who argue that the United States must deploy troops in Bosnia to preserve NATO confuse means and ends. NATO, or any other alliance, is merely one means to an important end—protecting the security of the American people. The preservation of an alliance should never become an end in itself.

President Clinton should notify the West European powers that, previous statements to the contrary, the United States will not risk American lives in Bosnia for any reason. That action might well have some unpleasant diplomatic repercussions. But the president ought to weigh those against the likely repercussions, including political ones, if body bags from an ill-conceived NATO peacekeeping mission come home to Dover Air Force Base. Few Americans are likely to be impressed by the argument that it was worth suffering those casualties to preserve the unity of NATO.

This article originally appeared in the *Washington Times*, October 25, 1995.

Beware of Entanglements

President Clinton's speeches during his European trip have been dripping with nostalgia for the "glory days" of the Marshall Plan and the creation of NATO in the late 1940s.

Invoking images of that era is designed to make the case that the United States can promote security, stability and prosperity in Eastern Europe today just as it did in Western Europe a half century ago.

Clinton's reasoning confirms that nostalgia is a poor basis for foreign policy.

There are tenacious but inaccurate myths about the Marshall Plan and America's overall role in Western Europe during the early years of the Cold War. According to the conventional wisdom, Western Europe might still be wallowing in poverty and despair had it not been for the Marshall Plan and other manifestations of U.S. "leadership."

George Mason University economist Tyler Cowen debunked such myths years ago, showing that no correlation existed between the amount of Marshall Plan aid specific nations received and their subsequent rates of economic growth. Their domestic economic policies were the decisive factor.

True, the Marshall Plan and the creation of NATO prodded the Western Europeans to bury their differences and work together. But the presence of a powerful and aggressive adversary, the Soviet Union, was even more important in fostering unity.

It is wishful thinking to assume that a vaguely defined aid program and the enlargement of NATO can promote similar harmony and stability in Eastern Europe under vastly different conditions.

Even if one accepts the argument that U.S. leadership was crucial in pacifying Western Europe, there is little prospect of comparable success in Eastern Europe. Many of the sources of conflict in Western Europe had been ebbing long before the Marshall Plan and NATO.

The Anglo-French antagonism, the complicated dynastic rivalries and a host of other issues that once plagued the western portion of the Continent had already receded into history. The principal remaining source of tension—the Franco-German territorial feud over Alsace-Lorraine—had also been decisively resolved with Germany's crushing defeat in World War II.

By contrast, Eastern Europe remains a cauldron of boundary disputes, ethnic and religious rivalries and fragile, unstable political and economic systems. The process of nation building in Eastern Europe today resembles that in Western Europe two or three centuries ago, with all the attendant turbulence.

Clinton's attempt to recreate Washington's Western European policy of the late 1940s in a volatile Eastern Europe is dangerously misguided.

America is far more likely to become entangled in Eastern Europe's problems than it is to be the region's savior.

This article originally appeared in *USA Today*, May 30, 1997.

The Three Booby Traps of NATO Expansion

Both the Clinton administration and the Senate Republican leadership are using a full-court press to get an immediate Senate vote on NATO expansion. Senators should resist such pressure for a rush to judgment before addressing the numerous problems associated with NATO expansion.

Proponents frequently act as though NATO is a democratic honor society that the nations of Central and Eastern Europe should be able to join. But NATO is a military alliance, and the decision to extend U.S. security guarantees to new members is serious business.

Three lethal booby traps await the United States if NATO expansion goes forward.

Any Enemy of My Ally Becomes My Enemy

Before senators welcome Poland, the Czech Republic and Hungary into NATO's ranks, they should assess potential conflicts that might embroil those countries. It would be a sobering exercise. Relations between Poland and neighboring Belarus, already tense, are rapidly deteriorating. Belarus recently recalled its ambassador from Warsaw and has banned Polish priests from entering the country. President Alexander Lukashenko ominously accuses the Polish minority in Belarus's western provinces of disloyalty.

Hungary has troubled relations with three of its neighbors—Romania, Slovakia and Serbia. Slovakia's prime minister continuously slanders the large Hungarian minority in his country and late last year proposed a population transfer that would send tens of thousands of ethnic Hungarians back to Hungary.

Relations between Hungary and Serbia are even worse. Indeed, the treatment of the Hungarian minority in Serbia's province of Vojvodina mirrors Belgrade's repression of the Albanians in Kosovo. Vojvodina has the potential to explode just as Kosovo has now done.

Thus, NATO expansion could entangle America in numerous murky, parochial disputes among Central and East European countries. Do Americans really want U.S. troops in the middle of a conflict between Hungary and Slovakia, or Hungary and Serbia, or Poland and Belarus? Yet NATO expansion entails precisely that sort of danger.

Poisoning the Relationship with Russia

The conventional wisdom is that, since the signing of the Founding Act between Russia and NATO, Moscow no longer opposes NATO expansion. Nothing could be further from the truth. A recent op-ed by Russia's ambassador to the United States makes it clear that Russian leaders regard even the first round of expansion as an unfriendly act. Any subsequent round, especially one that tried to incorporate the Baltic republics, would risk a military collision with a nuclear-armed great power.

Indeed, the Founding Act itself could become a source of recrimination. U.S. officials insist that the agreement gives Russia "a voice, not a veto" over NATO policy, but that is not the way Russian officials have interpreted the Founding Act. President Boris Yeltsin assured the Duma that the act gave Russia a veto over invitations to new members beyond the first round as well as over future "out-of-area" NATO missions, for example in the Balkans. U.S. and Russian officials cannot both be right.

Russia is reacting badly even to the initial round of expansion. Moscow has responded to NATO's encroachment by forging closer ties with both Iran and Iraq and undermining U.S. policy throughout the Middle East. Still more worrisome are the growing political and military links between Russia and China. Moscow and Beijing speak openly of a "strategic partnership," and China has become Russia's largest arms customer—something that would have been unthinkable a few years ago.

If the United States drifts into a new cold war with Russia because Washington insists on giving security guarantees to a collection of small Central and East European states, that will go down in history as a colossal policy blunder.

A Financial Black Hole

NATO and the Clinton administration now insist that the alliance can be expanded for a paltry $1.5 billion over 10 years. That conclusion differs sharply from an earlier Congressional Budget Office (CBO) estimate of $61 billion to $125 billion over 15 years and the Pentagon's own original estimate of $27 billion to $35 billion over 13 years. The latest NATO and administration projection doesn't even pass the straight-face test. It is a politically driven document that reflects the inability of the proposed new members and the unwillingness of the West European countries to pick up the real financial tab.

Johns Hopkins University professor Michael Mandelbaum aptly describes NATO expansion as "the mother of all unfunded mandates." If expansion is not merely an exercise in empty political symbolism, even the CBO estimate could prove to be conservative. Moreover, none of the estimates takes into account the probable costs of subsequent rounds of expansion, yet administration leaders insist that they will occur.

In light of those troubling facts, the Senate should at least conduct a lengthy, comprehensive debate on NATO expansion, not rush through the proceedings as if the issue was akin to designating National Wildflower Week. After all, the decision may determine whether American troops someday have to fight and die in Eastern Europe.

This article originally appeared in *The Hill*, March 18, 1998.

The "New NATO" Creates Instability in Europe

The decision taken by NATO leaders in 1997 to invite Poland, Hungry, and the Czech Republic to join the alliance was a watershed event. For the first time, NATO undertook security responsibilities in Central and Eastern Europe. Although the alliance did not embark on a second round of membership expansion at its Washington summit meeting in April 1999, additional enlargement seems likely at some point. President Clinton and Secretary of State Madeleine Albright emphasized that NATO membership is theoretically open to any European democracy. Albright has gone even further, asserting that no democratic country will be excluded because of where it is located on the map—a clear reference to the aspirations of the three Baltic republics and a display of brazen contempt for Russia's sensitivity about the issue.

While NATO enlarges its membership, another equally momentous change has been taking place in the alliance. When NATO was first established in 1949, it was explicitly designed to defend the territorial integrity of its member-states. Indeed, Article 6 of the North Atlantic Treaty described the region to be covered, lest there be any implication that the United States was undertaking to protect the colonial holdings of its new West European allies.

NATO forces never fired a shot in anger during the Cold War and the alliance's first military operation did not involve the defense of a member from attack. Instead, that initial mission took place in Bosnia, with NATO aircraft bombing Bosnian Serb positions and the alliance trying to prop up the Muslim-dominated government in Sarajevo. Later, NATO took responsibility for implementing the Dayton Accords by deploying a peacekeeping contingent in Bosnia, where it remains today.

New Mission

Not content with the futile and seemingly endless nation-building mission in Bosnia, NATO is meddling in the conflict between Serbia and its restive, predominantly Albanian province of Kosovo. The bombing campaign against Serbia is an even more dramatic expansion of NATO's post–Cold War mission. At least in the case of Bosnia, the alliance was asked to take military action by the Bosnian government (albeit a regime of dubious legitimacy that controlled less than half the country's territory). In the latest intervention, NATO has launched air strikes on a sovereign state that had not attacked or threatened to attack an alliance member or, for that matter, even a neighboring state. NATO, in other words, now asserts the right to bomb a country for refusing to accept an alliance-dictated peace settlement to an internal dispute in that country.

Defenders of the Balkan interventions insist that a new NATO—something more akin to a Euro-Atlantic collective security organization than to a traditional military alliance—is evolving and indeed must evolve if NATO is to address Europe's real security concerns in the post–Cold War era. That attitude is evident in President Clinton's comment during a May 1997 speech that "NATO, initially conceived to face a clear-cut and massive threat, is now a lighter, more flexible organization adapted to its new crisis management and peacekeeping missions. This alliance that is renovating itself is no longer that of the Cold War." On another occasion he stated, "It will be an alliance directed no longer against a hostile bloc of nations, but instead designed to advance the security of every democracy in Europe—NATO's old members, new members, and non-members alike." There is little doubt that the Clinton foreign policy team sees the missions in Bosnia and Kosovo as a model for future NATO enterprises. Indeed, the transformation of NATO's focus has been both breathtaking and alarming. NATO was once an alliance to keep Western Europe—a major strategic and economic prize—out of the orbit of an aggressively expansionist superpower, the Soviet Union. It has now become the babysitter of the Balkans.

As the leader of the "new NATO," the United States is assuming expensive and thankless responsibilities. The Bosnia mission has already cost American taxpayers nearly $12 billion, and the meter is still running. NATO's intervention in Kosovo could prove even more costly. The administration already asked Congress for $6 billion in emergency funding to cover America's share of the war's expense through the end of the 1999 fiscal year. The GOP-controlled Congress contends that $6 billion is woefully inadequate to rectify the strain the air campaign has imposed on the U.S. military and insists that some $11 billion is needed. If NATO escalates the war by introducing ground forces, the costs could skyrocket. And, as in Bosnia, even if the United States and its allies "win," the "victory" will simply be a prelude to expensive peacekeeping and nation-building efforts for Kosovo and its neighbors that would likely keep the United States entangled in the Balkans for decades.

Even more ominous, the out-of-area adventures in the Balkans do not fully satisfy the ambitions of some "new NATO" enthusiasts.

Former secretary of state Warren Christopher and former secretary of defense William Perry suggest that the alliance become an instrument for the projection of force wherever in the world the West's "collective interests" are threatened. In a moment of exuberance, Albright stated that NATO should be prepared to deal with unpleasant developments "from the Middle East to Central Africa."

The key rationale for a new NATO focused on out-of-area missions is to prevent the specter of "instability" in Europe (and perhaps beyond)—especially in the countries recently liberated from communism. Aside from the important question of whether the United States should incur the costs and risks of pursuing such an amorphous goal, NATO's strategy has been counterproductive in any case. The alliance's air war against Serbia has created further instability in the Balkans. Belgrade's response to the air strikes was to intensify ground operations against secessionist forces in Kosovo, leading to a massive outflow of refugees that has overwhelmed the meager financial and logistical resources in neighboring Macedonia and Albania. The influx of Albanian Kosovar refugees also threatens to disrupt Macedonia's delicate ethnic and political balance, and the war itself has led to bitter domestic controversies—including violent demonstrations against the alliance. NATO's bombing raids have destroyed numerous bridges on the Danube, effectively closing southeastern Europe's most important waterway to commerce. That action has already had a serious adverse impact on the fragile economies of Bulgaria and other countries.

Russian Fears

Worst of all, the "new NATO" is rapidly poisoning relations with Russia. Russia reacted badly even to the initial round of enlargement, arguing (correctly) that it violated Western pledges at the time of Germany's reunification that NATO would not move eastward. Russians across the political spectrum are determined to prevent additional rounds of expansion. The defense minister recently warned NATO that admitting the Baltic republics would cross a "red line" that no Russian government could tolerate.

If NATO'S intrusion into Eastern Europe wasn't enough to alarm the Russians, the United States and other NATO members are trying to establish a zone of influence along Russia's southern flank. Through the Partnership for Peace program, NATO has already conducted joint military exercises with Kazakhstan. The U.S. general who commanded that mission boasted that it showed the United States' ability to deploy effective military power in any region of the world. Turkey and the United States have engaged in a multiyear effort to channel the new oil production of the Caspian Basin through a pipeline that would run from Azerbaijan to the Turkish port of Ceyhan. U.S. officials have leaked statements to the media emphasizing that an important motive for that pipeline route is to undercut both Iranian and Russian influence in the region. Azerbaijan has asked to join NATO, and Azeri leaders have suggested that the United States establish a military base in their country. Although U.S. officials decline that invitation, they hint that American forces might be willing to use bases that remain under Azeri control. Finally, at the NATO summit meeting in April, the foreign ministers of the alliance issued a statement expressing NATO's concern about the continuing violence in the Caucasus and urged Georgia, Armenia, and Azerbaijan to settle their differences. That was a not terribly subtle declaration that the Caucasus, like the Balkans before it, is now a region in which NATO has a legitimate interest. Such developments were hardly calculated to reassure the Russians about the alliance's allegedly benign intentions.

Growing Anti-Western Sentiment

Moscow's reaction to NATO's military coercion of Serbia has been far more strident than its response to the alliance's political inroads on Russia's western and southern flanks. That should not be surprising. The bombing campaign discredited the West's soothing assurances that Russia had nothing to fear from NATO's enlargement because NATO was a purely defensive alliance. Whatever else one might conclude about the intervention in the Balkans, it shows conclusively that NATO is now a proactive, offensive military association.

That point was not lost on the Russians. Prime Minister Yevgeny Primakov turned his plane around in midflight across the Atlantic when it became clear that the alliance would proceed with air strikes even as he was scheduled to be in Washington for high-level talks. Alliance leaders could scarcely have chosen a more graphic way of displaying disdain for long-standing Russian interests in the Balkans or for Russia's status as a great power.

The Kremlin has responded to the attack on Serbia with the kind of shrill rhetoric not heard since the worst days of the Cold War. Large and sometimes violent anti-NATO demonstrations have erupted in Moscow and other cities. Pro-democratic Russian political leaders such as Yegor Gaidar, Grigory Yavlinsky, and Alexei Arbatov have warned their friends in the West that there is now an unprecedented degree of genuine anti-Western (especially anti-American) sentiment among the Russian people. Those leaders fear that NATO's actions may produce another surge of domestic support for communist and ultranationalist factions.

NATO leaders appear to be succumbing to the temptation to dismiss Russian anger as being of no great consequence. After all, given the pervasive economic woes in that country, the continuing dependence on financial aid provided by the Western-controlled IMF, and the disarray in Russia's military, there is no way that Moscow can challenge NATO directly. That is all true, but it would be a serious mistake to base U.S. or NATO policy on the assumption that Russia will remain weak forever. One should never equate a hibernating bear with a dead bear.

Moreover, even in its weakened state, Russia can take relatively low-cost, high-leverage actions that are calculated to make life difficult for the United States and its NATO allies. Moscow has already responded to NATO's encroachment by forging closer ties with both Iran and Iraq and undermining U.S. policy throughout the Middle East. Still more worrisome are the growing political and military links between Russia and China. Moscow and Beijing speak openly of a "strategic partnership," and China has become Russia's largest arms customer—something that would have been unthinkable a few years ago. Russia also concluded a deal to sell sophisticated S-300 anti-aircraft missiles to Cyprus, almost certainly realizing that the sale would provoke severe tensions between NATO members Greece and Turkey.

In response to NATO's coercion of Serbia, Russia has stepped up talks with China and India to create a counterhegemonic coalition implicitly directed against the United States and a U.S.-led NATO. While on a state visit to New Delhi, Primakov spoke of the possibility of a "triangular alliance" of those three powers to prevent global domination by any country. Even more worrisome than such diplomatic maneuvers is the Kremlin's decision to increase Russia's reliance on nuclear weapons—including tactical nuclear weapons. That step hardly advances the goal of people who had hoped that the post–Cold War world would be a more peaceful place than its predecessor.

If the United States and its NATO allies drift into a new cold war with Russia because the alliance insists on giving security guarantees to a collection of small Central and East European states and meddling in the convoluted disputes of the Balkans, that will go down as one of the most colossal policy blunders of all time.

The messy interventions in the Balkans and the growing tensions with Russia underscore an urgent need to reassess America's entire commitment to NATO. Ardent NATO supporters tend to regard the preservation of the alliance as a goal in itself. But the proper goal of U.S. foreign policy should be the protection of vital American interests. NATO (or any other institution) is merely a means to that end and ought to be retained only if the benefits of preservation decisively outweigh the potential costs and risks. It is not at all clear that the "new NATO" passes that test.

Proponents of American leadership of a new and expanded NATO typically argue that, whatever the costs and risks involved, they pale compared with those that would exist if the United States failed to stabilize Europe and were someday drawn into yet another massive European war. But U.S. policy should not be based on the need to prevent such a highly improbable scenario. There is no European power today or in the foreseeable future that has either the intention or the ability to replicate the campaigns for continental hegemony made by Nazi Germany or the Soviet Union—or even the more limited bid for preeminence made by Wilhelmine Germany in 1914.

From the standpoint of American interests, what matters in Europe is the conduct of the handful of major powers. As long as those states remain at peace with one another, and no menacing would-be hegemonic power emerges, there is no credible danger to America's security. Nor is there a danger to America's other important interest: keeping Europe relatively open to American trade and investment. Events involving small countries in Central and Eastern Europe may create annoyances, but they do not affect European stability or the overall configuration of power on the Continent. Becoming obsessed with problems such as the three-sided squabble in Bosnia or the status of Kosovo confuses the need for macrostability in Europe—

which is important to American interests—with the unnecessary and unattainable goal of microstability.

If trying to maintain peace in the Balkans and other strategic and economic backwaters is to be the mission of a new NATO, Americans need to seriously reconsider the wisdom of continued U.S. membership in the alliance. Such a mission should appeal only to masochists.

This article originally appeared in *The World and I*, August 1999. Reprinted with permission of *The World and I* © 1999.

4. Relations with the East Asian Allies

Introduction

Since the end of World War II, the United States has maintained an even more dominant position in East Asia than it has in Western Europe. Washington has enjoyed its status as the region's hegemon, and it has discouraged even friendly allies from playing substantial security roles—much less independent security roles. U.S. officials were largely responsible for the inclusion in Japan's constitution of Article 9, which renounces war and, if interpreted strictly, would seem to preclude even the existence of Japanese military forces.

As the Cold War with the Soviet Union intensified, Washington did encourage a more liberal interpretation of Article 9, and Japan gradually acquired the ability to at least assist with its own defense. It was not until the mid-1990s, however, that U.S. officials explicitly embraced the idea of having Japan assist in the general defense of the East Asian region. Even then, the expansion of Japan's security role was strictly limited and conditional—reflecting the wishes of both U.S. and Japanese leaders. Under revisions to the guidelines of the "mutual" defense pact between Tokyo and Washington adopted in 1997, Japan agreed to provide nonlethal logistical support to U.S. military operations in East Asia even if the conflict did not involve an assault on Japanese territory. That role was expanded modestly in 2002 when the Japanese Diet passed anti-terrorism legislation providing for such nonlethal logistical support outside the East Asian theater.

However, Japan is still a long way from having its Self-Defense Forces play an active military role in East Asia, much less in more distant regions. Tokyo continues to markedly underinvest in defense, devoting a paltry 0.9 percent of gross domestic product to the military. And that is the way the United States seems to prefer it. U.S. officials have frequently expressed private (and sometimes even public) objections to any suggestion that Japan play a significantly more assertive military role. Japan's long-standing policy of free riding on America's security guarantee appears to be popular with that country's political establishment and population as well.

Japan is hardly the only U.S. ally in East Asia to free ride on the United States, however. South Korea is equally brazen in such behavior. South Korea continues to depend heavily on U.S. protection. Seoul spends a mere 2.5 percent of its GDP on defense—less than does the United States—despite having as its neighbor one of the most unpredictable and ruthless regimes on the planet, Stalinist North Korea. It is not as though South Korea is incapable of providing for its own defense. South Korea has twice the population of North Korea and an economy more than 30 times larger. Seoul *chooses* to remain dependent on Washington, and U.S. leaders allow (if not encourage) that dependence.

As I noted in several articles, the free-riding phenomenon creates a needless burden for American taxpayers, but that is not the most serious problem with U.S. policy in East Asia. Far worse is the reality that Washington's hegemonic policy needlessly places American lives at risk. The current policy makes America the point man in any major security crisis that erupts in East Asia. Moreover, there is no guarantee that Washington's allies, which have benefited so much from the U.S. security guarantee, would back the United States in a crisis. During the Taiwan Strait tensions in early 1996 and again during the spy plane incident between the People's Republic of China and the United States in April 2001, America's East Asian allies declined to support the U.S. position publicly—much less provide tangible military aid.

America may be East Asia's hegemon, but it is a lonely and thankless hegemony. It would be a far better policy for Washington to insist that Japan, South Korea, and other allies finally take primary responsibility for the security of their own region.

ANZUS Is Now an Alliance in Search of a Purpose

ANZUS, the military alliance linking Australia, New Zealand, and the United States, is beset by mounting turmoil and ill will. In its pursuit of an uncompromising anti-nuclear policy, New Zealand's Labour government, headed by Prime Minister David Lange, bars atomic-powered and nuclear-armed American naval vessels from its ports. The United States has responded by excluding New Zealand from military exercises and otherwise freezing it out of intra-alliance affairs for more than a year. U.S. leaders charge the Lange government with "shirking" its alliance responsibilities and are denounced in turn for engaging in "overbearing," even "totalitarian," behavior.

While relations between the United States and Australia have not yet reached such a nadir, serious stresses trouble that front as well. The Australian government refuses to allow military facilities located in its territory to be used for developing the MX missile or the Strategic Defense Initiative, programs that Prime Minister Robert Hawke's Labour party strongly opposes. Hawke also vocally supports New Zealand's ultimate objective of making the entire South Pacific a nuclear-free zone, much to the dismay of the United States.

This wrangling underscores a growing divergence of strategic assumptions among the three alliance signatories. New Zealand and Australia perceive few existing or probable threats to their security. While they would like to preserve the political framework of ANZUS as a long-term "insurance policy" against adverse security developments, they no longer deem it prudent to assume the risks inherent in a close military association with a nuclear superpower.

Conversely, the United States sees ANZUS as merely one piece in a global security mosaic created during the 1940s and 1950s. Allowing even a minor strategic partner to redefine its "core" alliance responsibilities, as New Zealand has done, would undermine the entire basis of collective defense. Crucial allies, such as Japan and West Germany, might be tempted to engage in similar conduct, eventually causing America's elaborate system of alliances to unravel. It is this fear that impels the Reagan administration to adopt its uncompromising position regarding New Zealand's maverick tendencies.

The quarrel with New Zealand, while perhaps distressing, should provide the catalyst for a badly needed review of America's global strategy. Ideally, that review would include a reassessment of the entire collective defense doctrine, which has gone unexamined and unchallenged far too long. At the very least, it should serve as an occasion to reconsider the 35-year-old military association with Australia and New Zealand.

The South Pacific is simply not an area involving vital American strategic interests, so it is difficult to fathom why a U.S. alliance of any sort is needed there. U.S. policymakers must confront the reality that ANZUS is part of an obsolete security strategy, a relic of the early Cold War. Today, ANZUS is an alliance in search of a purpose.

The United States should take immediate action to terminate the ANZUS treaty, but it is vital that this step be taken for the right reasons. ANZUS is not failing because one member callously seeks to "shirk" its alliance obligations or refuses to bear a "proper share" of the West's collective defense burdens. Such thinking is either naive or exploitive, for it assumes that America's perceived strategic needs are—or at least ought to be—shared by all other Western nations. ANZUS is no longer viable because the security interests of the three signatories are fundamentally incompatible.

Above all, the United States should promote the demise of ANZUS with a maximum of grace. Trade sanctions against New Zealand, as suggested by several members of Congress, would be especially provocative and counterproductive. Such punitive measures would undermine the Lange government's laudable free-market initiatives and would needlessly poison relations with an otherwise friendly country.

While it is desirable for all concerned that the United States and its ANZUS associates cease being military allies, there is no reason to become economic adversaries. A strategic divorce is necessary, but American policymakers should endeavor to make it an amicable one.

This article originally appeared in the *Houston Post*, May 2, 1986.

Atlas of the Pacific

Since the end of World War II the United States has borne virtually all of the responsibility for maintaining the security of the Pacific Basin. It is an enormously expensive undertaking, costing American taxpayers some $40 billion a year.

At one time it might have been possible to justify such a burden, given the economic and military weakness of the other nations in the region. But that is no longer the case. The aptly termed "economic miracle" of the Pacific Basin should enable several of those nations to assume primary responsibility for their own defense. Japan has emerged as the world's number two economic power, South Korea has become an economic dynamo, and market-oriented reforms have awakened China, Asia's slumbering giant.

In such an environment, the fear that gradual U.S. disengagement from the region would lead to Soviet domination is misplaced. China already confronts the Soviet army along the lengthy Sino-Soviet border and refused to be intimidated even in the early and mid-1970s, when it was far weaker than it is today. Nor is it likely that such proud and powerful nations as Japan, Australia, South Korea, and Indonesia would tamely accept Moscow's dictation. Even if the Soviet Union sought to achieve hegemony—and recent events clearly signal a more accommodationist strategy—the East Asian nations would be far more likely to form an anti-Soviet coalition than to be "Finlandized." Medium-sized powers typically seek to balance a large expansionist state rather than bandwagon with it.

The East Asian nations will have little incentive to take responsibility for their own defense, however, as long as the United States is willing to bear that burden. U.S. officials foolishly cling to military arrangements that were established nearly four decades ago to meet the perceived dangers of an entirely different era. For example, the United States maintains 43,000 troops in South Korea to defend it against North Korea. Yet South Korea has a population twice as large as that of its communist adversary and a gross national product *five times* as large. Surely a nation with those characteristics no longer needs to be an American protectorate.

Even more unjustifiable is Washington's willingness to continue subsidizing the defense of Japan. Whereas the United States spends more than 6.6 percent of its gross national product on defense, Japan spends barely 1 percent.

Nor is it merely the huge disparity in spending that underscores the inadequacy of Tokyo's military role. Except for helping to defend the air and oceanic approaches to the home islands, Japan does precious little to maintain the security of the Far East, much less assume wider responsibilities. Although South Korea is far more relevant to Japan's security than to the security of the United States, American, not Japanese, forces help to defend it. Likewise, the Soviet naval buildup in the western Pacific during the past decade has been countered by Washington, not Tokyo. And American ships guard the Persian Gulf oil routes that are Japan's petroleum lifeline, while Japan's naval forces arc conspicuous by their absence.

The generous U.S. defense subsidy to Pacific Basin countries is especially foolish given today's more competitive international economic environment. American firms that once dominated global markets must now contend with ferocious competition—often from companies located in Far Eastern nations. Washington's willingness to subsidize the defense of those nations penalizes American firms and gives an artificial advantage to their foreign competitors. High taxes, the diversion of research and development funds to the military at the expense of civilian products, and the siphoning of civilian engineering and managerial talent into military work are among the adverse domestic consequences.

The Bush administration has unprecedented opportunities and incentives to reassess America's military commitments to the other nations of the Pacific Basin. Their rapid economic progress signifies that there is no longer a need for America to be the Atlas of the Pacific, bearing the region's entire security burden on its shoulders. It is the administration's duty to the American people to devolve that burden to the other Pacific Basin nations in an orderly but determined fashion.

This article originally appeared in the *Orange County Register*, March 20, 1989.

South Korea Does Not Need Eternal U.S. Protection

During his recent visit to South Korea, President Clinton went out of his way to stress the permanence of Washington's military commitment to that country. He assured South Korea's National Assembly that the 36,000 U.S. troops would remain "as long as the Korean people want and need us here."

Unfortunately, that is not the first time Clinton has indicated that the extent and duration of America's security commitments should be determined by the wishes of countries receiving U.S. protection. When pressed at a June news conference to justify the continuation of Washington's expensive NATO obligations after the disintegration of the Soviet Union, the president cited the eagerness of East European nations to join NATO as evidence that the alliance was still crucial.

In both cases, Clinton employs not only the wrong standard but a foolish and dangerous one for determining U.S. military commitments. The issue is not whether current or aspiring protectorates of the United States desire U.S. security guarantees. It is, after all, not surprising that nations living in dangerous international neighborhoods might want a friendly superpower to provide some insurance—especially when they have to pay little or nothing for that insurance.

The pertinent issue is whether such commitments are in the best interest of the American people. In the case of Korea, the United States is preserving an obsolete Cold War–era obligation that is both unnecessary and potentially lethal.

When the United States approved the Mutual Security Treaty with Seoul in 1954, South Korea was a war-ravaged country incapable of defending itself from an aggressive North Korea. Today the situation has changed beyond recognition. South Korea has twice the population of its communist adversary and a technologically sophisticated economy 11 to 12 times larger. Clearly, Seoul can afford to build whatever military forces it needs.

The strategic context is also totally different. During the Cold War, it was plausible to argue that a North Korean attack on South Korea would have been a crucial component of a general offensive by the Soviet Union or China—a bid for dominance in East Asia.

That premise is no longer valid. Moscow and Beijing have rapidly distanced themselves politically and militarily from North Korea's retrograde Stalinist regime and worked to establish close economic ties to the South. Neither China nor Russia has the slightest interest in fomenting a new round of fighting on the Korean peninsula.

Given those radically changed circumstances, a war between North and South Korea—as terrible as it might be for the inhabitants—would be a parochial struggle involving those two states. It would not necessarily have wider strategic significance, and it would impinge only on peripheral, not vital, U.S. security interests.

Even most defenders of the alliance with Seoul now grudgingly concede that South Korea could build the conventional forces needed to defend itself against its northern nemesis and that South Korea's strategic importance to the United States is not what it was during the Cold War.

They insist, however, that North Korea's apparent nuclear ambitions—evidenced by Pyongyang's threat to withdraw from the

Nuclear Non-Proliferation Treaty—require that the U.S. troop presence be preserved or even strengthened. Clinton apparently subscribes to that view; he repeatedly cited the possible nuclear threat from North Korea to justify the U.S.–South Korean alliance.

Contrary to Clinton's belief that the prospect of a nuclear-armed North Korea reinforces the need for Washington to maintain its military presence on the peninsula, it should increase the incentive for disengagement. The only thing worse than risking a conventional war to protect a small client state would be to risk a nuclear conflict. That level of risk should never be tolerated except to defend America's most vital security interests.

Clinton and his advisers ought to ask themselves how it benefits the American people to make 36,000 U.S. troops (as well as additional forces deployed elsewhere in East Asia) hostages in a parochial conflict that could go nuclear.

The Korean situation underscores the larger point that what is best for a client state may not be best for the United States. Indeed, South Korean political leaders have stated that they would want U.S. troops to remain even if North Korea collapsed and political reunification of the peninsula took place. The reason is simple: They fear possible expansionist designs by China, Russia and Japan.

Such attitudes imply a permanent U.S. military presence in Korea. Only when the South Koreans came to trust the North Koreans, the Chinese, the Russians and the Japanese could the United States withdraw its troops—in other words, never.

That is the expensive and risky enterprise to which President Clinton is committing America when he pledges to keep U.S. forces in Korea as long as the South Koreans want them. It is an expense and a risk that the American people can ill afford.

This article originally appeared in the *Cleveland Plain Dealer*, July 26, 1993.

Policing East Asia: The Downside

U.S. officials insist that the United States must maintain a large military presence in East Asia. Without that presence, they contend, national rivalries would reignite, arms races would ensue and the region would become dangerously unstable, thereby threatening important American economic and security interests. The conventional wisdom holds that only the United States can play the role of regional stabilizer and pacifier.

Two generations of American policymakers have stifled independent initiatives by even friendly East Asian countries. The United
States virtually imposed Japan's "peace constitution" after World
War II and still encourages Tokyo to rely heavily on the U.S.-Japanese
alliance rather than take responsibility for its own defense. Washington also pressured Taiwan and South Korea to abandon embryonic
nuclear weapons programs in the 1970s. More recently, the Bush
administration torpedoed Tokyo's suggestion for a modest "security
dialogue" between Japan and the Association of Southeast Asian
Nations.

Although America's dominance has contributed to East Asia's
stability, the recent tensions between mainland China and Taiwan
demonstrate that the policy has an alarming drawback. In essence,
the United States has volunteered to be on the front lines of every
regional military crisis. That is an exceedingly dangerous strategy.

Numerous pundits and policy experts have insisted in recent
weeks that Washington must inform Beijing that we "stand behind
Taiwan" militarily. Those armchair warriors, however, rarely go
beyond such banal generalities. Their reluctance to spell out the
substance of their proposed policy—and the possible consequences—is understandable. Assuming the commitment is not
merely bluff and bluster, it means that the United States must be
willing to fight a major war, if necessary, against China to protect
Taiwan's de facto independence.

Beijing might back down if faced with a demonstration of American "resolve," but that outcome is far from certain. Not only could
the United States find itself embroiled in a perilous military confrontation, it might have to wage the struggle virtually alone. Although
Taiwan would undoubtedly contribute to its own defense, assistance
from Washington's other East Asian "friends" would be problem-
atic, at best.

Japan, in particular, would almost certainly stand on the sidelines.
That is especially troubling since Japan is the logical regional strategic counterweight to China. It has both the population base and the
economic strength to play the role of a great power. But Japanese
officials insist that the peace constitution allows the nation's "Self-
Defense Forces" to be used in combat operations only if Japan itself
is attacked. Indeed, Tokyo rejected a U.S. request at the height of
the crisis over North Korea's nuclear program in 1994 to dispatch

minesweepers to assist American naval forces should the confrontation with Pyongyang escalate.

America thus finds itself under pressure to protect Taiwan and otherwise contain China's expansionist ambitions while Japan and other East Asian states, which have far more important interests at stake, remain safely in the background. That is a thoroughly unhealthy situation for the United States.

Instead of insisting on remaining East Asia's pacifier, Washington should adopt a fundamentally different strategy. America's objective ought to be a reasonably stable balance of power among the principal East Asian nations.

An activist Japan is an essential part, indeed the single most important component, of that balance-of-power system, but such countries as South Korea, Taiwan, Indonesia and Australia also have important roles to play. Both Taiwan and South Korea need to develop more robust defenses to deter any aggressive inclinations on the part of their communist neighbors. Indonesia, Australia and other midsized states can from time to time put their military weight into the regional balance to prevent any major power from achieving a dominant position. The recent defense treaty between Indonesia and Australia is a laudable sign of such prudent strategic thinking.

The United States has some important East Asian interests and cannot be indifferent to the region's fate. No reasonable person would suggest that the United States adopt a Fortress America strategy. But having some interests in the region and being willing to make a contribution to its stability are a far cry from volunteering to be the point man in every crisis. The United States should be the balancer of last resort, not the intervener of first resort, in East Asia's security equation.

U.S. officials may be comfortable with Washington's existing "smothering" strategy, but keeping the noncommunist East Asian countries so heavily dependent on the United States for their security is increasingly dangerous. It perpetuates a massive power vacuum that inevitably will be filled by either the United States or China. At best, that means a Cold War–style rivalry that goes on for decades. At worst, it means a calamitous military collision.

This article originally appeared in *Real Money* magazine, Spring 1996.

United States Should Examine One-Sided, Archaic Military Pact with Japan

The U.S. military alliance with Japan no longer serves the best interests of either country.

That arrangement, with America as military patron and Japan as Washington's compliant security dependent, was created in a bygone era when Japan lacked the economic strength or the political confidence to play an assertive role in international affairs and the emotional wounds of World War II were still fresh.

U.S. leaders need to adopt a new policy based on the realities of the post–Cold War world.

Washington continues to subsidize Japan's defense at the expense of American taxpayers.

That subsidy, which has amounted to approximately $900 billion (in 1995 dollars) since the early 1950s, is a powerful incentive for the Japanese to continue free riding on the U.S. security guarantee. And Japan's much-touted host-nation support of $5 billion a year actually covers only a fraction of the cost of U.S. security obligations in East Asia.

The financial consequences are detrimental to the interests of the American people.

Japan's defense budget is less than one-fifth of America's, even though Japan is the world's second largest economic power. Tokyo's defense expenditures, never robust, have now fallen to an anemic 0.9 percent of GDP and are projected to decline even further in the coming years.

It costs each American more than $1,000 a year to support the military, whereas it costs each Japanese a mere $360.

Moreover, Washington's policy encourages an unhealthy dependent mentality and enables Tokyo to evade political and military responsibilities in East Asia, even when Japan has important interests at stake.

Japanese officials admit that, in the event of war, Japanese military units would not join U.S. forces in combat operations unless Japan itself were attacked. Tokyo would merely provide financial and (possibly) logistical assistance.

Americans should ask whether it is reasonable for U.S. military personnel to be put in danger to deal with security problems that are far more relevant to Japan than they are to the United States.

The prospect of American troops' dying in Korea, the Taiwan Straits, or the South China Sea, while the Japanese merely hold America's coat, is appalling.

To be sustainable, an alliance must be clearly worthwhile to both parties if deterrence fails and a war has to be waged. An arrangement in which one party must assume nearly all of the costs in blood and treasure while the other party reaps the benefits is unstable as well as unjust. Yet that is the reality of the U.S.-Japanese alliance, and an East Asian military crisis would immediately expose that fact.

U.S. leaders foolishly perpetuate Japan's security dependence.

Washington's East Asian policy is held hostage to the exaggerated fears of Japan's neighbors, who oppose a more active military role for Tokyo. A lingering undercurrent of distrust toward Japan in U.S. policy circles has also been a major motive.

Such fears are misplaced. The Japanese are not congenital aggressors.

Imperial Japan's expansionism in the 1930s and 1940s, as horrible as it was, arose from a specific set of conditions that bore little resemblance to the current or any reasonably foreseeable situation.

Both East Asian and U.S. officials must overcome the simplistic assumption that Japan's military role must inevitably be one of extremes—either the rampant imperialism of a half century ago or the self-effacing dependency of the post–World War II era.

Were it not for the American security blanket, modern Japan would probably play a role somewhere between those two extremes. In other words, Japan would act as a typical prosperous, conservative great power.

A new U.S. policy toward Japan is badly needed. Washington should seek a mature relationship between equals and recognize that Japan, as the principal great power in East Asia, must take a more significant role in the region's security affairs.

Indeed, Washington's policy should be to view Japan as an essential component of a regional balance of power and the front-line state for promoting stability and containing expansionist threats.

The United States should withdraw its forces from Japan and other countries in East Asia over the next five years and keep smaller forces based in Guam and other U.S. territories. The U.S.-Japan alliance ought to be replaced by a more limited, informal security relationship.

America should be the balancer of last resort, not the intervener of first resort, in East Asia's security equation.

This article appeared in the *Washington Times,* November 17, 1995.

U.S.-Japan Defense Accord Preserves Old Inequities

American and Japanese officials contend that new defense guidelines announced last month will redefine and reinvigorate the alliance between the two countries.

The guidelines actually preserve long-standing inequities in the security relationship and create the illusion rather than the reality of meaningful change.

Japan will remain America's military welfare dependent.

The principal revision authorizes Japanese logistical support for U.S. military operations in "areas surrounding Japan"—a phrase that is never defined—that are relevant to Japan's own security.

Until now, Japanese officials have argued that Article 9 of Japan's constitution precludes such involvement unless Japan itself is under attack.

Despite the hype on both sides of the Pacific, the reforms fall far short of establishing an equal security partnership between Japan and the United States. In the event of an East Asian conflict that does not involve an attack on Japanese territory, Japan will merely provide logistical support for U.S. troops and allow U.S. forces to use facilities in Japan for their operations.

There is no suggestion that Japan's Self-Defense Forces will participate in combat missions alongside their U.S. allies.

Such a one-sided relationship ought to be unacceptable to American political leaders. Perhaps more important, it will be unacceptable to the American people if there is a crisis in East Asia.

There is something grotesquely unfair about expecting U.S. military personnel to risk their lives to repel an act of aggression that threatens the security of East Asia while Japan merely provides such things as fuel, spare parts, medical supplies, and body bags for American casualties.

However important the freedom and stability of East Asia may be to the United States, they should be far more important to Japan. Therefore, Japan needs to act like a normal great power and take primary responsibility for defending its interests and maintaining the stability of its region.

The new defense guidelines do nothing to end Japan's status as a U.S. military dependent; they merely allow Japan to be a more active and helpful dependent.

Incredibly, the anemic reforms contained in the new guidelines have attracted ferocious opposition. The changes are "really nothing" admits former ambassador Hasahiko Okazaki, one of Japan's leading foreign policy thinkers, yet he warns that "there will be a tremendous fight" to win the Diet's approval.

Washington's international military welfare programs foster a dependent mentality on the part of U.S. allies. Japan is a prime example.

An entirely new approach is required. Japan does not need to do more to support a U.S.-directed security strategy in East Asia. Japan needs to determine its own destiny and do whatever the Japanese people believe is necessary to protect the country's interests.

That means that Japan has to become a serious, independent factor in East Asia's security equation. Whatever the virtue of Article 9 may have been when the United States pressed Japanese political leaders to adopt it after World War II, the article is now an obstacle to a worthwhile and equitable U.S.-Japanese relationship.

The impetus for meaningful change will probably have to come from Washington. Japan benefits too much financially from its reliance on the U.S. security shield to relinquish that lucrative subsidy willingly. (Japanese officials have admitted that the loss of the U.S. alliance would require Japan to spend an additional $25 billion to $50 billion a year on defense.) Relying on the United States to guarantee the stability of East Asia also spares the Japanese political elite and population from a serious domestic debate about Japan's regional role.

Finally, Japan's security dependence eliminates the need to confront the diplomatic difficulties with its neighbors that would arise if Tokyo decided to adopt an activist policy. Given those incentives, it is not surprising that Japan would resist anything more than marginal changes in the U.S.-Japanese alliance.

Although the status quo might be in Japan's best interest, it unfairly places the United States on the front lines of virtually every East Asian crisis. The U.S.-Japan alliance is a wholly one-sided arrangement, and that defect will not be remedied by the cosmetic changes embodied in the new defense guidelines.

This article originally appeared in the *Baltimore Sun*, October 23, 1997.

Make Missile Defense a Pay-for-Use Deal

North Korea's launch of a multistage ballistic missile last summer generated interest throughout East Asia in defending against incoming missiles. Who knows where President Kim Jong Il might aim one?

More recently, reports that China was building up missiles across the strait from Taiwan generated still more interest. Japanese officials have already decided to include funds for anti-ballistic missile research in their upcoming defense budget. Yet to be decided in Tokyo is whether they'll spend even more to participate in the deployment of a U.S.-coordinated missile defense shield. South Korea and Taiwan also have shown some interest in joining such a system.

Given North Korea's unpredictability and longer-term concerns about China, the desire of other East Asian countries to get under an American-sponsored missile defense shield is understandable. But providing such an umbrella is not necessarily in our best interest.

Instead of building a U.S. missile defense system to protect friends and clients in Asia, Washington should simply sell the hardware to friendly countries so they can deploy their own systems. Not only would that make more sense financially, it would reduce the risk of unpleasant diplomatic and strategic side effects. Financially, a policy of getting Japan, South Korea and possibly Taiwan to help fund a U.S.-controlled missile defense program invites "free riding." The stronger our apparent commitment to such a system, the more likely it is that the other partners will try to saddle American taxpayers with most of the bill. We've run into the free-riding problem again and again with the members of NATO.

Even worse, allowing East Asian allies to hunker down behind a U.S. missile defense shield would perpetuate, and probably make even worse, the already unhealthy security dependence they have on America. South Korea, for example, continues to rely on the United States for key components of its national defense, even though it has a population twice as large as that of North Korea and an economy nearly 30 times greater than the North's.

Despite facing a heavily armed and unpredictable totalitarian neighbor, South Korea responded to the economic downturn caused by the East Asian financial crisis by reducing its already inadequate defense budget. In the event of war, Seoul envisions a U.S. troop deployment almost as large as its own current active-duty force. Japan's long-standing security dependence on the United States is equally striking, and the much-touted new U.S.-Japanese defense guidelines will not change much. In the event of an East Asian conflict that does not involve an attack on Japanese territory, Japan will merely provide nonlethal logistical support (fuel, spare parts and medical supplies) for U.S. troops and allow U.S. forces to use Japanese facilities. The revised defense guidelines do not end Japan's status as Washington's military dependent; they merely allow Japan to be a somewhat more helpful dependent.

The last thing the United States should do is create a new opportunity for security dependence on the part of Japan and South Korea. Yet that is the inevitable effect of shielding them with a U.S.-run missile defense system.

Perhaps the most serious objection to a U.S. regional missile shield is the adverse effect such an initiative would have on America's relations with China. Even if U.S. officials decided to exclude Taiwan from coverage, Beijing would react badly. Chinese leaders would regard the deployment of a regional missile defense system as an unambiguous signal that the United States intended to adopt a military containment policy against China.

At best, Washington's commitment to such a shield would severely damage Sino-American relations; at worst, it could lead to a Cold War–style confrontational relationship. Including Taiwan in the system would virtually guarantee the latter scenario. Indeed, that step would entail more than a small risk of an armed conflict with China in the future. True, Chinese officials would hardly be thrilled about a U.S. decision to sell missile defense hardware to its East Asian neighbors—especially if sales to Taiwan were approved. But at least that strategy would not create the impression that the United States was laying the foundation for a regional military alliance directed against China. A U.S.-controlled shield would inevitably create that impression.

Making missile defense hardware available at full cost to friendly governments that believe it is necessary for their security is, therefore, a better option on both financial and strategic grounds.

This article originally appeared in the *Los Angeles Times*, March 28, 1999.

Our Guardian Angel: Why Not Let It Rest in Peace?

During their recent meeting in Washington, Prime Minister John Howard and President Bill Clinton predictably reaffirmed the importance of the U.S.-Australia security relationship. Clinton had previously expressed that sentiment even more explicitly in a speech to the Australian parliament, insisting that the alliance is "not just for this time, it is for all time."

Such an attitude ignores George Washington's wise admonition that the United States should have neither permanent friends nor permanent enemies. Commitments that make sense under one set of international conditions may become irrelevant or even counterproductive when conditions change. Revealingly, proponents of the U.S.-Australia alliance rely more on nostalgia, especially the joint effort to repel Japanese aggression in World War II, than on post–Cold War strategic justifications. But nostalgia is a poor basis for foreign policy.

It is not clear that the U.S.-Australia alliance had much relevance even during the Cold War. ANZUS, the strategic pact linking the United States, Australia, and New Zealand, was outmoded the day it was signed. There was no need to counter a major Soviet military presence in the South Pacific, because one never emerged. ANZUS was actually an insurance policy against a new round of Japanese aggression, but with the Imperial Fleet resting at the bottom of the Pacific and the "peace constitution" imposed on Tokyo, the alliance was a classic example of preparing to fight the last war. Long before ANZUS became moribund following New Zealand's refusal in 1984 to countenance the presence of nuclear-armed or nuclear-powered U.S. ships, it lacked any strategic relevance.

A similar lack of relevance characterizes the annual Australia-U.S. Ministerial Consultations (AUSMIN). AUSMIN might gratify the egos of high-level civilian and military officials in both countries, but substantive rationales are sparse.

No one should be opposed, of course, to close diplomatic, cultural and economic relations between Canberra and Washington. But there is scant evidence that a security association enhances such ties.

After all, the existence of AUSMIN certainly did not prevent the Clinton administration's recent imposition of quotas and stiff tariffs on lamb imports from Australia for the next three years. Indeed, the incentives seem to flow in the opposite direction. Although

117

Howard stated that he and other Australians were "very disappointed and upset" about the decision, he quickly added that Canberra could not allow the incident "to contaminate a broader relationship, certainly not the security relationship." In other words, the prime minister was willing to sacrifice even an important Australian economic interest on the altar of the alliance with the United States.

The nostalgic U.S. security tie to Australia is merely one manifestation of Washington's intellectually sclerotic strategy for dealing with East Asian security issues. The only good thing that can be said about ANZUS and AUSMIN is that they aren't especially dangerous. Australia is highly unlikely to become involved in an armed confrontation with any of its neighbors in the foreseeable future and call on the United States for assistance. That is not the case with Washington's other security obligations throughout the region.

For example, Washington's alliance with South Korea could easily entangle the United States in another war on the Korean peninsula. Just last month, South Korean naval forces exchanged fire with North Korean vessels in disputed territorial waters. Washington then sent U.S. warships into the area to show solidarity with its ally, thereby becoming embroiled in a spat between the two Korean states over petty stakes that should not matter a whit to any American.

America's mutual defense treaty with the Philippines entails less obvious but scarcely less dangerous risks. It is no secret that Manila's renewed enthusiasm for military ties to the United States is a direct result of the ongoing territorial dispute between Manila and Beijing over the Spratly Islands—a dispute punctuated by skirmishes in the vicinity of Mischief Reef. Officials in the Philippines openly advocated the recently ratified Visiting Forces Agreement on the grounds that it would help secure Washington's backing for Manila's claims to the Spratlys. Although that perception may be erroneous, the continued existence of the Cold War–era defense treaty with the Philippines could nevertheless entangle America in the murky Spratlys squabble.

By contrast, the alliance with Australia is merely irrelevant, not dangerous. Yet maintaining an unnecessary security obligation even if there is little intrinsic risk to the United States is ill-advised. The perpetuation of such arrangements encourages an unhealthy dependent mentality on the part of allies and clients.

The East Asian countries need to develop a more mature attitude about security issues—especially the need to balance China and to make it difficult for Beijing to pursue any hegemonic ambitions. Such realistic thinking will not, indeed probably cannot, take place as long as Washington continues pursuing its smothering strategy. Since the end of World War II, the United States has consistently discouraged any manifestation of military self-reliance on the part of its East Asian friends.

For example, Washington still keeps Japan as a barely trusted junior security partner, a tethered status that is not significantly altered by the much-hyped revised U.S.-Japan defense guidelines recently approved by the Japanese parliament. Those changes merely allow Japan to be slightly more active in providing logistical support to U.S. military efforts in East Asia.

The smothering strategy not only perpetuates security obligations that are no longer in America's best interest, it creates a brittle bipolar regional strategic environment. If Washington persists in its course, in another two decades (at most) American military power will be the only significant barrier to a hegemonic China.

Having been spared the need to deal with security issues on their own—and in many cases having been discouraged by Washington from developing adequate military capabilities and responsibilities—China's neighbors will be unable to provide the needed strategic counterweight. But relying on a distant patron for protection from an ever-stronger regional power will be a high-stakes gamble for Australia and all the other countries of East Asia.

America's alliance with Australia is an example of the short-sighted U.S. insistence on remaining East Asia's nanny. That is why, despite the lack of any immediate risk it might pose to the United States, the security relationship should be terminated. Such a dramatic action would be a wake-up call, not only to Canberra but to other capitals throughout East Asia.

It is time for Australia and its neighbors to assume responsibility for their own defense and, even more important, for the overall security and stability of their region instead of relying on the United States.

This article originally appeared in the *Australian Financial Review*, July 16, 1999.

Japan, However Reluctantly, Reawakens

Japanese prime minister Yoshiro Mori's comment earlier this year that his nation is "a divine country with the emperor at its center" triggered a surge of apprehension in East Asia and the United States that aggressive Japanese nationalism is making a comeback. Although Mori's remarks were imprudent, Japan is simply beginning to behave like a normal country again after a U.S.-encouraged political and strategic slumber lasting more than half a century.

Instead of always relying on the United States to take care of security problems in East Asia, Tokyo is beginning to show some independent initiative. That change is long overdue and should be accepted—indeed, encouraged—by the United States and Japan's democratic neighbors in the region. A strong, more assertive Japan is an essential component of East Asian security.

Several events during the mid and late 1990s forced Japan to begin taking security issues more seriously: Beijing's attempted bullying of Taiwan in 1995–96, North Korea's missile launch in August 1998 and Washington's flirtation with a U.S.-China "strategic partnership"—a naive venture that peaked during President Clinton's visit to China in June 1998.

Tokyo's actions, though, have been modest and cautious. After the tepid U.S. reaction to the North Korean missile launch, Japan decided to create a robust, independent intelligence gathering and evaluation capability, including a network of spy satellites. Japanese officials also began to take more interest generally in developments on the Korean peninsula, as evidenced by Tokyo's active diplomatic posture in the months leading up to the recent summit between North Korea and South Korea.

Potentially more significant, Japan is on the verge of deciding to let its naval Self-Defense Forces participate in multilateral efforts to eradicate piracy in the Strait of Malacca. The Liberal Democratic Party, the dominant party in Japan's governing coalition, has indicated for the first time that it is willing to discuss modifying Article 9 of the Japanese constitution. As generally interpreted, that article prohibits Japan from using military force except in response to an attack on its own territory.

These developments suggest that Japan wishes to begin playing a strategic role commensurate with its status as an economic great power. Other actions, though, convey a continuing hesitation. For example, Tokyo declined to contribute military personnel to the international peacekeeping force in East Timor, despite the obvious Japanese stake in promoting stability in Indonesia.

Worse, Japan appears content with perpetuating its subordinate status under the revised defense guidelines for the U.S.-Japan alliance adopted in 1997. The revisions authorize Japan, for the first time, to provide logistical support for U.S. military operations involving a crisis in East Asia that does not include an attack on Japan. Despite considerable propaganda on both sides of the Pacific, however, that change is relatively modest. The revised guidelines in no way suggest that Japanese combat forces will join their American counterparts in responding to a crisis in, say, the Taiwan Strait—much less that Japan can take the initiative in repelling an act of aggression directed against a neighbor.

Unfortunately, Washington prefers such an anemic security role for Japan: The U.S. desire to keep Japan on a short leash was evident in the comments of Clinton administration officials following the preliminary negotiations on the revised guidelines. Those senior officials stressed that they did not expect Japanese forces to fight alongside U.S. forces in an East Asian crisis, nor did they desire such a commitment.

Such reflexive distrust of Japan is unhealthy for all concerned. Both the United States and Japan's East Asian neighbors need to recognize that the Japan of the early 21st century bears almost no resemblance to the aggressive, militaristic Japan of the 1930s. Today's Japan is a stable, democratic country with an enormous economic stake in the regional and global status quo. Those who fear the rebirth of Japanese militarism are chasing ghosts.

Japan needs to become a normal great power in every respect. Developments on the Korean peninsula ought to matter more to Japan than to the United States. Likewise, discouraging Beijing from forcibly absorbing Taiwan should be a high priority for Japanese leaders, since such an act of aggression would change the entire balance of power in the region.

Contrary to those who warn of resurgent Japanese nationalism, the danger is not that Japan will seek to do too much too soon in the security arena. Given the growing signs of turmoil in East Asia, the real danger is that Japan will do too little too late.

This article originally appeared in the *Los Angeles Times*, September 1, 2000.

With Friends like These . . .

Critics of the Bush administration's diplomatic compromise with China over the spy plane incident worry that Washington conveyed weakness and damaged its credibility with East Asian friends and allies. But if anything, it is the credibility of those countries as friends and allies that has been damaged, given the statements and actions of East Asian leaders in response to the crisis.

Vocal support for the U.S. position was notably absent. Even Washington's treaty allies in the region—including Japan, South Korea, Thailand and the Philippines—declined to say that a U.S. apology to Beijing was unwarranted. Only Singapore's elder statesman, Lee Kuan Yew, unequivocally supported the U.S. position. Japan's tepid, ambiguous stance epitomized the reaction of America's so-called friends and allies. Kazuhiko Koshikawa, a spokesman for Prime Minister Yoshiro Mori, said, "We strongly hope this case will be settled in an appropriate and acceptable manner." Beijing could take as much comfort as Washington from such a comment.

This is not the first time America's East Asian allies have abandoned the United States in the midst of a crisis. Indeed, that sort of behavior has become a pattern. The motto of the East Asian governments appears to be that they will always stand behind the United States—about as far behind as they can get.

Their behavior in this episode is disturbingly reminiscent of their actions during the 1996 crisis in the Taiwan Strait. As China conducted provocative missile tests in the strait, the United States dispatched two aircraft carrier battle groups to waters near Taiwan. The reactions of the allies were most revealing. South Korea and the Philippines emphasized that their mutual security treaties with the United States did not cover contingencies involving Taiwan. Other countries contented themselves with the banal response of urging restraint on both sides. Japan went no further than to express "understanding" of the reasons for the naval deployment.

Those incidents underscore a potentially dangerous flaw in U.S. East Asian strategy. Throughout the Cold War, Washington could operate with confidence that its security clients would not form close economic ties with America's strategic adversaries. In other words, there would be no serious tension between the economic interests of those allies and their security relationship with the United States.

The situation today is much more ambiguous. A chilly relationship (to say nothing of an armed confrontation) between the United States and China would put the East Asian countries in a difficult position. Most of them have extensive investments in China and maintain lucrative trade ties.

122

That accounts for their repeated ambivalence. In essence, the East Asian allies seek the best of both worlds. They view the United States as an insurance policy to protect them from Chinese aggression or intimidation, if that problem should arise. But they don't want to incur Beijing's wrath—or even jeopardize their commerce with China—by endorsing a hard-line U.S. policy on any issue.

That may be a smart (albeit cynical) strategy for them, but it puts the United States in a most unappealing position. As East Asia's protector, the United States might find itself involved someday in a perilous military confrontation with China over Taiwan or some other issue. Even worse, it might have to wage the ensuing struggle virtually alone. American leaders would be wise to rethink a strategy that puts all the burdens and obligations for East Asia's security on the United States while the countries that benefit from U.S. protection seem inclined to stand on the sidelines whenever a crisis erupts.

This article originally appeared in the *Washington Post*, April 18, 2001.

Japan Taking Small Strides to Partake in World Affairs

The Japanese Diet has taken a much-publicized step toward having Japan play a meaningful security role in the 21st century. Over the vehement opposition of pacifist legislators, the Diet passed Prime Minister Junichiro Koizumi's anti-terrorism bill that would allow Japan's Self-Defense Forces (SDF) to support the U.S.-led war against Osama bin Laden. Three Japanese naval vessels are now on their way to take up positions in the Indian Ocean.

It is a worthwhile measure, and it stands in marked contrast to Tokyo's policy during the 1990–91 Persian Gulf War. During that crisis, Japan confined its role to "checkbook diplomacy," paying some US$13 billion of the war's cost but otherwise declining to assist the international coalition that forced Saddam Hussein's troops out of Kuwait.

One should not overstate the importance of the anti-terrorism legislation, however. It is still a relatively timid venture into the realm of the world's security affairs. Japan must do far more if it hopes to be taken seriously as a political and military player.

The most disappointing aspect of the anti-terrorism measure is that it confines Japan's role to noncombat, logistical support. That restriction reflects the same unfortunate timidity contained in the 1997 changes to the defense guidelines for the U.S.-Japanese alliance.

Those guidelines were an improvement on their predecessor. For the first time, Japan agreed to have the SDF play a role in repelling a security threat in East Asia, even if Japan itself were not under attack. But as in the case of the later anti-terrorism bill, the SDF was only to provide logistical support for U.S. combat operations.

That limitation needs to end. Article 9, the "pacifist clause" in Japan's constitution, has outlived whatever usefulness it may have had when it was adopted at the insistence of the United States after World War II.

Japan is the only major power that refuses to play a security role commensurate with its political and economic status. Even Germany, the other principal defeated power in World War II, has recently sent peacekeeping troops to the Balkans and has now agreed to send 3,000 combat personnel to participate in the war against bin Laden. Tokyo cannot forever confine its security role to one of cheerleading and logistical support.

The standard argument against Japan playing a more active military role is that it would upset its neighbors in East Asia. The nations of that region, it is said, still remember the outrages committed by imperial Japan during the 1930s and 1940s and would react badly to any manifestations of "Japanese militarism."

But that argument oversimplifies reality. True, a few countries (most notably South Korea) are still utterly paranoid about Japan. China also opposes any military role for Japan. Indeed, if Beijing had its way, the Japanese SDF would not even exist. But China's strident objections are self-serving; PRC officials realize that an active, assertive Japan would be a major obstacle to Beijing's own ambitions to become the dominant power in the region.

Other East Asian countries are beginning to mute their objections to Japan playing a more active security role. Successive Australian governments have said that the time has come to bury the fears about renewed Japanese militarism. Singapore earlier this year offered Tokyo the use of its naval facilities—a strong signal that it accepts the reality that Japan no longer poses a threat. Similar accommodating statements have been emanating from the Philippines over the past year.

Those changes are gratifying. They show a recognition that the era of Japanese imperialism ended more than a half century ago and that 21st-century Japan bears no resemblance to the rapacious, expansionist Japan of that earlier era. Modern Japan is a conservative, status quo power that would be a stabilizing force against aggression, not a source of aggression.

Japan needs to seize the opportunity afforded by the changing attitude of its neighbors. It is time for the SDF to play a realistic security role in East Asia and beyond. No rational person would object if Tokyo provided combat forces for the struggle against Osama bin Laden and his terrorists. It is time for Japan to fully rejoin the ranks of the great powers.

This article originally appeared in the *Taipei Times*, November 23, 2001.

5. Relations with China

Introduction

In the years since the Nixon administration initiated contact with the People's Republic of China, two opposing camps have emerged regarding U.S. policy toward that country. One camp consists of the advocates of "engagement." They believe that extensive economic relations and an ongoing diplomatic dialogue with Beijing will foster ever greater economic reforms in China and eventually produce a peaceful and increasingly democratic country. Arrayed against that faction are the proponents of an explicit or implicit containment policy. Members of the containment camp argue that China remains a totalitarian state, that it has expansionist ambitions in East Asia, and that over the long term it will be an adversary of the United States.

I have always been a member of the engagement faction in the policy debate, but I've remained more cautious than some others in that camp. Too many advocates of engagement implicitly embrace a capitalist version of the Marxist doctrine of historical inevitability. According to their reasoning, engagement will create irresistible economic changes within China that will gradually but inexorably undermine the Communist Party's political monopoly. They point to other countries throughout East Asia—most notably South Korea, Taiwan, and Indonesia—where economic liberalization led to political liberalization—and argue that the same process will occur in China.

They may well be right. Certainly, economic engagement maximizes the likelihood of such a benign outcome. Trying to isolate China is clearly not a realistic option. Even if the United States could succeed in a policy of strict containment (and given the attitude of other countries in East Asia, that would be difficult), it would likely produce a hostile, insular PRC. After all, Washington pursued a policy of isolation from 1949 to 1971, and the China of that era was far worse than the current version.

But proponents of engagement are too confident about the out-come of their policy. The possibility exists that China will retain a highly authoritarian political system even if it embraces further economic liberalization. Those who doubt that such an amalgam is possible need to consider the case of Singapore. For more than three decades that country has maintained one of the world's most open economies; it has also maintained an extremely authoritarian politi-cal regime.

There is also no guarantee that even a democratic China would necessarily be a peaceful, nonexpansionist China. The history of international affairs suggests that some caution is warranted in adopting that conclusion. Rising great powers—even democratic great powers—have tended to be assertive, if not aggressive, in their regions. One need only recall that the United States in the late 19th and early 20th centuries was not the best of neighbors to other countries in the Western Hemisphere.

Because there can be no certainty about what kind of China will emerge in the coming decades, I have argued that the United States needs to adopt a hedging strategy. America should by all means continue to engage the PRC economically and diplomatically. At the same time, Washington needs to subtly encourage the develop-ment of a balance of power in Asia so that a limit will be placed on any expansionist ambitions Beijing may harbor. That is not the same as pursuing a U.S.-led containment policy. Washington does not need to pressure other countries in the region to contain China. They will follow their own security instincts. U.S. officials merely need to stop stifling the strategic ambitions of key countries (especially Japan) and stop encouraging the nations of East Asia to rely on the United States for their security. Fostering such reliance creates a dangerously brittle regime of deterrence wherein a decade or two from now the only power standing in the way of the PRC's domi-nance in East Asia will be the United States. No one should wish for that situation.

The most volatile issue in the U.S.-PRC relationship is, of course, the status of Taiwan. As on the larger question of engagement or containment, I have tried to articulate a middle position between those who would sacrifice Taiwan to maintain cordial ties with China and those who would use American military force, if necessary, to defend the island's de facto independence. Rejecting both options,

I have suggested a policy of extensive arms sales to enable Taiwan to provide for its own defense. At the same time, despite my sympathy for Taiwan's capitalist democracy, I strongly oppose putting American lives at risk to defend Taiwan's security.

Move beyond Cold War Theories

China's recent saber rattling about Taiwan has caused numerous pundits, policy experts, and politicians to advocate a firm U.S. military commitment to defend Taiwan's de facto independence. But Americans must ask themselves whether they really would be willing to assume the risk of a confrontation with a nuclear-armed power over such an issue.

Proponents of a policy of deterrence blithely assume that Beijing would back down if faced with a clear demonstration of American "resolve." That is a lesson drawn almost entirely from America's Cold War experience. The conventional wisdom is that aggressors will be deterred from molesting a U.S. ally or client whenever Washington provides an unambiguous security commitment.

But the assumption that the deterrence of Soviet aggression during the Cold War can be replicated in a much more complex post–Cold War international system is dubious.

Three factors are especially important in determining whether extended deterrence—attempting to deter an attack on an ally or client—is likely to succeed: the importance of the stakes to the protector, the importance of the stakes to the "aggressor," and the extent of the aggressor's inclination to gamble.

All three factors worked to Washington's advantage to an unusual degree in its confrontations with the Soviet Union.

America's security guarantees were largely confined to Western Europe and northeast Asia. Both regions were considered crucial to America's own security and economic well-being, and U.S. policymakers were determined to prevent them from coming under the control of the Soviet Union. It was therefore credible to leaders in the Kremlin that the United States would be willing to incur significant risks—even the possibility of a nuclear war—to thwart a Soviet conquest.

Conversely, while those regions would have been a significant strategic and economic prize for the Soviet Union, neither area was essential.

Fortunately for the United States, the Soviet leadership tended to be relatively risk averse. Most of Moscow's challenges occurred on the periphery, primarily in the Third World. Although Soviet leaders occasionally tested the U.S.-led alliance network (especially over West Berlin), they did not put their prestige on the line to such an extent that a tactical retreat became impossible.

As the possible confrontation between the United States and China over Taiwan makes clear, there are crucial differences in all three deterrence factors. Taiwan may have some importance to the United States, since it is a significant trading partner and a sister democracy. Nevertheless, its relevance to American economic and security interests hardly compares with the central position U.S. policymakers thought the Western European and northeast Asian powers occupied during the Cold War.

The problem is that Chinese officials probably understand that point as well. Soviet leaders may have considered it credible that the United States would risk nuclear war to keep Western Europe and northeast Asia out of the Soviet orbit. But it is far less likely that the Chinese believe that Washington will incur the same risk merely to defend Taiwan.

While Taiwan's importance to the United States is at a lower level, the island's importance to China is much greater than Western Europe or northeast Asia was to the Soviet Union. To Beijing, Taiwan is not merely a political and economic prize; the status of the island is caught up in issues of national pride and prestige. Along with Hong Kong, Taiwan is a reminder of China's long period of humiliation at the hands of outside powers. When such potent emotions are engaged, even normally dispassionate political leaders do not always act prudently or even rationally.

In its casual dissemination of nuclear weapons technology, the Chinese leadership already has given some indication that it may be less risk averse than was the old Soviet hierarchy. The comment of an anonymous high-level Chinese official that Beijing did not fear U.S. intervention because "American leaders care more about Los Angeles than they do about Taiwan" was a none too subtle threat. Perhaps the comment was mere bluster, but it is equally possible that China does not regard a U.S. attempt at deterrence in this case as credible.

At the very least, it is risky to assume that the United States can invariably deter great-power coercion of small U.S. clients around the world. Washington's successful deterrence of the Soviet Union may have been an aberration, a combination of luck and an unusual convergence of factors. If that is the case, applying the supposed lessons of the Cold War in confrontations with other major powers could lead to a humiliating retreat or a disaster.

This article originally appeared in the *Los Angeles Times*, March 3, 1996.

Trade Is Wrong Weapon

There is growing sentiment in Congress and elsewhere for a hard-line U.S. policy toward China. One manifestation has been the annual controversy about whether the United States should continue China's most-favored-nation trade status. Critics seek to condition extension on improvements in Beijing's human rights record and a host of other issues. A more recent variation is to oppose China's membership in the World Trade Organization unless concessions are forthcoming.

Both are deeply flawed strategies.

The temptation to use trade as leverage, especially on human rights, is understandable. Beijing's brutality toward dissidents offends anyone who values individual freedom. The United States cannot allow moral outrage to govern its trade relations, however. Repression is all too common in the world, and the United States would have to sever commercial ties to numerous nations. How could we purchase oil from Saudi Arabia, for example?

Americans who want to withhold most-favored-nation status and World Trade Organization membership to coerce the Chinese government into being more cooperative and democratic advocate precisely the wrong policy.

Such actions would primarily injure the sectors of China's economy that are the most dynamic and have the most extensive connections to the outside world. Those sectors are dominated by younger, cosmopolitan Chinese who view the aging communist autocrats in Beijing with thinly disguised distaste and impatience. We should strengthen such potential sources of change and power, not weaken them by restrictive trade regulations.

That is not to say that Washington ought to ignore human rights abuses—or other, equally troubling aspects of Beijing's behavior, including a growing belligerence toward its neighbors and a careless (at the very least) policy on arms transfers.

But such problems should be handled in the realm of diplomacy. Linking trade to the resolution of those disputes merely creates further friction in an already tense U.S.-China relationship.

Finally, it needs to be emphasized that the freedom to buy or sell products and services without arbitrary government interference is itself an important human right—for Americans as well as Chinese. Trade should not become a pawn in a game of global political chess.

This article originally appeared in *USA Today*, February 20, 1997.

A Risky Game of Chicken

As Taiwan approaches the first presidential election that the ruling Kuomintang Party (KMT) might lose, tensions between Beijing and Taipei are likely to rise. U.S. policy has unfortunately made the situation even more flammable.

Indeed, reports are circulating that Richard Bush, head of the American Institute, Washington's unofficial embassy in Taipei, has told Taiwan to cease its provocative behavior, lest the United States find itself pulled into a conflict in the Taiwan Strait. Without a change in Washington's policy, however, such warnings are likely to remain unheeded.

Taiwanese president Lee Teng-hui triggered a new escalation in tensions with his call for conducting Beijing-Taipei relations on a "state-to-state" basis.

China's response was predictably hostile; the People's Republic of China has established two missile bases near its coast, with the weapons apparently targeted on Taiwan. Taipei officials, including Vice-President Lien Chan, responded by calling for development of a fleet of long-range missiles to deter potential invaders.

President Lee indicated that his country already possessed some offensive missiles and warned that such mainland cities as Beijing, Shanghai, and Nanjing would suffer "terrible consequences" if the PRC attacked Taiwan. This appears to be a not very subtle hint that Taiwan possesses, and is prepared to use, nuclear weapons or other weapons of mass destruction in response to any attack.

Although responsible officials in neither capital want war (and certainly not a nuclear war), the possibility of a mistake is real. Beijing is suffering from an economic slowdown and political uncertainty; assertion of sovereignty over Taiwan is one of the few things on which most mainland Chinese agree.

Likewise, given Vice-President Lien's otherwise lackluster presidential campaign, the KMT's tough stance towards Beijing may be its best hope for retaining power in the March election.

As a result, the potential for a military confrontation seems dangerously high. Yet the Clinton administration's policy is both incoherent and dangerous. By misleading both parties, the United States risks increasing the chances of war.

In Washington the debate has been disappointing. Richard Bush has reiterated the administration's line: firm support for a "one-China" policy and equally firm criticism of Taipei's attempt to act

133

independently. The readiness to appease Beijing was evident when an unnamed administration official criticized President Lee's comments on state-to-state relations and his failure to offer "a little bit more of an outstretched hand to get dialogue going."

At the same time, the administration has been inconsistent in its policy towards weapons sales to Taiwan. Yet for all the explicit calls for restraint, the United States has implicitly promised to defend the island state.

This is a dangerous mix. By rejecting Taiwan's attempt to enhance its status, Washington has undercut its own credibility in threatening military intervention. The administration's affirmation of Beijing's position encourages the PRC to act more belligerently. Yet Washington's implicit defense guarantee encourages Taipei to expect U.S. military support in the case of trouble.

The result could be a risky game of international chicken, leading to a formal declaration of independence.

Unfortunately, although Republican critics of administration policy are more consistent, they are also more dangerous. GOP congressmen are pushing the Taiwan Security Enhancement Act, which would enhance the military relationship between Taiwan and the United States. Some conservative activists want to formally recognize Taiwan as the Republic of China. They would threaten to use force if Beijing acted against Taipei.

The risks of such an approach are many. China probably would sever diplomatic relations with the United States and, despite its modest military, could not easily ignore a U.S. decision to recognize Taipei, let alone a Taiwanese declaration of independence. A measured Chinese response—seizing some essentially indefensible Taiwanese offshore islands, for instance—would force Washington to choose between humiliating retreat and dangerous escalation. In neither case could the United States count on the support of Japan, South Korea, and the Philippines, all of whom emphasize that their "mutual" defense treaties with the United States do not cover contingencies in the Taiwan Strait.

The United States should adopt a new policy of conflict avoidance. Taiwan's future should be up to Taiwan's people, not the communist rulers in Beijing. But responsibility for defense, like the decision on independence, should be left with Taipei.

Washington should make clear that Taiwan will pay the price for miscalculating any move towards independence. The capitalist and democratic island is a valuable friend, but America has at stake no interests that justify risking war with the nuclear-armed PRC.

Washington should, however, sell Taipei the weapons that would allow it to defend itself.

Obviously, the PRC would be foolish to confront the United States militarily. But nationalism sometimes causes nations to do stupid things, and Beijing rationally believes Washington has less at stake in Taiwan than does China.

Although the Clinton administration has proved sadly ready to go to war, so far its adversaries have been pitiful. Conflict involving the PRC would be vastly different.

Washington needs to extricate itself from potential conflict before war erupts in the Taiwan Strait.

This article, coauthored with Doug Bandow, originally appeared in the *Australian Financial Review*, February 24, 2000.

The United States Should Adopt a Flexible Policy toward Beijing

An increasingly angry and divisive debate is taking place in the United States about policy toward China. The Clinton administration as well as business-oriented elements within the Republican Party advocate extensive "engagement" and seek ways to accommodate the Beijing regime. Those factions not only support China's membership in the WTO, they opposed Taiwan's request to purchase four Aegis destroyers and seek to block passage of the Taiwan Security Enhancement Act. Arrayed against them is an alliance of conservative Republicans and liberal human rights activists who advocate a hard-line policy of "containment" toward the PRC.

Unfortunately, the debate is taking place in an inevitable fog of uncertainty about Beijing's intentions or likely behavior in the future. The root of the problem is that there is simply no way to know whether the PRC will be a peaceful, status quo power or an aggressively revisionist power. Significant factors push Beijing in both directions.

Precisely because of that uncertainty, the United States must not lock itself into a strategy based on expectations of either friendship or an adversarial relationship with China. Instead, Washington should adopt a hedging strategy—a set of principles that are likely to work reasonably well no matter what type of regime holds power in

135

Beijing a decade or two from now or, equally important, what kind of great power the PRC turns out to be in terms of its international conduct.

Although China's extensive economic ties with its Asian neighbors (and with the United States) are an important incentive for status quo behavior, there are other factors that produce incentives for aggressive revisionism. Most important, China is still nursing grievances about the humiliations and territorial amputations that occurred during its period of weakness in the 19th century and the first half of the 20th century.

That is why the return of Hong Kong acquired an importance that transcended even the territory's considerable economic value; it was a symbol of China's restored national pride. The return of Macau is another step, but it is far from certain that China's leaders will consider the process complete unless Taiwan is absorbed and Beijing's territorial claims in the South China and East China Seas are vindicated.

Some experts argue that the PRC does not harbor expansionist ambitions and wants to concentrate on internal economic progress. Even if that is true at the moment—and Beijing's saber rattling at Taiwan raises some doubts—the existence of such an array of unresolved problems points to less pleasant possibilities.

Moreover, the history of international relations shows that rising great powers, especially those with territorial claims, typically pursue assertive, if not abrasive, policies. One need only recall the behavior of the United States throughout the 19th century and the early years of the 20th century.

There is no way to know yet whether China will replicate such behavior, but it is unduly optimistic to assume that American and Chinese security interests are so compatible as to warrant a strategic partnership—as the Clinton administration naively assumed in 1997 and 1998.

Moreover, if those policy experts and political leaders who contend that the interests of the two countries are likely to conflict are correct, choosing the PRC as a strategic partner would be an act of folly. Indeed, if the concerns about China's future strategic behavior have even the slightest merit, the United States should be pursuing precisely the opposite course: creating an incentive structure for other regional powers or groups of powers to counterbalance the PRC.

UCLA political science professor Deepak Lal notes the potential arenas in which U.S. and Chinese interests are likely to clash—as well as Beijing's ongoing effort to increase the capabilities of its ballistic missile forces, which he concludes is aimed at building an effective deterrent against the United States—and argues that Washington's behavior toward India makes no strategic sense.

"If the strategic interests of China and the United States are so clearly at odds, it would seem bizarre to penalize the one country in the region that might provide a strategic counterweight," he contends.

Even if one does not fully agree with Lal's assessment of Beijing's behavior, his observation about India's potential as a partial strategic counterweight has merit. Other analysts note that Japan could likewise play a counterbalancing role—indeed Japan would probably be an even more important factor in Asia's strategic equation. Russia, Vietnam, Korea, a well-armed Taiwan and other powers would also likely be relevant players in the overall balance of power.

Although it is important for the United States to avoid the extremes of containment or strategic partnership in its relations with China, it is even more important for the United States to adjust its overall Asia policy. That requires new thinking, something that has not been in abundance among U.S. policymakers.

The best course from the standpoint of American interests would be to encourage the emergence of multiple centers of power in Asia. The existence of several significant security actors would complicate the calculations of the PRC—or any other power that might have expansionist ambitions. Otherwise, Washington is creating the blueprint for a brittle bipolar security environment in East and South Asia in which the only security actors that will matter a decade or two from now are the United States and the PRC. The likely outcome would be either a war between China and the United States or China's emergence as the new regional hegemon.

Encouraging the evolution of a multipolar strategic environment is not the same as adopting a provocative, U.S.-led containment policy against China, however. Washington does not have to be the godfather of a vast anti-PRC alliance. If U.S. officials stop smothering Japan and other allies in an effort to perpetuate their security dependence on the United States and refrain from berating India for wanting to be a first-class military power, China's neighbors will draw their own conclusions about Beijing's ongoing and probable behavior and adopt policies accordingly. Washington merely needs to get out of the way of that most normal of processes in the international system.

Encouraging—or at least accepting—the evolution of a balance of power designed to contain any PRC expansionist ambitions is also different from regarding China as an implacable foe of the United States. Washington ought to treat China as simply another great power and cultivate a normal relationship, recognizing that the interests of the two countries will sometimes coincide and sometimes conflict. Cooperation needs to be fostered in the first case, and an effort to contain adverse effects must be made in the latter.

A normal relationship is inconsistent with attempts to isolate the PRC economically, much less adopt an overt containment policy. The latter approach would be especially unwise. A policy based on the assumption that China will inevitably become an aggressor and a mortal enemy of the United States could easily create a tragic, self-fulfilling prophesy.

Embracing the goal of multipolarity, of course, would mean relinquishing America's own hegemony in East Asia. Washington would have to be content with a status of "first among equals" in the region, and that would entail some loss of control. But a hegemonic role is probably not sustainable over the long term in any case. It is a manifestation of national arrogance to think that the United States can forever dominate a region that contains nearly a third of the world's population and that, despite a brief stumble, is becoming an increasingly sophisticated center of economic and technological output.

Only an unusual convergence of circumstances following World War II—the eradication of Japan as a political and military player, China's exceptional weakness, and the final stages of decay in the various European colonial empires—enabled the United States to establish a hegemonic position in the first place and maintain it for more than a half century. It defies both logic and history to assume that hegemony can be maintained for another half century.

U.S. leaders can adjust gracefully to the emergence of a more normal configuration of power in the region, or they can resist change to the bitter end. If they choose the former course, the United States will be able to influence the nature of the new multipolar strategic environment in Asia and seek the maximum advantage for American interests. The U.S.-PRC relationship would then be merely one component of a complex mosaic of relationships throughout the region, and there would be a significant opportunity for the United States to pursue a policy that avoided the extremes of viewing the PRC as a strategic partner or a new enemy. The danger of a U.S.-PRC military clash would substantially decline, and Washington would be able to develop a policy toward China that was prudent, sustainable, and beneficial to American interests.

If U.S. leaders choose the course of stubborn resistance to change, the United States will ultimately end up either in an armed struggle with the PRC for dominance in East Asia or be compelled to relinquish power to the region's new hegemon. The opportunity for the emergence of a relatively stable regional balance of power involving several major players will have been lost, and America's strategic and economic interests will be less rather than more secure.

This article originally appeared in the *Taipei Times*, May 8, 2000.

China: Emerging Partner or Threat?

Is China a rising colossus that intends to bully its neighbors and dominate Asia? Should Washington adopt a more hard-line policy toward China on trade, human rights and national security issues? Or is China a country that has already moved far along the road to a market economy and a more open society and is committed to being a stabilizing, cooperative power?

Those are the questions U.S. policymakers must examine as they consider whether to establish permanent normal trade relations with China and support its accession to the World Trade Organization.

The United States and other countries are betting that China's accession to the WTO will make China a more open society and eventually lead to democratic rule as well as a more stable and peaceful international policy by Beijing. But, while free trade is necessary for peace, it is not sufficient.

The Chinese Communist Party may be willing to sacrifice substantial gains from trade in order to protect its power and privilege. The challenge for the United States is to exploit opportunities for further gains from trade while moving toward a constructive partnership with China, but at the same time protect vital U.S. interests.

Unfortunately, the U.S. policy debate thus far has been largely a contest between the Clinton administration's muddled and inconsistent approach and the extremely confrontational approach advocated by many conservatives. The latter strategy risks creating a self-fulfilling prophecy of China's becoming an enemy. Indeed, a growing chorus of voices in the U.S. Congress and the U.S. foreign policy community argues that China is a belligerent dictatorship and an implacable future enemy of the United States.

It is true that no one can be certain how China will behave on security issues in the future. Unlike Nazi Germany or the Soviet Union, however, China is not a messianic, expansionist power; it is a normal rising (or reawakening) great power. That can be difficult enough for other countries to deal with at times, but such a country does not pose a malignant security threat.

The best course is to treat China as a normal (albeit sometimes repressive and prickly) great power but avoid the extremes of seeing China as either enemy or strategic partner. The United States would also be wise to encourage other major countries in Asia to think more seriously about how they intend to deal with a rising China. A collection of diffident, militarily weak neighbors, wholly dependent on the United States for protection, is not likely to cause Beijing to behave cautiously.

The Taiwan issue remains an especially dangerous flash point. Any move toward formal independence by Taipei would surely provoke military action by Beijing. China's strong economic dependence on Taiwan's prosperity, however, means that military action must be seen as a last resort. Moreover, the election of Chen Shui-bian and the defeat of the long-dominant Nationalist Party are stern reminders to the CCP that its own future is highly uncertain.

Beijing's biggest dilemma is how to allow the productive nonstate sector to grow and at the same time prevent an erosion of the party's power as market participants demand greater civil liberties and a meaningful political voice. The domestic tension created by opening China's economy to the outside world while preventing meaningful political change has to be released sooner or later. Gradualism appears to have worked reasonably well thus far, but the inefficiency of China's nonstate sector is apparent and corruption is rampant. Wholesale privatization would help solve the problems of inefficiency and corruption but would undermine the last vestiges of party power. So the challenge for China's leadership is stark.

Cutting off—or even limiting—trade with China in the hope of improving human rights would be self-defeating. Isolating China would strengthen the party and the state while harming the nascent market sector and reducing economic freedom. If free trade is restricted, the probability of conflict between China and the United States will also increase. That is why it is essential for peace and prosperity that the U.S. Congress vote in favor of permanent normal trade relations with China and support its accession to the WTO.

The best concise answer to the question of whether China will be a constructive partner or an emerging threat in the early 21st century was given to us by an independent scholar in Beijing. In his view, the answer will "depend, to a very great extent, on the fate of liberalism in China: A liberal China will be a constructive partner; a nationalistic and authoritarian China will be an emerging threat." The United States must prepare for both possibilities, but its policies should avoid needless snubs and provocations that would undermine the prospect for the emergence of a democratic, peaceful China.

This article, coauthored with James A. Dorn, originally appeared in the *Japan Times*, May 15, 2000.

Taiwan and the United States Have Rival Goals

As they prepared to take office, policymakers in the administration of President Chen Shui-bian suggested that the United States become a "facilitator" to restart a meaningful cross-straits dialogue. ROC spokesmen emphasized that they were not asking Washington to play the role of a mediator—merely that U.S. officials might exploit their own contacts in Beijing to help dissipate the pervasive atmosphere of suspicion there.

Washington politely declined to be a facilitator—officially. However, recent actions, including comments by Secretary of State Madeleine Albright during a visit to Beijing, suggest that the United States is playing that role unofficially. There is little doubt that Albright and others are gently prodding Beijing to conduct talks with Taipei. On the other side of the strait, there are indications that Chen's brief, abortive flirtation with an ambiguous version of the "one-China" formula was encouraged by the United States.

Having the United States play the role of facilitator, officially or unofficially, is unwise for both Taiwanese and U.S. interests. It would heighten Washington's already worrisome exposure to a complex, emotional and dangerous dispute. Moreover, it would do so in a manner that would likely undermine the independence and security of the ROC.

First of all, there is a very fine line between facilitation and mediation. As the Middle East peace process demonstrates, the United States, because of its prestige, power and influence, is invariably expected to take a more active role in negotiations. That same "slippage" into the role of hyperactive mediator might well occur if Washington becomes involved in diplomatic maneuvers between Taipei and Beijing.

Even worse, the Middle East peace process shows that the United States can be manipulated by the more unscrupulous party to pressure the other side into making (sometimes unwise) concessions to prevent a breakdown in negotiations. In recent years, the Clinton administration has responded to Arab demands by repeatedly escalating the pressure on Israel, and Jerusalem has ended up making the overwhelming majority of concessions.

The receptivity—indeed, enthusiasm—in Beijing to the original facilitator proposal raises the troubling possibility that the regime sees the potential of the United States playing a similar role in pushing Taipei to be more "accommodating."

That belief may well be accurate. The Taiwanese ought to understand that while U.S. and ROC policy objectives may overlap in many areas, there are significant differences that Beijing can exploit. Most U.S. policymakers and opinion leaders would like to see Taiwan's political system and market economy continue to flourish. But Washington's primary objective is to make certain that the "Taiwan issue" does not lead to a breach of the peace in East Asia. In addition, the rapidly growing economic ties between the United States and China, now in excess of US$80 billion annually, have created a powerful lobby in the United States determined to prevent any disruption in that lucrative relationship.

Although saber rattling by Beijing typically produces stern warnings from Washington not to use force against Taiwan, such incidents also typically cause U.S. officials to intensify pressure on Taipei not to do anything "provocative"—such as insist on the ROC's right to greater recognition.

Indeed, the desire in Washington to prevent the "Taiwan issue" from leading to greater tensions has led to some dubious initiatives.

Perhaps the most notorious was the reported "trial balloon" by Assistant Secretary of State Stanley Roth proposing an agreement in which Taipei would accept Beijing's version of a "one-China" concept in exchange for an explicit nonaggression pledge from the Chinese authorities.

Put bluntly, U.S. leaders regard Taiwan as a problem that must be "managed" so that it doesn't cause a crisis in U.S. relations with Beijing and lead to a war in East Asia. For the people and government of Taiwan, preventing the escalation of tensions is also an important objective. But it is not the most important. Preserving the independence and freedom of Taiwan is even more crucial.

When Taiwanese officials ask the United States to play the role of diplomatic intermediary, they implicitly assume that U.S. and ROC objectives are virtually identical. That is simply not the case. It is a dangerous illusion to believe that Washington would never sacrifice Taiwan's interests to advance broader U.S. policy goals— notably, preserving a stable and peaceful relationship with the PRC. Asking Washington to become a facilitator risks having Taiwan delivered to the tender mercies of the Beijing government on the installment plan.

This article originally appeared in the *Taipei Times*, July 10, 2000.

Appeasing China, Humiliating Ourselves

Clinton administration officials once again have their lips firmly planted on Beijing's boot. The latest occasion for unnecessarily appeasing the Chinese government is a brief stopover Sunday in Los Angeles by Taiwanese president Chen Shui-bian, en route to visiting several Central American countries that maintain diplomatic relations with the Republic of China. Since Beijing insists that the Republic of China ceased to exist following the communist revolution in 1949, and that Taiwan is nothing more than a rebellious province, Chinese leaders lodged a shrill diplomatic protest over Chen's presence in Los Angeles.

Instead of brusquely dismissing Beijing's protest, the Clinton administration went out of its way to be accommodating. While declining to bar Chen from landing at Los Angeles International Airport, administration officials hastened to assure the Chinese government that Chen was making only a "brief" transit stop and that he would hold no meetings and conduct no public activities while on U.S. soil. In reality, Chen plans to stay overnight in Los Angeles, and a California businessman hoped to give a reception in his honor. Several journalists—and even some members of Congress—have also asked to meet with Chen.

The State Department has done everything possible to prevent such interaction. Indeed, its conduct was so intrusive that Rep. Dana Rohrabacher (R-Calif.) accused the department of attempting to "quarantine" Chen and deny him the rights to freedom of speech and assembly.

The administration's conduct is disgraceful but not surprising. It is reminiscent of the policy adopted more than five years ago when then–Taiwanese president Lee Teng-hui requested a visa to attend a reunion at his alma mater, Cornell University. The administration's initial response to objections by the Chinese regime was to offer assurances that the visa request would be denied. Only after Congress overwhelmingly passed a resolution demanding that Lee be allowed to come to the United States did the administration beat a hasty retreat.

The proper response to Beijing's attempts to block the visits of Lee and Chen would have been a firm rebuff. Indeed, the episodes created an opportunity to throw a favorite objection made by Chinese officials back in their faces. The Beijing government habitually responds to U.S. protests about its egregious human rights record by denouncing "interference in China's internal affairs." Yet Chinese leaders don't hesitate to try to dictate America's visa policy or decide whether a traveler in transit can set foot on American soil.

U.S. officials should have told their Chinese counterparts that such matters are none of Beijing's business. The Chinese regime would have a legitimate objection if—and only if—executive branch policymakers held official meetings with a Taiwanese leader. Otherwise, any resident of Taiwan should be able to visit the United States, speak at public gatherings, give interviews to journalists, and even meet with members of Congress without interference. If Beijing doesn't like such manifestations of a free society, too bad.

The administration's excessively deferential behavior toward China not only betrays important American values; it is potentially dangerous. Chinese leaders are impressed with quiet displays of strength and pride; they have justifiable contempt for fawning behavior. Unfortunately, the Clinton administration has all too often engaged in the latter.

In addition to its campaign of diplomatic appeasement regarding the Lee and Chen visits, the administration acquitted itself poorly in May 1999 in responding to attacks on the U.S. embassy in Beijing following NATO's inadvertent bombing of the Chinese embassy in Belgrade. It was certainly appropriate for Washington to apologize— once—for the bombing and to offer generous compensation to the victims and their families. It was troubling, though, to see U.S. officials apologizing to China again, and again, and again.

Even worse, the administration responded to the violent, week-long attacks on the U.S. embassy and the U.S. ambassador's residence—clearly conducted with the connivance of the Beijing regime—with nothing more than anemic diplomatic protests. The proper response would have been to recall the ambassador (who was scheduled to retire in any case) and, more important, announce that appointment of his successor would be delayed until Beijing apologized and made explicit assurances that it would provide appropriate protection for embassy property in the future. Other contacts between the two governments should have been curtailed as well, to show Washington's displeasure.

Such actions would have made it clear to Beijing that the United States was not about to be bullied and intimidated. Unfortunately, the administration's actions conveyed precisely the opposite message.

Few people would dispute that it is important for the United States to maintain a cordial relationship with China. But there is a big difference between that goal and having U.S. officials abase themselves when China's communist rulers make outrageous demands or engage in outrageous conduct. The Clinton administration seems incapable of grasping that distinction.

This article originally appeared in *National Review Online*, August 14, 2000.

Arms Policy Playing into China's Hands

As tensions continue to simmer between the People's Republic of China and Taiwan, the Bush administration will come under increasing pressure to provide Taiwan with a firm security guarantee. That could be dangerous and put the United States directly at risk. Instead, the United States should increase arms sales to Taiwan and encourage other countries to do the same.

One of Beijing's top priorities is to cut off Taiwan's access to sophisticated military hardware. It's working. As late as 1991, some 20 countries supplied Taiwan with arms. Today, the United States is virtually the only supplier. Israel was once a leading supplier but stopped in 1992 when it opened diplomatic relations with China. Israel today is an important supplier of cutting-edge military equipment and technology—to China. Germany agreed to stop arms sales to Taiwan in 1993. France, which had sold 60 Mirage fighters to Taiwan, stopped in 1998.

Chinese officials make it clear to countries with arms industries that "good" relations and lucrative economic ties with China depend upon those countries' willingness to end military sales to Taiwan. Few governments contemplate defying Beijing's wishes.

Even the United States has bowed to the pressure. Although the 1979 Taiwan Relations Act obligates Washington to provide Taiwan with defensive weapons, Washington's performance has been erratic. Indeed, in the August 1982 U.S.-China communiqué, the Reagan administration promised to decrease and ultimately eliminate arms sales to Taiwan. American officials have insisted that the pledge was contingent on Beijing's commitment to avoid using force to resolve the Taiwan issue. Chinese leaders interpret the communiqué provision as an ironclad, unconditional U.S. pledge to phase out arms shipments.

Washington today is wary of Taipei's arms purchase requests for fear of angering Beijing. The Clinton administration's decision this year reflected that timidity. Washington agreed to sell Taiwan a long-range early-warning radar system, advanced medium-range air-to-air missiles (AMRAAMs), Javelin anti-tank missiles, and Maverick air-to-surface missiles. But Taiwan didn't get most of the items it asked for, including the centerpiece of its request, the Arleigh Burke–class Aegis destroyers, as well as diesel submarines and P-3 Orion patrol aircraft. Indeed, among the top six items on Taipei's list only one—Maverick missiles—was approved. Washington did sell AMRAAMs to Taiwan. But the fine print in the deal says that the missiles stay in America unless Washington releases them in response to an emergency. In other words: After you're attacked we'll let you have a weapon to defend yourself.

Such timidity plays into Beijing's strategy to isolate, weaken and ultimately strangle Taiwan. If Taipei is to deter China from using coercion on the issue of reunification, Taiwan must be able to purchase modern armaments, now and in the future.

Beijing claims that if Taiwan agrees to reunification, the Taiwanese will be able to retain their government, economic system and military for an extended period. But this last pledge is meaningless unless Taiwan has access to modern weapons. Otherwise, the Taiwanese will be in the same position as Poland in 1939, which had the best horse cavalry in Europe. That did little good against Nazi Panzer tanks.

This does not mean that Washington should approve every request. Taipei's desire for diesel submarines, for instance, seems ill-advised and a waste of money. (Taiwan's military would be better off increasing the number of P-3 aircraft for antisubmarine missions in its next request.) But U.S. officials should approve most weapons systems Taiwan seeks and stop worrying about whether such actions will annoy Beijing. As far as China is concerned, any arms sale to Taiwan is unacceptable.

In its own self-interest, Washington should be more open to Taiwan's arms requests. A well-armed Taiwan is better able to deter Beijing from contemplating the use of force to achieve reunification. Conversely, a Taiwan armed only with obsolete weaponry may prove an irresistible temptation to hard-liners in Beijing. An effective Taiwanese deterrent makes it less likely that the United States will ever be called on to rescue Taiwan. That is definitely in America's best interest.

This article originally appeared in the *Japan Times*, December 24, 2000.

The Chinese Military Budget Still Pure Fiction

China recently made a surprise announcement that it would boost military spending this year by 17.7 percent—the biggest inflation-adjusted increase in two decades. The large increase, Finance Minister Xiang Huai-cheng stated, was needed to "meet the drastic changes in the military situation around the world." Critics understandably found both the size of the increase and the justification cited for it alarming. Some China watchers even speculated that the PRC might be gearing up for a military confrontation with the United States in a few years.

But another point should also have received attention. The "official" defense budget figure of US$17.195 billion is pure fiction. Virtually all experts believe that the real level of military spending is somewhere between US$35 billion and US$55 billion. Much of it is either concealed in other budget categories or is off budget entirely.

Why does Beijing persist in presenting a military budget that is so obviously phony? The most likely reason is that PRC leaders want to keep others guessing about the actual extent of spending. After all, the range of even expert calculations is quite large. A US$55 billion budget can produce considerably more military capability than a US$35 billion budget. Another reason may be that, having published false spending figures for years, Chinese officials would now find it politically embarrassing to offer honest figures.

Whatever the motive, Beijing is making a serious mistake in perpetuating such fraudulent budgeting. It breeds suspicion. Not only the United States but China's neighbors in Asia have reason to wonder what the PRC is hiding—and why.

Ironically, the actual level of military spending is not all that terrifying. The lower end of the range would put the PRC's outlays at virtually the same level as those of Britain, France and Germany. Even the higher end would mean that the PRC is spending only a little more than Japan's US$45 billion. Even the highest of the estimates is dwarfed by the U.S. $300 billion budget.

There is little doubt that China is modernizing its military and intends to have a first-class force someday. There is also some reason for concern about Beijing's strategic goals in East Asia—especially regarding Taiwan. But a military budget somewhere between US$35 billion and US$55 billion is not the massive spending one would expect from a country determined to embark on an expansionist binge.

The PRC would be wise to allay the suspicions and worries of its neighbors. An essential first step is to be honest about its military budget. Not only should Beijing be forthright about the actual level of spending contemplated but it should restate the figures in previous budgets for at least the past five years. That is what corporations seeking to regain the public's confidence must do if they have misstated revenues and earnings because of dubious accounting methods. We should expect no less of a nation that says it desires the world's trust and confidence.

Transparency about defense spending and the country's defense doctrine would be the most effective rebuttal possible to critics who argue that China harbors aggressive intentions. Beijing needs to come clean about its actual military outlays and do so without delay.

This article originally appeared in the *Taipei Times*, April 4, 2001.

Undue Bill from China

The United States has offered to pay China $34,000 to cover costs associated with the April collision of a U.S. reconnaissance plane and a Chinese fighter jet. "We have arrived at what we think is a fair figure for services rendered and assistance in taking care of the aircrew and some of the materials and contracts to remove the EP-3 plane," stated Pentagon spokesman Rear Adm. Craig Quigley.

Beijing, however, is not at all happy with the offer of a $34,000 payment. Instead, Chinese government officials are demanding at least $1 million as compensation.

Washington's offer is foolish and Beijing's demand is outrageous. The United States should not pay even one dollar. Giving any payment would reward China for conduct that violated international law in multiple ways.

It is perfectly legal to conduct electronic surveillance of another country from international airspace. (The wisdom of conducting such flights so close to the territory of a notoriously prickly power such as China is another matter.) And there is no question that the U.S. plane was in international airspace at the time the collision occurred. Both Beijing and Washington placed the plane at approximately 60 to 70 miles off the shore of Hainan island. Under international law, a country's territorial waters and airspace extend only 12 miles from shore. The plane entered Chinese airspace only after it was damaged by the collision and needed to make an emergency landing.

That collision would never have occurred if the reconnaissance plane had not been illegally harassed by the Chinese fighter.

The actions of Chinese authorities after the collision were even more disturbing. The decision to enter the plane and remove the crew for questioning may have been warranted by the unusual circumstances of the EP-3's arrival. But detaining the crew and preventing them from having access to U.S. embassy officials for nearly 72 hours was a flagrant violation of international law. And declining to release the crew for nearly two weeks verged on creating a hostage incident.

The Bush administration already swallowed its pride by offering expressions of regret (i.e., a "half apology") for the episode. Although the administration was under no obligation to make such a concession, U.S. officials probably had no choice if they wanted to get the crew back in a timely fashion and prevent a further deterioration in U.S.-Chinese relations. Likewise, the administration could have done little to prevent Chinese authorities from insisting that the plane be cut up and shipped back to the United States in crates unless Washington was willing to escalate the confrontation.

Making compromises and accepting unpleasant realities is sometimes a necessary part of diplomacy. But rewarding a regime for egregious behavior is going far beyond what is necessary. The Bush administration should never have offered financial compensation. And given Beijing's insulting demand for even more money, the administration should immediately rescind the offer.

This article originally appeared in the *Washington Times*, August 17, 2001.

6. Relations with the Soviet Union and Russia

Introduction

I had the opportunity to write on U.S. policy toward the Soviet Union only during the final years of the Cold War. During that period, I tried to draw a distinction between defending legitimate American security interests and needlessly getting involved in proxy struggles with the USSR in obscure portions of the Third World. One arena where a firm U.S. policy was needed was in the Western Hemisphere. In various articles, I urged U.S. leaders to firmly resist Moscow's efforts to establish client states in Latin America. That strategy did not require the United States to overthrow leftist regimes merely because they were Marxist, but it did mean making it clear to the leaders of such regimes that establishing close political or military ties with America's Cold War adversary would not be tolerated.

Once the Soviet Union disintegrated, the relevant issues changed dramatically. During the early and mid-1990s, the conventional wisdom in the United States was that Washington needed to provide Moscow with generous quantities of foreign aid. I challenged that view, arguing that unless Russia adopted market-oriented economic policies and firmly established the rule of law with adequate protections for property rights, outside aid would be utterly wasted. Events later in the decade proved that point. Even today, Russia is in a sort of economic limbo. Russian leaders privatized most (although regrettably not all) of the major state industries, but the privatization process was highly politicized and rife with scandal. The rule of law is still disturbingly weak, and, as a result, both domestic and foreign investors have hesitated to establish large positions in the Russian economy.

On the security front, the United States frequently behaves as if it doesn't take Russia seriously as a great power. The expansion of

NATO eastward toward the Russian border hardly seems a friendly act. Likewise, the growing U.S. presence in Central Asia and the Caucasus suggests that Washington is taking advantage of Russia's weakness to set up shop in Moscow's geopolitical backyard. Although relations between the two countries have improved since the September 11 terrorist attacks (in part because Russia seeks U.S. backing for its counterinsurgency campaign against secessionist rebels in Chechnya), it is uncertain whether that thaw will endure. The United States has an opportunity to bury the Cold War relationship with Moscow and develop a new, cooperative relationship, but thus far U.S. leaders seem to be exploiting that opportunity only intermittently.

How Now to Counter Moscow?

The U.S.-Soviet competition for dominance in the Third World has exhibited a consistent pattern throughout the Cold War era. Moscow has relied heavily on political subversion to install and maintain Leninist clients in countries deemed strategically important. The United States has countered those efforts by assisting incumbent anti-communist governments in a variety of ways. Lately Washington has gone on the offensive, with the Reagan Doctrine, and it now seeks to help insurgents dislodge pro-Soviet regimes.

The results of that intense jockeying for power have been less than satisfying for both superpowers. It might appear that the Soviet Union has scored a number of geopolitical triumphs, the communist victories in Cuba, Vietnam, Ethiopia and Angola being the most obvious examples. But Moscow has discovered that such victories entail enormous and seemingly endless financial drains.

Fidel Castro's Cuba, one of the world's foremost economic basket cases, survives only by the grace of an annual Soviet subsidy of nearly $1 billion. Vietnam may provide the Soviet Union with a strategically important naval base at Cam Ranh Bay, but it too is a billion dollar welfare recipient. Moscow continues to pour military and economic aid into Angola to help the government of José dos Santos stave off the determined insurgency of Jonas Savimbi's UNITA rebels. An even worse situation exists in Afghanistan, where the USSR had to commit its own military forces in order to prevent the collapse of a client.

Complex Entanglements

The American record also has been disappointing. Washington's long-standing policy of sponsoring authoritarian regimes has earned the United States enmity throughout the Third World. It has also created complex entanglements, as demonstrated by Washington's current effort to dissuade Pakistan from acquiring a nuclear weapons capability while using that country to channel military aid to the Afghan rebels. The policy has been expensive; the United States has provided nearly $160 billion in economic assistance and tens of billions in military aid to Third World nations during the past four decades. Moreover, the Vietnam debacle demonstrated how costly an attempt to preserve a vulnerable client could be in terms of American lives.

Both Moscow and Washington of late have signaled alteration of their Third World policies in an attempt to overcome such drawbacks. Especially since Mikhail Gorbachev's ascension to power, the Soviet Union has adopted more subtle techniques. Its new strategy is apparently to de-emphasize attempts to install Leninist regimes while accelerating efforts to garner political and economic influence with noncommunist governments. Moscow has flirted with that approach before, most notably during the Khrushchev years, when the USSR provided developmental aid programs to India and Egypt. Those measures, though, were a mere appendage to the Soviets' principal Third World strategy: political and military subversion.

This time economic overtures appear to constitute a far more important component of Soviet strategy, perhaps even the dominant one. That is not to suggest that Moscow will abandon its client states. There may be some retrenchment, but the major change is that Moscow is now reluctant to take on new dependents, preferring to adopt more indirect methods of enhancing Soviet geopolitical clout.

During the past two years Moscow has engaged in several significant initiatives. It has negotiated commercial treaties with Kiribati and Vanuatu, far-flung island nations whose strategic location and mineral wealth have not been lost on the Kremlin. Those treaties gave the Soviet Union important access to the Central Pacific. Soviet officials have also courted various Persian Gulf states, and Moscow capped its diplomatic offensive by concluding a major economic development agreement with Iran. It has made serious efforts to improve relations with nations as diverse as China, Indonesia and Argentina.

Conversely, Moscow is showing signs of losing its enthusiasm for incompetent Leninist clients. Mr. Gorbachev is exerting increasing pressure on the East European satellites to emulate the Soviet Union's economic reforms in order to revitalize their moribund economies. The desire to escape at least some of the burdens of empire is also becoming apparent with respect to Third World clients.

The Kremlin's relations with Marxist Mozambique have cooled dramatically in recent years, and its growing frustration and impatience with its Afghan dependent have become obvious. Another indication of Moscow's desire to stanch its financial hemorrhage came this summer when Nicaragua, an incipient client, requested increased shipments of low-priced petroleum. Not only did the

Kremlin refuse to oblige, it informed the Sandinistas that the existing level of shipments might not be maintained.

The recent shift in America's Third World policy has been somewhat less dramatic. It has chiefly taken the form of a more selective endorsement of authoritarian clients. The 11th-hour abandonment of Ferdinand Marcos in favor of Corazon Aquino, the encouragement of democratic reforms in South Korea, and the covert support for opponents of Gen. Manuel Noriega in Panama all represent examples of that trend.

Washington's receptive posture toward democratic alternatives is refreshing, but it seems to stem largely from a belated realization that indiscriminate support for autocrats has been counterproductive. It is apparently not a response to the Soviets' new strategy in the Third World, because other aspects of America's Third World policy demonstrate little awareness of the change in Moscow's approach and even less of the ramifications. Indeed, elements of that policy give the Soviets unnecessary opportunities to expand their influence.

The Reagan Doctrine can rekindle Third World fears of U.S. "imperialism" at a time when Moscow is adopting a lower political profile. Washington's blundering military intervention in the Persian Gulf region has enabled the Soviet Union to reap diplomatic benefits, at least in Iran, just by remaining on the sidelines. (The enthusiasm of some Arab states in the region may prove transitory.) Soviet political and commercial penetration of the Central Pacific was facilitated by U.S. insensitivity toward fishing rights, French nuclear testing, and other issues important to those island nations.

Worst of all, the United States has pursued a variety of protectionist trade practices that are injurious to Third World producers. U.S. restrictions on the importation of textiles, sugar, bauxite and other products have been devastating the economies of those nations and they have reacted with bitterness and anger. Demonstrations of anti-American sentiment explicitly or implicitly linked to trade issues have occurred in Thailand, South Korea, Fiji, Australia and Costa Rica. U.S. officials are being dangerously naive if they assume that the Soviets are not sufficiently adroit to fish in such troubled waters. Particularly in the Pacific Basin and Latin America, they are already doing so.

If the United States does not alter its Third World strategy, it will play directly into the hands of the Soviet Union. Clumsy military

interventions and such imitative subversion measures as the Reagan
Doctrine are not even well suited to countering the kind of heavy-
handed foreign policy pursued by Mr. Gorbachev's predecessors.
Against a more sophisticated Soviet approach they will fail utterly.

Promote Capitalist Values

A three-pronged strategy would allow the United States to avoid
such egregious errors and counteract Soviet Third World initiatives
without incurring undesirable political or military entanglements.
First, the United States must practice as well as preach the virtues
of free trade. Second, the Reagan administration should intensify
its ideological offensive to promote capitalist values in addition to
furthering its geopolitical objectives. Moscow hopes to demonstrate
the vitality of socialism and bolster its waning appeal in the Third
World. It is imperative to prevent that discredited economic doctrine
from enjoying a resurgence.

Finally, Washington must abandon debilitating or counterproductive measures. It should especially avoid funding bilateral and multilateral aid programs that merely encourage Third World nations to
embrace the failed principles of centralized planning. Nor need the
United States become the arbiter of Third World debt problems and
fashion a comprehensive "solution." Debtor nations and private
Western creditors can more effectively resolve short-term difficulties
on a case-by-case basis; long-term solutions await the adoption of
market reforms in the debtor countries, reforms that current U.S.
trade and foreign aid policies tragically delay.

This tactical triad offers the United States the best hope of coping
with a subtle and varied Soviet policy in the Third World. Washington should welcome the opportunity to compete with Moscow in
the ideological and economic realms, where the Soviets will operate
at a tremendous disadvantage, given their rigid domestic system.
It is an ideal chance to demonstrate the superiority of democratic
and capitalist principles throughout the Third World.

This article originally appeared in the *Wall Street Journal*, October 13, 1987. Reprinted
with permission of the *Wall Street Journal* © 1987 Dow Jones & Company, Inc.

Back to a Monroe Doctrine

The debate over U.S. policy in Central America features competing
liberal and conservative fantasies. Liberals have become wedded to
the Arias peace plan while conservatives continue to romanticize

the politically murky Nicaraguan insurgents as the "democratic resistance," and argue that the United States has a moral obligation to assist such "freedom fighters."

Critics of the Reagan administration are excessively optimistic that the Nicaraguan conflict can be solved through negotiations. History offers exceedingly few examples of bitter civil wars ending in negotiated settlements, and despite the much touted cease-fire, it is a forlorn hope that the Sandinista regime will bargain away its monopoly of power. At the same time, despite widespread disenchantment with the Ortega government's illiterate economic policies, the Contras have failed to overcome their own political liabilities and galvanize the Nicaraguan populace into an effective revolutionary force.

The policy debate also fails to define the true nature of U.S. security interests in Central America and the rest of the Caribbean Basin. Liberals and conservatives both concentrate too narrowly on individual nations at the expense of a regional perspective, and even worse, the internal politics of a particular country typically becomes the litmus test.

Similar Misguided Obsession

Although Nicaragua has been the most frequent object of concern, we are now seeing a similar misguided obsession with Panama's domestic affairs, as the United States employs economic coercion in an effort to oust military strongman Manuel Noriega. Even if Washington succeeds, it will do so at the cost of irreparable damage to Panama's economy and a potent legacy of nationalist resentment directed at "Yankee imperialism."

The internal composition of a foreign government actually has little relevance to legitimate U.S. security interests. Washington has experienced few qualms about dealing with (indeed, sometimes sponsoring) dictatorships in Central America or elsewhere in the Third World. The United States did not insist on democracy for Nicaragua during the long Somoza dynasty, or for Haiti throughout the brutal reigns of François and Jean Claude Duvalier. Nor is it convincing to argue that, while America might be able to endure "traditional" authoritarian regimes, Marxist dictatorships are intolerable. Washington's cordial relations with Yugoslavia, China and Mozambique belie that notion.

157

But it is equally erroneous to assume that a tiny nation such as Nicaragua cannot pose a security threat. Under certain conditions it can, especially by becoming a base of operations for a larger hostile power—the Soviet Union. It is this issue—the nature and scope of political and military ties to the USSR by small nations in the Caribbean Basin—that should be but rarely is the focus of debate about the administration's policy.

The original principles of the Monroe Doctrine may offer some guidance. That doctrine did not attempt to dictate the internal political composition of governments in the Western Hemisphere, but it did stress that any attempt by a European power to gain control over a Latin American nation would be considered "the manifestation of an unfriendly disposition toward the United States." Unfortunately, during the early years of the 20th century the Monroe Doctrine became a pretext for Washington to act as the hemispheric disciplinarian concerning the internal affairs of Latin nations, leading to a plethora of interventionist episodes.

That transformation was most unwise, but even worse was the tacit abandonment of the Monroe Doctrine in the early 1960s when Cuba became a military client of the Soviet Union. Indeed, U.S. policy toward Cuba since that time symbolizes the failure to properly define America's vital interests in the Caribbean. For nearly three decades, Washington has railed against the Castro regime's odious ideological sins and responded with a host of ineffectual measures including a trade embargo and, at least initially, a CIA-organized army of Cuban exiles. As if to underscore an inability to learn from its predecessors' mistakes, the Reagan administration has pursued a nearly identical strategy with respect to Nicaragua.

The United States should instead emphasize a more pertinent grievance: the extensive economic and military ties that have made Cuba a Soviet surrogate and threaten to do the same for Nicaragua. (Although Reagan administration officials have invoked that argument, it tends to become lost in the more frequent verbal static about Nicaragua's domestic affairs.) Americans have ample reason to be concerned when Cuba receives more than $4 billion annually in aid from Moscow (which Havana has used to build a powerful military apparatus) and in exchange serves as the Kremlin's principal geopolitical pawn. Likewise, Moscow's economic and military assistance to Nicaragua, which approached $1 billion during 1987, is creating precisely the extensive linkage to a nonhemispheric power that the Monroe Doctrine pledged the United States to prevent.

A more explicit U.S. security policy for the entire Caribbean Basin—a new Monroe Doctrine—is overdue. It should not merely stress, as the Kennedy administration did during the Cuban missile crisis, that the introduction of Soviet nuclear weapons into the region—or the establishment of conventional military bases for that matter—would constitute an intolerable threat.

Even less egregious actions on Moscow's part are cause for concern given the Caribbean Basin's proximity to the American homeland. Cuba's willingness to allow the Soviet navy to use port facilities significantly strengthens the operational capability of that force in the Western Atlantic and Gulf of Mexico. Nicaragua's desire to create an 800,000-man army equipped with modern Soviet weapons and, perhaps, to obtain sophisticated MiG aircraft may not pose an immediate threat to the United States, but it would seriously upset the military balance in the region, with unpredictable consequences.

A new Monroe Doctrine must underscore to Nicaragua and Cuba as well as their patron that Soviet surrogates will no longer be tolerated in this hemisphere. In recent months, the Gorbachev government has shown signs that it is weary of the financial drain caused by supporting inept Leninist dependents. The impending withdrawal from Afghanistan is the most recent and startling indication. A firm U.S. position that Moscow's ties to its two hemispheric clients must be reduced dramatically would be an acid test for the Kremlin to demonstrate whether the desire to shed such burdens is genuine.

A carrot is needed with the stick, however. The normalization of economic relations with Cuba and Nicaragua as well as a pledge not to interfere in their internal affairs would be important incentives for other regimes to accept an otherwise bitter geopolitical situation. Although critics might contend such an approach betrays the democratic cause, it merely recognizes the reality that the United States cannot bring democracy to Cuba or Nicaragua short of massive military intervention. And few Americans wish to pay that price.

Of course, Washington must be willing and able to enforce its security demands. One of the advantages of a security-based strategy is that it maximizes the chances of attaining a domestic consensus if coercive action should prove necessary. Conversely, American public opinion would be bitterly divided regarding intervention for lesser reasons, and the presence of a sizable anti-war faction would undermine such an initiative from the outset. Military coercion undoubtedly entails risks and should be undertaken only if the Soviet Union insisted on maintaining its network of clients and those clients spurned normal political and economic relations with the United States in order to remain Moscow's vassals. Such an outcome would be strong evidence of a Soviet-led drive to threaten the United States. If that is the reality, most Americans would prefer to confront the problem directly rather than indulge in illusions about benign Soviet intentions.

Even in this worst-case scenario, it should be possible to achieve "core" security objectives without the costly invasions and prolonged occupations that would be necessary to secure ideological conformity. As foreign policy analyst Alan Tonelson has suggested, a judicious application of air and naval power against recalcitrant Soviet clients would probably be sufficient. Unless the Kremlin leadership is irrational, the USSR would be no more likely than it was in 1962 to risk a full-blown military confrontation with the United States in a region where Soviet forces would operate at a severe disadvantage.

Alternatives More Dangerous

Although a new Monroe Doctrine is not risk free, the alternative strategies are ultimately far more dangerous. Liberals would tolerate regimes that are not only undemocratic but also Soviet clients, with all the attendant regional security problems. Conservatives would embark on a quixotic crusade to impose freedom and democracy by force of arms. One need only think of Haiti—paradoxically a prime concern of liberals—to contemplate how many American dollars and lives might be sacrificed in such endeavors.

A strategy based upon the Republic's essential security interests would neither court unnecessary interventions nor tamely accept a menacing proliferation of Soviet surrogates. It would tolerate repugnant ideologies among neighboring countries but not allow an Old World imperialist state to project its power into this hemisphere. Good policy in the 1800s and now.

This article originally appeared in the *Wall Street Journal*, May 4, 1988. Reprinted with permission of the *Wall Street Journal* © 1988 Dow Jones & Company, Inc.

Be Wary of Soviet "Peace Plan" for Central America

During his recent trip to Nicaragua, Soviet foreign minister Eduard Shevardnadze unveiled a comprehensive peace plan for Central America. On the surface, his proposal seems to represent a refreshing willingness on Moscow's part to ease tensions in the region and decrease its sponsorship of the Sandinista regime.

On a deeper level, however, his peace offensive is a subtle ploy to legitimize and institutionalize an expanded political role for Moscow in the Western Hemisphere.

At the heart of Shevardnadze's plan is his call for the withdrawal of all military advisers from and the closure of all foreign military bases in Central America. The peace of the region, he insisted, requires an "equilibrium of forces," which he defined as the balance that will be achieved when "each country in Central America has armed forces sufficient for its defense goals and nothing more."

Even on their face, those seemingly benign proposals should be viewed with caution by U.S. policymakers, because they contain some disturbing ambiguities. What, for instance, constitutes a "base"? In the past the Soviets have insisted that their extensive access to Cuban port facilities does not meet that definition. The crash last week in El Salvador of the Nicaraguan plane bearing Soviet-made missiles shows that the Cuba supply line is active. Similarly, would "military advisers" include the Cuban "technicians" and other so-called civilian advisers who have descended on Nicaragua since the Sandinista revolution?

Despite such ambiguities, Shevardnadze's plan is likely to attract considerable support in the United States. After all, critics of Washington's current Central America strategy will contend, the initiative implies Soviet support for reducing the Sandinista government's large military establishment, which has been an important objective of U.S. foreign policy.

That is a valid point, although it is not especially surprising that Moscow might be willing to make such a concession. Military aid to Nicaragua and other clients has become a serious drain on the Soviet treasury—something that the USSR can ill afford given the magnitude of its internal economic woes.

Moreover, Moscow's concession comes with an unacceptably high price tag. Shevardnadze's concept of a military equilibrium in the region is not self-implementing. Indeed, he stressed that the United

States and the Soviet Union should help the Central American nations define military sufficiency and stability. It is his vision that the superpowers would act as joint guarantors of a regional agreement on the equilibrium of forces. That aspect of his proposal is a Trojan horse for an increased, albeit more subtle, Soviet political role in Central America and, ultimately, one must anticipate, throughout the Western Hemisphere.

Shevardnadze's plan is consistent with the style of Soviet foreign policy that has emerged since the ascension of Mikhail Gorbachev; that approach relies on supple diplomacy rather than bluster and crude subversion techniques to advance Soviet interests.

In that respect it is a decided improvement on the pre-Gorbachev era, and it suggests that the Soviet Union is now conducting itself as a conventional great power instead of a renegade state motivated by an expansionist totalitarian ideology. Nevertheless, it is unwise for the United States to docilely accept the expanded influence of an adversarial great power—even a conventional one—in a region that has long been regarded as essential to American security. Washington's resistance to an extensive Soviet presence in the hemisphere is further justified because Moscow has few, if any, valid interests in this part of the world.

Conversely, the Soviets do have security concerns in some other regions, and U.S. leaders should acknowledge them instead of reflexively clinging to a global containment strategy established during the most virulent stages of the Cold War. For example, both Southwest Asia and the Middle East are important to the USSR because of geographic proximity as well as other factors. Moreover, that situation would exist even if a noncommunist government were in power. Attempting to exclude all Soviet influence from those areas is impractical as well as counterproductive.

The Soviet Union also has significant security (as well as economic and political) interests in Europe. As Henry Kissinger, Christopher Layne and other experts have stressed, it is necessary to formulate a settlement that will enable the two superpowers to disengage their military forces and accommodate the vast political and economic changes taking place in Eastern Europe. Such an arrangement is imperative if the now often predicted end of the Cold War is to become a reality. Negotiating a European political settlement will require Moscow's full cooperation, which is likely only if there is an explicit Western recognition of Soviet security interests.

162

The Soviet Union, however, has no comparable legitimate interests in the Western Hemisphere. There is no need or justification for a Soviet role, joint or otherwise, in Central America. The region is several thousand miles from the Soviet homeland, and it is one in which Moscow has meager economic stakes. Shevardnadze's "peace plan" is an attempt to legitimize an unwarranted intrusion into a region that has been an important American security zone since the proclamation of the Monroe Doctrine in the 1820s. U.S. officials should politely but firmly repel that attempt.

This article originally appeared in the *San Diego Union*, December 1, 1989.

Nix on Post-Soviet Aid

Policymakers should resist the siren calls of Richard Nixon and others who propose massive aid programs for the former Soviet Union. Even if an outpouring of funds would actually benefit the recipients, it would not be in the best interests of the American people. A nation with an overtaxed citizenry, a chronic federal budget deficit that may reach $400 billion this year and a growing array of domestic ills should not be seeking new ways to spend money on other countries.

Further, grandiose assistance schemes would probably harm rather than advance the causes of democracy and market economies in the Commonwealth of Independent States. The record of foreign aid programs throughout the Third World during the past four decades is dismal. Third World countries are littered with white-elephant development projects costing billions. Even worse, Western aid frequently has bankrolled authoritarian political policies and the disasters inflicted by centrally planned economies. Why should we assume that the results would be different in the CIS?

Instead of adopting wasteful aid proposals, the USA should open its market to the products of the CIS republics, enabling them to earn badly needed hard currency. The Bush administration's decision to authorize the importation of Russian space and nuclear technologies is a positive step. Nevertheless, the USA maintains a virtual iron curtain against imports as diverse as steel and textiles from both the CIS and the new democracies of Eastern Europe. Those barriers should be abolished immediately.

Except for helping to fund the dismantling of nuclear weapons in the CIS, which clearly increases the security of the American

163

people, the USA should pursue a policy of trade, not aid. That strategy would benefit all parties.

This article originally appeared in *USA Today*, March 13, 1992.

Aid to Russia Is Futile

All Americans want to see Russia make the transition from communism to democratic capitalism, but those who insist that the USA must provide a generous aid package to guarantee that outcome embrace two faulty assumptions.

The first fallacy is that actions taken by us would have a decisive impact on political and economic trends in Russia. That attitude greatly overestimates Washington's influence and reflects a pervasive conceit that all problems in the world have a "made in the USA" solution.

To make a successful transition, the Russian government must accelerate rather than slow the pace of economic reform. Massive privatization of industry and agriculture, an immediate end to all price controls and the establishment of a legal system that protects property rights are the essential steps.

If the Yeltsin government adopts that course, Russia will attract private foreign capital. Conversely, if Moscow continues to pursue a "half-pregnant" reform strategy, the economy will stagnate and the political future will be bleak.

The second fallacy is that government-to-government aid would advance the goal of a market economy. Given the dismal record of foreign aid programs throughout the Third World over the past four decades, it is astonishing that anyone still advocates that strategy. At best, aid sent to Russia would be wasted; at worst, it would encourage Moscow to adopt the same counterproductive policies as previous aid recipients.

The emergence of an authoritarian Russia would be an unpleasant development, but the outcome of the current political and economic struggle will be determined by internal, not external, factors. Russia is not a lump of clay to be sculpted by U.S. policymakers.

This article originally appeared in *USA Today*, December 22, 1992.

Back Off on Russia Aid

An audible sigh of relief can be heard in Washington now that Boris Yeltsin has apparently won the showdown with his political opponents. Predictably, there are calls to accelerate the delivery of U.S. economic aid to Russia to prop up the Yeltsin government and forestall a new bid for power by hard-line elements. A more cautious policy is warranted. Indeed, the Clinton administration may be making a serious mistake in linking U.S. interests so tightly to Yeltsin's political fortunes. His victory in this round does not guarantee that he will prevail in the long run. The resurgence of the "former" Communists in Lithuania and Poland could be repeated in Russia.

Furthermore, it is not clear how strong Yeltsin's own commitment is to market reforms and democracy. Reformers have complained repeatedly about the zig-zag course of Yeltsin's economic policy. His attitude toward democracy is even more suspect. Yeltsin's fondness for ruling by decree, his stifling control of the Russian news media and his appointment of a former KGB official who was in charge of harassing dissidents in the 1980s as the new chief of Russia's security apparatus are not encouraging signs. It will be most embarrassing to U.S. officials if Yeltsin turns out to be an autocratic "reform czar" instead of a democratic leader.

Flooding Russia with economic aid would be unwise in any case. U.S. foreign aid programs throughout the developing world have fostered command economies and bloated public bureaucracies. Aid money would strengthen those entrenched bureaucratic forces in Russia that are the most opposed to reform. Such "help" might doom any hope that the Russian people have of making the transition to democratic capitalism.

This article originally appeared in *USA Today*, October 5, 1993.

Ruffling Russia's Feathers a Bad Idea

President George W. Bush insists that he wants a new, cooperative relationship with Russia. The Cold War has been over for a decade, he emphasizes, and the United States no longer regards Russia as an adversary.

Those are noble words, but the Bush administration's actions in recent months belie such sentiments. As a result, the United States may be squandering a historic opportunity for an improvement in U.S.-Russian relations.

Moscow's reaction to the September 11 terrorist attacks appeared to create such an opportunity. Not only did Russian president Vladimir Putin vehemently denounce the attacks, but he gave the United

States substantive assistance in a variety of ways. Most crucially, Putin made it clear to the governments of the Central Asian republics that Russia did not object to a temporary U.S. military presence in the region to wage the war in Afghanistan. Without Russia's approval, the United States would have found it far more difficult to gain the cooperation of those governments, since they would not have wished to incur Moscow's displeasure. And without the use of former Soviet military bases, the United States would have had a much more difficult time prosecuting the war.

Russia helped the United States in other ways. For example, Moscow resisted pressure from the Organization of Petroleum Exporting Countries to cut its oil output to revive sagging global oil prices. As the world's second largest oil producer, Russia had a crucial role to play. Instead of responding favorably to OPEC's requests, Moscow maintained production at high levels—a position favored by the United States. Among other benefits, the Russian decision reduced the danger of an oil price spike as the United States waged war in Afghanistan and hinted darkly of possible future operations against Iraq—developments that would normally have caused jitters in world oil markets.

How has the Bush administration rewarded Russia for its cooperation? One of the administration's first initiatives was to announce America's withdrawal from the Antiballistic Missile Treaty, which Moscow had long regarded as the centerpiece of its relationship with the United States on arms control issues. The decision gave new ammunition to elements in Russia's political elite who argue that the United States seizes every opportunity to exploit and humiliate Russia in its weakened condition.

The administration then took two other provocative actions in rapid succession. First, U.S. officials let it be known that the United States intended to maintain a long-term military presence in the Central Asian republics. This was a classic double cross, and Russian officials were none too happy about Washington's action. The subsequent statement by U.S. military officials that the United States does not intend to keep forces in Central Asia "permanently" relieves Russian anxieties barely at all.

Those Russians with a sense of history recall that the United States said the same thing in 1951 about not stationing troops in Europe permanently when it sent four Army divisions to the Continent as part of a new NATO force. Five decades later, those troops are still there.

Second, the Bush administration played a duplicitous game with regard to agreed upon reductions in offensive nuclear weapons. At their most recent summit meeting, Bush and Putin had agreed to cut the number of warheads to a level between 1,700 and 2,200 warheads for each country. But U.S. officials have now announced that most of the reduction will not come from actually destroying surplus warheads. Instead, the excess warheads will simply be put in storage. Russian leaders have reacted angrily to this gambit, arguing that all cuts in offensive arsenals must be "irreversible," and that means destroying, not storing, warheads.

Such insensitive U.S. actions have rapidly revived Russian suspicions about Washington's global ambitions. The danger is not that Russia will launch a new offensive arms race or plunge the two countries into a new cold war. Thus far, Moscow's response has been surprisingly restrained. Russia clearly prefers a close, cooperative relationship with the United States and is not willing to close the door on that possibility by resorting to intemperate outbursts or crude retaliatory measures.

But if Washington continues to take unfair advantage, Russia can and probably will pursue other options. Moscow is already cultivating closer ties with such countries as Iran and China.

This article originally appeared in the *Charlotte Post*, February 21, 2002.

7. Middle East–Persian Gulf Policy

Introduction

The intertwined issues of U.S. Middle East and Persian Gulf policy have become a monumental headache for the United States. Despite more than three decades of U.S. mediation, punctuated by an assortment of high-profile peace initiatives, the Israeli-Palestinian dispute seems no closer to resolution than it did immediately following the Six Day War in 1967. Last year, President Bush's national security adviser, Condoleezza Rice, summed up the situation when she observed that the United States "cannot make bread out of a stone."

As I pointed out on several occasions over the past decade, the root problem is that the Israelis and the Palestinians are locked in an intractable struggle over core issues of identity. Neither side is willing to make the concessions that would be necessary to break the impasse. Progress may occur occasionally on peripheral matters, but whenever the central issues, such as the West Bank settlements or the status of Jerusalem, are addressed, a breakdown in negotiations inevitably occurs. The upsurge in the cycle of Palestinian terrorist attacks and Israeli reprisals during the past year makes any meaningful progress even more remote.

As difficult as it may be emotionally for U.S. policymakers to stand aloof from the fray, that is in fact the best policy from the standpoint of American interests. The Israeli-Palestinian dispute may have had a marginal bearing on U.S. security during the Cold War when the Soviet Union sought to exploit that conflict to establish a dominant position in the Arab world. But in the post–Cold War era, there are no global security ramifications to the Israeli-Palestinian feud. It may be of overwhelming importance to the parties involved, and perhaps to neighboring states, but in terms of its strategic importance it is indistinguishable from a score of ugly ethnic and religious conflicts elsewhere in the world. America can and should make it clear to both the Israelis and the Palestinians that it will be up to them to decide whether to live in peace or perpetuate an endless cycle of violence.

The Persian Gulf entanglement has proven equally frustrating. Those of us who opposed the Gulf War in 1991 warned that, while the United States might score a decisive military victory, it would be merely the beginning of an interminable American mission in one of the most volatile and dangerous regions of the world. That fear has been justified. More than a decade later, the United States is still stuck in its role as nanny of the Persian Gulf. Contrary to widespread expectations, Saddam Hussein's regime in Iraq did not collapse following its defeat in the Gulf War. Washington has remained in the Persian Gulf as Saddam's jailer. Lacking any worthwhile ideas, the United States enforces an embargo that has devastated millions of innocent Iraqis while barely inconveniencing the regime. That embargo, which is simultaneously cruel and ineffectual, has earned the United States the hatred of much of the Muslim world.

Launching another war to oust Saddam from power might solve one problem, but it would create a whole new set of problems. As I noted in various articles, it would make the United States ultimately responsible for the future of post-Saddam Iraq. Issues such as regional secession movements, religious extremism, and instability in the region as Iran sought to exploit Iraq's demise as a strategic counterweight could create headaches that might even surpass the current ones.

Alternatives to the current policy exist, if U.S. officials are willing to consider them. I noted as far back as 1990 that the Iraqi military was not the equivalent of Germany's military juggernaut in World War II; it was a large, but ill trained, force that primarily served as an instrument of Saddam's system of domestic repression. Even at the time of the Gulf War, Saddam's neighbors had more military personnel and hardware at their disposal than he did. That gap has grown in the intervening years. Therefore, the ingredients are in place for a containment policy run by the states in the region.

That is even true with regard to the most difficult issue: Iraq's capabilities in the area of weapons of mass destruction (WMD). Israel's possession of 150 to 300 nuclear weapons makes it unlikely that Iraq will attack that country with WMD. (The only exception might be if the United States seeks to remove Saddam from power and he concludes he has nothing to lose.) Iraq's other neighbors need to contemplate what weapons they might need to effectively deter Iraq from engaging in WMD blackmail.

The proliferation of such weapons is obviously not an optimal outcome, even if they are used solely for deterrent purposes. But the alternative is to have U.S. forces deployed indefinitely in the Persian Gulf, with the likelihood that sooner or later they will be drawn into a confrontation with Iraq or another expansionist power (probably Iran). That scenario is much worse from the standpoint of America's security interests.

Bush Jumped the Gun in the Gulf

The Bush administration's decision to dispatch American troops to the Arabian peninsula was a knee-jerk, Cold War reaction that the president and the rest of us may soon regret. We now confront a crisis that may ultimately escalate into full-scale combat costing $1 billion a day and untold numbers of lives. In essence, the Bush administration has made the United States the point man in the Middle East, a dangerous and thankless status that prudent statesmen would seek to avoid.

Throughout the Cold War, our leaders insisted that the United States is the only power capable of preventing aggression. However, that belief was based on the assumption that the Soviet Union or a Soviet surrogate would be the source of aggression and that only a superpower could thwart the other superpower and its agents.

Unfortunately, that attitude has persisted into the post–Cold War era, in which global political and military conditions are vastly different. Moscow is no longer a likely source of expansionist threats. As the Persian Gulf episode demonstrates, smaller, regional powers with their own agendas are now the probable candidates.

But the more limited nature of such threats also means that other regional powers should be able to contain them. There is no longer even a plausible case for the United States' being the planetary policeman, taking responsibility for all security burdens.

That point is especially relevant to the Persian Gulf. Washington responded reflexively to Iraq's invasion, adopting a high-profile leadership role with all the attendant costs and risks. No one in the Bush administration even considered alternatives to our barging into the region.

There was, in fact, little need for the dangerous step of introducing U.S. combat forces. The administration's equation of Saddam Hussein with Adolf Hitler—with the implication that Mr. Hussein had an ability to achieve virtually unlimited expansionist objectives—was fundamentally flawed. Much has been made of Baghdad's million-man army, but Iraq is still a small Third World nation with a population of barely 17 million. While oil rich, it has an economy impoverished by the costly war with Iran. This is hardly the foundation for a sustained expansionist push.

Moreover, Iraq's neighbors were quite capable of limiting its expansionism (although probably not of compelling it to disgorge

Kuwait). Iran, Syria, Jordan, Saudi Arabia and Turkey have more than 1.8 million troops, outnumbering Baghdad's forces by nearly two to one. Moreover, Iraq has 5,500 tanks to its neighbors' 9,900. Baghdad has only 513 combat aircraft, compared with the nearly 1,300 of its potential foes.

Those figures do not include the additional forces that other regional powers, such as Egypt, could bring to bear. Nor do they take into account the support—especially naval support—that could be provided by outside powers, most notably Japan and the members of the European Community, who rely far more heavily than the United States on Middle East oil.

We assume that President Hussein had designs on Saudi Arabia. But he could not have invaded Saudi Arabia without stretching his forces on the southern front dangerously thin. This would have left Iraq exceedingly vulnerable to Syrian, Iranian and even Turkish counterattacks. This was a danger that Mr. Hussein could not afford to ignore.

The Bush administration never allowed time for such interested parties to deal with Iraqi aggression on their own. Nor did it give the Arab League a chance to formulate a political solution. The fear was that either Iraq would take Saudi Arabia without effective resistance or that, in the event of determined opposition, the resulting regional conflagration would cut off oil supplies.

But the U.S. buildup—on a scale that portends offensive operations against Iraq—also puts oil supplies at grave risk. Even worse, the dominant American presence enables Saddam Hussein to portray himself as an Arab hero standing up to Western neocolonialist invaders.

The administration also feared that, even without an invasion of Saudi Arabia, Iraq would dominate OPEC, threatening the West with high oil prices and disruptions in supply. But that would be strange behavior indeed for a country in economic ruin and $80 billion in debt. More likely, it would seek to maximize its oil revenues, which means providing a steady supply at prices low enough to discourage widespread conservation and alternate fuels.

As Washington rushed into the conflict it seemed almost grateful for the opportunity to demonstrate America's continuing global leadership in a post–Cold War setting. Asserting such "leadership" may gratify the egos of policymakers obsessed with maintaining a hyperactive American military role despite the demise of the Cold War. It may also serve the interests of the national security establishment, which desperately needs a justification for $300 billion military budgets. It may even be an occasion for gratitude on the part of nations that were spared the risks and costs of defending their own vital interests (although one should not count on such gratitude).

But a major military deployment that costs more than $15 million a day and risks a shooting war that would cost $1 billion a day— not to mention producing a steady stream of casualties—does not serve the interests of the American people.

This article originally appeared in the *New York Times*, August 18, 1990. Reprinted with permission.

Don't Rush into Folly in the Gulf

The beat of Persian Gulf war drums has suddenly become very loud. Reiterating that Saddam Hussein is another Hitler, the administration is now hinting that the mistreatment of U.S. hostages in Iraq and Kuwait will be used as a pretext for war.

The United States is again sliding inexorably into a war the Congress has not sanctioned. Since 1945, American presidents have committed U.S. troops to two major wars (Korea and Vietnam) and a host of lesser conflicts (most recently Panama, Grenada and Lebanon) without asking Congress to declare war. Dusting off the imperial presidency's supposed prerogatives, the Bush administration has categorically refused to promise that it will seek congressional authorization before initiating hostilities against Iraq. Congress should act now—before it is too late—and prohibit the use of U.S. forces in offensive actions against Iraq unless Congress expressly approves.

By making the president commander in chief while reserving to Congress the power to declare war and ratify treaties, the Framers issued—in constitutional scholar Edward S. Corwin's oft-quoted observation—an invitation for the two branches to struggle for supremacy in conducting foreign policy. Nevertheless, until the end of World War II, it was clearly understood that a president could not commit U.S. forces to a major conflict without the consent of Congress.

The Cold War's exigencies upset the delicate constitutional balance. To meet the perceived communist threat in a world that was viewed as bipolar both geopolitically and ideologically, the United

174

States became a national security state—permanently mobilized for war in order to contain communism worldwide. Executive branch authority increased dramatically while congressional power eroded (and, to a large degree, was abdicated voluntarily). In a nuclear world, it was said, the president needed a free hand to respond quickly to global crises.

In the Persian Gulf crisis, however, there are no compelling arguments for allowing the administration to start a war without first obtaining congressional consent. Americans and their elected representatives have the time to debate Washington's Persian Gulf policy, a debate too important to be left to street demonstrations staged by aging 1960s radicals. The Persian Gulf crisis is not a Cold War superpower confrontation with all the possibilities of sudden escalation to the nuclear level that such a clash could entail. There is no imminent danger to America's territorial integrity, to its physical and economic security or even to the global balance of power. Thus, none of the conditions cited during the Cold War as support for unconstrained presidential authority to use the military apply in this case. This crisis has dragged on more than three months, and there is time to reflect before making the fateful decision for war in the gulf, a conflict that may not end quickly and will assuredly cost American lives.

A sober assessment of U.S. policy objectives in the gulf is needed. Will vanquishing Iraq really bring stability to that perennially volatile region? Will the anti-Iraq coalition hold together if the United States strikes Iraq first? What impact will an American-initiated war have on moderate Arab governments—and on Arab populations? How will Washington's policy affect U.S.-Israeli relations?

Beyond the issues pertinent to the immediate crisis, Bush's whole notion of a "new world order" needs to be scrutinized. In the post–Cold War era, it is far from clear that America must remain the world's policeman, or that it can afford to do so. In this sense, the Persian Gulf crisis provides the opportunity for a new, full-scale "Great Debate" about America's purposes and world role.

Wars are easy to start but often difficult to end. Thus the hard questions—about the nature of America's security interests, the feasibility of Washington's objectives, and the relationship of military means to policy ends—must be asked before the shooting starts.

In its historic 1966 hearings, the Senate Foreign Relations Committee asked the right questions about U.S. policy in Vietnam. But it was too late to halt the march of folly in Southeast Asia, because vast numbers of American troops had already been committed to combat. Congress should not make that mistake again. Morally and constitutionally, it is time for Congress to assert its foreign policy prerogatives—especially the power to declare war—in the Persian Gulf crisis.

This article, coauthored with Christopher Layne, originally appeared in the *Los Angeles Times*, November 6, 1990.

U.S. Role Can Make Peace Harder to Attain

Secretary of State James Baker's Middle East trip has kindled expectations that the USA will be able to achieve a breakthrough in the long-standing dispute between Israel and its Arab neighbors. Those expectations are unrealistic. Despite the sense of U.S. omnipotence that has emerged from the military triumph in the Persian Gulf, some problems are beyond Washington's ability to solve. The Arab-Israeli conflict is one.

The USA's high profile actually gives the adversaries an incentive to posture rather than confront the substantive issues.

Arab governments insist that because Washington is Israel's principal sponsor and protector, the USA can "deliver" an acceptable settlement. That fiction spares them from having to recognize Israel and conduct direct negotiations.

Israeli leaders play a similar game. Confident the USA will never abandon Israel, they exhibit a continuing intransigence on the central issue of a Palestinian homeland. Washington's support enables them to avoid hard choices about territorial concessions that are necessary to secure a lasting peace. Instead, they prefer to keep the Palestinians in a condition of political limbo.

Proponents of U.S. activism cite the Camp David Accords as an example of what mediation can accomplish. But those agreements occurred because both Israel and Egypt were fully committed to reaching a settlement. Cairo was tired of the debilitating costs of an endless confrontation and wanted to regain the Sinai. Israel was willing to withdraw from the Sinai if that concession would split the Arab coalition and secure peace on its southwestern flank.

The current situation is fundamentally different. The remaining issues impinge on core Israeli security concerns and involve lands imbued with historical significance for the Jewish state. Combined with Palestinian demands for an independent state on those same lands, this leaves little room for compromise.

The USA is creating expectations it cannot fulfill. Arab members of the anti-Iraq coalition expect to be rewarded for supporting Washington. That reward, in their view, should include U.S. pressure on Israel to make major concessions. Conversely, Israel expects to be rewarded for not responding to Iraq's Scud attacks and disrupting the anti-Saddam coalition, specifically an easing of pressure on the Palestinian question.

Washington is now encountering some of the subtle costs of creating the coalition against Iraq. It is unlikely that the USA can satisfy the opposing demands of its Middle East allies. Indeed, by attempting to do so, it may ultimately antagonize both sides. A settlement to the Arab-Israeli conflict, if it is ever achieved, must come from the parties themselves.

This article originally appeared in *USA Today*, March 13, 1991.

The United States Should Butt Out of Mideast Squabbles

The much-touted Middle East peace plan of Secretary of State James Baker has already begun to falter. Baker has encountered enormous difficulties just in getting the parties to agree on procedures for a regional peace conference.

Such intransigence bodes ill for the prospect of success once the thorny substantive issues must be addressed. Even if Baker eventually gets his peace conference, it is likely to produce few if any meaningful results.

Washington's latest round of diplomatic activism in the Middle East was based on two assumptions:

The Bush administration believed that because Israel and several major Arab nations were on the same side in opposing Iraq's expansionist ambitions, that cooperation would carry over into the postwar period and lead to progress on the long-standing disputes between Israel and its neighbors.

Some officials also assumed that the decisive victory by the U.S.-led coalition in the Gulf War would translate into greater diplomatic influence for the USA throughout the Middle East.

Neither premise was valid. Washington's diplomatic activism may, in fact, be counterproductive. Both sides exploit the USA's role to engage in posturing rather than conduct serious negotiations.

The Arab governments insist that Washington pressure Israel and "deliver" a settlement. Israel, for its part, can afford to be uncompromising, confident that its "special relationship" with the USA can weather any temporary diplomatic storms.

The USA should stop playing a game that serves no one's best interests, least of all its own. If the adversaries finally conclude that they wish to end the decades of hostility, Washington can help mediate an agreement. But the USA must stop acting as though it has more to gain from a peace settlement than do the disputants.

There should be no further hyperactive shuttle diplomacy to beg the parties to agree to a peace conference. Nor should there be any promises of financial aid to bribe them to conclude a peace that is in their own interests.

One other policy change is essential. The USA cannot hope to act as an "honest broker" and still be Israel's principal sponsor. It is time to end the $3 billion a year aid program to that country. Such largess not only encourages the Israeli leadership to be intransigent, but it makes U.S. taxpayers accomplices in the ongoing de facto annexation of the West Bank.

Israel may well conclude that continued control of the West Bank is justified from the standpoint of both historical and security considerations. But it should have to rely on its own resources to implement that policy. U.S. taxpayers should not be asked to finance the territorial expansionism or imperial ambitions of another country.

This article originally appeared in *USA Today*, May 17, 1991.

"Payoff" Was Illusion

The outcome of the USA's intervention in the Persian Gulf is reminiscent of a cynical medical joke: The operation was a success but the patient died.

Washington won a military victory with surprisingly few U.S. casualties, for which we can all be thankful. But the USA achieved few meaningful political goals, and the intervention created more problems than it solved.

Kuwait is busily persecuting Palestinians and other minorities as well as democratic reformers.

Iran is already exploiting the power vacuum created by the weakening of Iraq to expand its influence in the region, setting the stage for a confrontation with the USA over another alleged threat to oil supplies.

Washington has become the protector of the Kurds by stationing a rapid deployment force in Turkey for possible intervention, a step that could entangle the USA in Iraqi civil conflicts as messy as the ongoing turmoil in Yugoslavia.

Washington's attempt to encourage the gulf nations to create a collective security arrangement is in shambles. Those regimes have few incentives to assume the costs and risks of protecting their own security if they believe the USA will always come to the rescue.

The Bush administration did not even achieve its goal of removing "the new Hitler," Saddam Hussein. Washington's principal "accomplishment" was to restore the autocratic emir of Kuwait to a palace refurbished with gold-plated bathroom fixtures (courtesy of the labor of U.S. military personnel).

To attain that dubious objective, the USA put American soldiers at risk, slaughtered more than 60,000 Iraqis and increased the turmoil in an already volatile region.

Victory parades cannot disguise the fact that although the gulf intervention was a military success, it has been a political failure.

This article originally appeared in *USA Today*, July 29, 1991.

Don't Risk More Gulf Folly

War clouds are gathering again in the Persian Guff as the UN Security Council contemplates authorizing air strikes to punish Saddam Hussein for his defiance of inspectors searching for evidence of his nuclear and chemical weapons programs.

The USA should avoid a "Son of Desert Storm" operation. Even those who insisted that the Persian Gulf War served U.S. security interests cannot argue that a new round of coercion is necessary.

Iraq's military forces, which were never as potent as pro-war elements contended, have been broken and will take years to recover. Although Saddam's nuclear ambitions are worrisome, Iraq is not on the verge of becoming a nuclear weapons power. Most experts believe that Baghdad is years away from building a single crude nuclear device, much less deploying an operational arsenal.

The other argument for air strikes—that the United Nations' credibility is at stake—is even less compelling. Administration officials are in danger of believing their own propaganda. Although they obtained UN approval to expel Iraq from Kuwait, that was primarily a facade for a U.S.-dominated operation. Desert Storm was no more a genuine collective security enterprise than the "police action" in Korea 40 years earlier. In both cases, Washington merely used the United Nations for its own purposes.

It would be folly for the USA to waste lives in another military adventure that could further destabilize Iraq and the entire gulf region just to support the United Nations' pretensions as an effective global peacekeeping organization.

Washington's military victory in the Gulf War has already turned to political ashes, as evidenced by Baghdad's intransigence, the absence of democracy in Kuwait, and Iran's burgeoning power. Stirring those ashes would be pointless.

This article originally appeared in *USA Today*, July 24, 1992.

Policing Gulf Futile Policy

Iraq's latest troop movements raise fears of a second Persian Gulf War less than four years after the USA's overwhelming military triumph. That possibility—and one hopes it is just a false alarm—underscores the futility of Washington's policy of policing the Persian Gulf.

The problem with attempting to stabilize such a politically turbulent region is that even when a problem has been "fixed," it doesn't stay fixed.

The latest incident also demonstrates that those who assumed that Operation Desert Storm would chill the blood of aggressors around the world were naive.

Not only has that victory failed to deter the Serbs, Armenians, Abkhazians and others who have since resorted to force for territorial gain, it may not even have deterred Saddam Hussein.

How many times is the USA prepared to wage war and waste the lives of its military personnel to protect Kuwait and the other decrepit autocracies of the Persian Gulf? Even if this crisis does not flare into combat, sooner or later Iraq—or, more likely, Iran—will make another bid for preeminence in the region.

Is the USA really willing to police the gulf forever, despite the tremendous cost and risk?

The conventional wisdom is that the USA must do so to protect its oil supply. But respected economists, including Milton Friedman, James Tobin and David Henderson, have demolished that rationale.

Henderson, for example, has calculated that an Iraqi conquest of Kuwait and its neighbors would give Saddam control of only 23 percent of world oil production—with the ability to drive up oil prices by a maximum of 50 percent.

The cost to the USA of that development would be $30 billion a year. But Washington spends more than $40 billion each year just maintaining the forces needed to guard the security of the gulf and intervene in a crisis. Given that expense, the "cheap" oil of the Persian Gulf is an illusory bargain.

Washington accomplished little of lasting value with Desert Storm. This time the USA should let the odious regimes of the gulf region fight their own battles. Do not use American troops as their bodyguards.

This article originally appeared in *USA Today*, October 10, 1994.

United States Has No Role in Iraq

Saddam Hussein's successful military assault on the Kurdish city of Irbil underscores the bankruptcy of the United States' Persian Gulf policy.

The Clinton administration, under pressure to "do something," contemplates a "limited" military response and presses for a postponement of the United Nations agreement under which Iraq could resume sales of oil and use the revenue to purchase humanitarian goods for Iraqi citizens.

Both reactions are ill-advised.

The oil embargo has inflicted suffering on innocent Iraqis while barely inconveniencing Saddam and his cronies. There is no evidence that continuing such a cruel measure will produce a better result in the future.

Military action, even if confined to air strikes, would entangle the United States further in the complex thicket of Persian Gulf politics.

After the Gulf War, the United States pledged to shield the Kurds from Baghdad's coercion. But the Kurds have been fighting among themselves. One faction has openly allied itself with Iran; the other has sought the assistance of Saddam's regime—which prompted the attack on Irbil. Ironically, if the United States intervenes against Baghdad's forces, it helps strengthen Iran's influence in the region.

More than five years after the Gulf War, the United States' policy lacks any coherent rationale. In the name of preserving access to "cheap" Persian Gulf oil, we maintain extensive military forces to rescue an assortment of regional clients. But the cost of that commitment exceeds $40 billion a year—making gulf oil anything but "cheap."

Even worse, the United States has crawled into bed with some of the most odious, repressive governments and political factions in the world, thereby incurring the wrath of opposing (often equally odious) groups.

The bombings in Saudi Arabia highlight the danger to American troops as they become identified with one side in murky disputes. The United States is now deeply involved in quarrels, and even armed struggles, that it barely comprehends.

The situation involving the Kurds illustrates the point. Which Kurdish faction represents the values of democracy and justice— the pro-Iranian Patriotic Union of Kurdistan or Saddam's latest ally, the Kurdish Democratic Party?

It is unlikely that one American in 100 could venture an informed guess. The most probable answer is that neither faction even remotely embodies those values.

There is nothing at stake in the current struggle, or indeed the entire gulf region, that warrants risking American lives. Rather than retaliating against Baghdad for its attack on Irbil, the United States should disengage its forces from a dangerous and unrewarding commitment.

This article originally appeared in *USA Today*, September 3, 1996.

Misguided Missiles

Prominent Republicans, while endorsing President Clinton's decision to launch cruise missiles against Iraq, have caustically noted the president's failure to hold together the coalition of the Persian Gulf War. That failure, they say, reflects a growing lack of confidence in Washington's, or more precisely, Mr. Clinton's leadership.

It is true that the Gulf War coalition no longer exists. International backing for the latest American confrontation with Saddam Hussein was conspicuously meager. Only Britain gave early support. Germany, Japan, Israel and Kuwait offered belated and cautious endorsements. The other relevant European and Middle Eastern countries either remained silent or were openly critical.

But this lack of international support has little to do with American leadership or its absence. A far more important reason is that other governments believe that U.S. policy toward Iraq is misguided, potentially dangerous and undermines their interests.

That attitude is especially prevalent in the Middle East. Turkey and Saudi Arabia refused to let the Clinton administration use bases on their territory for raids against Iraq. Other countries apparently refused to grant overflight rights. Many Americans seem puzzled and angry that the principal beneficiaries of the Gulf War have been so uncooperative. But there are understandable reasons for their recalcitrance.

Most important, Turkey and the Persian Gulf states fear Iran far more than they do Iraq. They worry that if the United States continues to weaken Saddam Hussein politically and militarily, it could create a power vacuum that would prove irresistible to Iran. Thus none of the governments in the region has ever shown much enthusiasm for Washington's support of the de facto Kurdish state in northern Iraq or even for the limited protection given to Shiite secessionists in the south.

Another factor is that countries with troublesome human rights records—including Saudi Arabia and Turkey—are uneasy about the proposition that the use of force by a government within its own territory constitutes aggression that can justify an international military response. Several of our allies have restless ethnic or religious minorities with secessionist objectives and are thus unlikely to applaud the implied American support of Kurdish separatism in Iraq.

Finally, the Gulf States worry that endorsing American attacks on a fellow Arab country may further embolden their domestic critics who accuse them of being American lackeys. The U.S. military presence is a lightning rod for dissidents, as shown most recently by the bombing of the American barracks in Dhahran in June.

Governments in Egypt, Jordan and Bahrain have a precarious grip on power, and even the stability of Saudi Arabia is increasingly doubtful. The last thing such governments want is to strengthen their enemies by endorsing American attacks against Iraq.

A simple display of American "leadership" is unlikely to change the allies' minds. It is arrogance to assume that whatever happens in the world must be the result of American action or inaction. The

Persian Gulf states may want protection, but they will remain neutral or even denounce the United States when it seems necessary.

Americans should not expect gratitude, much less obedience, from such "friends." Nor should we think that the Gulf War coalition can be easily reassembled. If the United States insists on being the guardian of the Persian Gulf, it will be a lonely and often resented role.

This article originally appeared in the *New York Times*, September 12, 1996. Reprinted with permission.

This Isn't a U.S. Fight

Holding another conference in Washington to put the beleaguered Middle East peace process back on track is a mistake. Under no circumstances should the United States be drawn in yet again to play the role of mediator. All that will do is enable Israeli and Palestinian leaders to posture for their constituencies and use the United States as a scapegoat for any failure in the negotiations.

Even if a new accord is reached, it is likely to prove no more durable or meaningful than the previous agreements that have been shattered by the latest round of violence in the West Bank and Gaza.

There is little the United States can do to end the long-standing Palestinian-Israeli conflict. Peace is not a product that can be exported by Washington. The United States can neither bribe nor cajole unwilling parties to overcome their animosities and adopt a policy of constructive coexistence.

If a viable settlement to the dispute is over achieved, it will come about only when overwhelming majorities in both the Israeli and Palestinian communities become so weary of violence and hatred that they are willing to make the necessary mutual concessions. That day appears to be far away. True, there are many in both communities who desire peace, but the hard-liners increasingly have the power to sabotage their initiatives.

Washington should treat the Israeli-Palestinian struggle as merely one of many ugly parochial conflicts now taking place around the world. The end of the Cold War has eliminated whatever larger strategic significance such squabbles might once have had. The issues at stake in the West Bank and Gaza may be extremely important to the Israelis and Palestinians. Those issues, however, do not have substantial relevance to the security and well-being of America. We should adopt a policy of benign detachment toward the conflict. It is national arrogance to assume that every problem has a "made in Washington" solution. We should let the Israelis and Palestinians confront the reality that they must work out their problems or bear the consequences.

This article originally appeared in *USA Today*, September 30, 1996.

Oust Saddam ... and Replace Him with Whom or What?

U.S. policy toward Iraq has now shifted from containment to the goal of ousting Saddam Hussein from power. No matter how emotionally satisfying the option of removing a thug like Saddam may seem, that strategy is extremely ill-advised. It will make Washington responsible for Iraq's political future and entangle the United States in an endless nation-building mission beset by intractable problems.

Barring a coup against Saddam by one of his equally brutal and corrupt cronies, U.S. military forces would probably have to dislodge him. Some optimists argue that the so-called Iraqi democratic opposition in exile, especially the largest umbrella group, the Iraqi National Congress, can do the job with minimal assistance from the United States. That apparently was the logic motivating the 105th Congress to pass the Iraq Liberation Act and earmark $97 million to support efforts to undermine Saddam's regime. But few knowledgeable analysts take the Iraqi opposition's prospects seriously.

Gen. Anthony Zinni, commander of U.S. forces in the Persian Gulf, notes that anti-Saddam forces are rife with factionalism and show little independent initiative. Indeed, the opposition is a motley assortment of 91 groups running the gamut from Marxist revolutionaries to Islamic fundamentalists. The principal goal of most factions seems to have been extracting funds from a credulous U.S. Congress rather than waging an armed liberation struggle against the Baghdad regime.

That underscores the first major problem with a U.S. commitment to oust Saddam. Not only would American troops be needed to install a new government, but they'd have to protect it from authoritarian elements and create democratic institutions strong enough to survive the eventual departure of U.S. occupation forces. Otherwise, another military dictator, a "new Saddam," would emerge, and

Washington would face a renewed threat to its goal of peace and stability in the Persian Gulf region.

Installing and preserving a democratic Iraqi government would entail a nation-building mission of indefinite duration that would dwarf the effort in Bosnia. The Bosnia mission is now in its fourth year and has already cost U.S. taxpayers some $10 billion.

The unpromising prospects for a stable democratic system in Iraq should be sufficient to dissuade those who want the U.S. military to occupy Baghdad. But there are other problems. Most notably, there is the issue posed by two persistent regional secession movements: the Kurds in the north and the Shiites in the south. Washington would have to decide whether to commit itself to preserving the territorial integrity of Iraq or to give its blessing to the secessionists. Either option has a serious downside.

Holding Iraq together might take some doing. Attempting to force the Kurds and Shiites to remain under Baghdad's jurisdiction would probably provoke ferocious resistance. Washington would face the task of explaining to Americans why troops were dying in military campaigns to suppress the aspirations of populations that merely want to throw off the shackles of Iraq's Sunni Muslim elite. Yet endorsing the creation of independent Kurdish and Shiite states would have the United States presiding over the dismemberment of Iraq—an action Sunnis and others throughout the Islamic world would resent. Dismemberment would also eliminate the only significant regional military counterweight to Iran.

Furthermore, the establishment of an independent Kurdistan would create a thorny problem for Washington's ally, Turkey. A Kurdish republic would be an incitement for Turkey's Kurdish population—more than half of all Kurds living in the region. Ankara has waged a bloody war for more than 14 years to suppress a Kurdish insurgency in southeastern Turkey. Turkish forces have repeatedly entered northern Iraq since the Gulf War, taking advantage of the fact that Saddam's regime does not exercise effective control of the area. Turkey would find its difficulties multiplied if rebel forces could find sanctuary in a neighboring Kurdish state, and Turkish military incursions would be considered a violation of international law. None of this would matter if the United States hadn't declared the peace and stability of the Persian Gulf region to be a vital national interest. Trying to stabilize one of the world's most politically turbulent regions has proven to be a frustrating, open-ended objective.

Even if Iraq ceases to be a disruptive power, there are certain to be other crises: an Iranian bid for regional preeminence or a radical revolution against the Saudi monarchy, to mention the two most likely.

As ill-conceived as current U.S. policy may be, a decision to oust Saddam and become responsible for Iraq's political future would be far worse. The United States would then be the full-blown successor of the Ottoman and British Empires as the colonial overlord in the gulf region. No rational American should be willing to expend the blood and treasure such a mission would require.

This article originally appeared in the *Christian Science Monitor*, February 8, 1999.

Wearing Blinders on Turkey?

Massive anti-American demonstrations in Greece have stunned the Clinton White House, compelling the president to reschedule and shorten his visit to that country. The conventional wisdom is that the outpouring of rage against the United States is either typical fare from radical leftists, still furious about Washington's support of the military junta that ruled Greece from 1967 to 1974, or residual anger at NATO's war against Serbia, which was overwhelmingly unpopular among Greeks.

Both factors undoubtedly play a role, but there is another reason: annoyance at Washington's increasingly evident bias toward Greece's long-time rival, Turkey. Greeks are especially upset that U.S. policymakers ignore or excuse Turkey's behavior—even when Ankara's actions include military aggression, ethnic cleansing and pervasive human rights violations.

Washington's double standard is breathtaking. The United States was in the forefront of demands that NATO take military action against Serbia because of its ethnic cleansing in Kosovo. Yet U.S. officials have expressed only tepid and perfunctory criticism of NATO-member Turkey's ongoing occupation of Cyprus. Turkey invaded that country in 1974, occupied some 37 percent of its territory, expelled more than 165,000 Greek Cypriots from their homes, set up a puppet republic and brought in tens of thousands of colonists from the Turkish mainland. If Ankara's actions in Cyprus do not constitute ethnic cleansing, the term has no meaning.

The Cyprus episode is not Turkey's only disturbing behavior. For more than 14 years, Turkish security forces waged a violent counterinsurgency campaign against Kurdish separatist rebels in southeastern Turkey. Nearly 37,000 people perished in that struggle, which only now seems to be winding down. The main Kurdish rebel group—the pro-communist Kurdish Workers Party—clearly committed terrorist acts. But Human Rights Watch and other organizations have concluded that the Turkish military was responsible for the majority of civilian casualties. Turkey's counterinsurgency campaign also included the forced "depopulation" of some 3,000 Kurdish villages and the razing of at least 900 villages.

Given Ankara's track record on aggression and ethnic cleansing, Greeks cite the hypocrisy of the United States and its allies in allowing Turkish forces to participate in the war against Serbia. But Washington's double standard regarding Turkey extends further. U.S. officials insist that NATO is an alliance of democracies and any nation wishing to become a member must have a firm commitment to democratic practices. Yet Washington said little in 1997 when the Turkish military gave an ultimatum to the country's prime minister: resign or be overthrown. And U.S. officials do not have much to say when Turkish authorities routinely jail journalists and academics who have the temerity to suggest that there is an ethnically distinct Kurdish minority in Turkey—much less that the Turkish government ought to pursue a less repressive policy toward that minority.

In short, the Greeks are angry because it is all too evident that Turkey has become Washington's pet ally and that Ankara can get away with murder—sometimes literally. The underlying reason for the pro-Turkish bias was expressed candidly by U.S. Ambassador to the United Nations Richard Holbrooke. According to Mr. Holbrooke, Turkey is as important to the United States and NATO in the post–Cold War era as West Germany was during the Cold War. A government that regards Turkey as such an indispensable ally is not likely to let minor blemishes like military aggression, ethnic cleansing or contempt for democratic norms preclude a close relationship.

Washington's indulgent attitude is short-sighted as well as hypocritical. U.S. policymakers regard Turkey as a bulwark against Islamic radicalism and as a stabilizing influence in the Balkans, the Middle East and Central Asia. The first assumption is questionable, given the strength of radical Islamic elements inside Turkey; the second assumption is wholly fallacious.

Turkey shows signs of being a disruptive, revisionist power, not a stabilizing, status quo power. In addition to Ankara's intransigence regarding Cyprus, Turkey imposed a brutal economic blockade against Armenia and has threatened to use force to settle disputes with Syria. Worst of all is Ankara's conduct toward Greece. Turkish air force planes routinely violate Greek airspace and engage in other forms of harassment, and Ankara continues to press claims to Greek islands in the Aegean. Again, the United States not only fails to condemn such behavior, it is receptive to Turkey's dubious territorial claims.

Although there has been much press speculation about an improvement in Greco-Turkish relations as a result of humanitarian cooperation in the aftermath of the earthquakes that damaged both countries, the conciliatory actions have thus far been overwhelmingly one way. For example, Greece has dropped its opposition to Turkey's becoming a candidate for membership in the European Union. Turkey promptly pocketed that concession but has not reciprocated with concessions on Cyprus or any other issue.

It is, of course, not Washington's responsibility to compel Ankara to cease its offensive behavior. But the United States should at least not be Turkey's enabler. Unfortunately, Washington's flagrant double standard encourages Turkish officials' inflated sense of their country's strategic importance and may even encourage them to conclude that they can pursue aggressive measures against neighboring countries with U.S. acquiescence, if not tacit approval. The demonstrations convulsing Greece are at least partly a response to Washington's hypocrisy. It is a message the administration should heed.

This article originally appeared in the *Washington Times*, November 18, 1999.

Benign Detachment Is Best

Pressure is mounting on the Bush administration to become more "engaged" in the Israeli-Palestinian conflict. Recently, Egypt and Saudi Arabia as well as Yasser Arafat's Palestinian Authority have called on Washington to stop Israel from escalating its coercive tactics in the West Bank and Gaza. The administration should firmly resist the pressure to "do something."

When President Bush came into office, he and his advisers indicated they intended to back away from the intrusive, hyperactivist policy of the Clinton years. Their more restrained approach was based on the correct assumption that Washington could not facilitate a peace accord unless both parties were sufficiently tired of the violence and bloodshed to make essential concessions.

Unfortunately, neither side has reached that point. Hamas and other extremist factions in the Palestinian community resort to horrific acts of violence, including terrorist bombings, to further their cause. It isn't clear Arafat could rein in the extremists even if he wished to. For its part, the Israeli government of Ariel Sharon responds with attacks on alleged terrorist targets without much concern about innocent victims who may be caught in the crossfire.

That is not an environment conducive to a peace settlement. Both sides wish to manipulate Washington for their own purposes. It is perilously easy for a well-meaning U.S. mediation effort to burgeon into unrealistic expectations that the administration can produce a "made in Washington" solution. President Clinton nearly succumbed to such delusions of grandeur at Camp David.

Calls for renewed U.S. activism, including suggestions that the United States provide official monitors or observers, would put this country on a very slippery slope. There is no need for America to incur the risk of acquiring a Middle East headache.

The Israeli-Palestinian quarrel is merely one of many nasty ethnic and religious conflicts taking place around the world today. But in contrast to the Cold War era, when an aggressive major power, the Soviet Union, could have exploited that quarrel, the Israeli-Palestinian struggle no longer has global strategic implications. It is a parochial squabble that the United States can and should treat with benign detachment.

This article originally appeared in *USA Today*, August 9, 2001.

8. Policy toward the United Nations and Its Offspring

Introduction

Discussions of the United Nations often seem more akin to a theological debate than a rational policy debate. To partisans of the UN, the organization is the institutional conscience of humanity and represents mankind's last best hope for peace. Those individuals regard any criticism of the UN as evidence of an inadequate commitment to the goal of global peace, at best, and evidence of American know-nothing isolationism, at worst. Critics of the UN tend to reach equally overwrought conclusions. Right-wing, anti-UN polemics are filled with dire warnings of the impending imposition of a world government on freedom-loving Americans, and even the most innocuous UN initiatives are seen as evidence of such a plot.

My attitude toward the organization has always been roughly midpoint between those two extremes. The UN's record has scarcely validated the hopes of those who see the institution as the centerpiece of a new, far more peaceful, global security structure. Indeed, the point that stands out most starkly in the UN's 57-year history is the general irrelevance of the world body. It played virtually no role in the main episodes of the Cold War struggle between the United States and the Soviet Union, and it has been scarcely more relevant in the post–Cold War period. The marginal role the UN has played thus far in the U.S.-led war on terrorism is consistent with that record.

That underscores a crucial point: the United Nations has always been, is now, and is likely to remain a peripheral actor in world affairs. That is not to say the organization is worthless. It serves as a forum for the airing of grievances, and it has sometimes been a reasonably competent mediation and conciliation service. Finding a face-saving formula for the Soviet Union to withdraw from Afghanistan at the end of the 1980s, managing the transition to democracy in Namibia, and helping to foster a reconciliation of the feuding parties at the end of El Salvador's civil war are all examples of UN successes.

The world body has been far less successful when its partisans (or key governments on the Security Council) have pushed it to perform broader and more difficult missions. The peacekeeping fiascos in Somalia and Bosnia are instructive examples.

Americans should be content to have the United Nations play a modest, focused role in world affairs. We should be especially wary of proposals to significantly expand the UN's powers. Thus, schemes to give the UN the authority to levy a tax (however minor the specific tax might appear at first) or dilute the veto power of the five permanent members of the Security Council ought to be firmly opposed.

The same vigilance is needed with regard to certain offshoots of the United Nations. Washington wisely declined to have the United States join the International Criminal Court. Although its ostensible purpose is to bring war criminals to justice, the ICC as currently conceived is a dreadful body. Its proceedings will lack numerous due process guarantees that Americans take for granted. The ICC is the epitome of highly politicized international "justice."

Sending Troops Is Wrong

Calls for vigorous UN action to end the chaos and suffering in Somalia have become a growth industry. Some ambitious advocates of "humanitarian intervention" even suggest revoking Somalia's independence and placing the country under a UN trusteeship enforced by an army of occupation.

Although one can sympathize with such humanitarian impulses, an international military intervention would be a great mistake. It would risk repeating the Lebanon disaster of the early 1980s when the USA led a multinational force that attempted to impose order in that faction-ridden country. More than 250 Marines died in that futile effort.

The proposed intervention in Somalia is part of a larger campaign to expand the United Nations' power to preserve international stability. Universalizing internal or local conflicts, however, is a misguided policy. With the end of the Cold War, a host of long-submerged disputes is resurfacing. Those conflicts typically have deep historical roots and are impervious to solutions imposed from the outside. Such artificial political entities as Somalia and Bosnia are not viable, and attempts to hold them together are doomed to fail.

Even worse is the notion that as the "international leader," the USA must lead UN global policing missions. Accepting the costs and risks of intervention in parochial conflicts during the Cold War, when Soviet surrogates were often involved, was bad enough. It would be masochism for the USA to do so when the strategic rationale for such intervention has disappeared.

We should not waste U.S. lives or resources by leading ill-conceived UN crusades. The USA will gain nothing by trying to be a planetary nanny.

This article originally appeared in *USA Today*, November 16, 1992.

Intervention in Somalia Was a Mistake

As U.S. helicopter gunships and UN peacekeeping forces kill dozens of civilians in Mogadishu, even some supporters of the original decision to send American forces to Somalia acknowledge that something has gone terribly wrong. The perversion of what was hailed as the most noble of humanitarian missions proves again that policies must be judged by their consequences, not their intentions.

193

U.S. policymakers were undoubtedly sincere in wanting to alleviate the terrible suffering of the Somali people when they launched Operation Restore Hope in December 1992. But those who opposed the enterprise warned at the time that it would be impossible to intervene militarily for humanitarian purposes without getting caught up in the underlying political conflicts that had torn the country apart. Events of recent weeks have shown that such warnings were all too accurate.

If the United States had withdrawn its forces as soon as relief supplies were flowing, it might have avoided the worst of the potential entanglements. Instead, the Clinton administration foolishly agreed to keep 4,000 U.S. troops in Somalia to support the subsequent UN goal of pacifying the country and achieving a political reconciliation among the feuding clans. That decision has now put American military personnel in the middle of a situation that increasingly resembles Beirut during the early 1980s.

U.S. forces have joined with units from other UN member-states to hunt down Mohamed Farrah Aidid and smash the military capability of his faction. Both U.S. and UN officials portray Aidid as the principal villain in the Somali conflict and appear to be operating under the illusion that destroying him would make possible a lasting political settlement. In reality, it would merely strengthen the relative positions of other, equally odious warlords.

Not surprisingly, Aidid and his supporters regard the UN-directed operation as a manifestation of Western imperialism, and they strike at the peacekeeping forces whenever the opportunity arises. Innocent civilians in Mogadishu invariably get caught in the crossfire. Moreover, as the most visible and effective component of the UN occupation force, American troops are increasingly the target of Somali wrath.

The UN's objective was arrogant and pretentious from the outset. UN supporters were duped by their own propaganda when they believed that the organization could restore a society as badly fragmented as Somalia's and dictate a political accord. U.S. policymakers were equally shortsighted when they signed on for that mission. Cases such as Somalia and Bosnia illustrate that some countries are simply not politically viable—a point that UN officials, with their insistence on preserving the territorial integrity of member-states at all costs, habitually refuse to recognize.

It is imperative that the Clinton administration and the American people learn some valuable lessons from the Somalia fiasco. First, even the initial intervention was a colossal mistake. Washington should explicitly acknowledge its blunder and then take immediate steps to extricate the American troops before they are drawn deeper into the fighting and casualties mount. Ironically, as bad as developments have been in Mogadishu, the worst may lie ahead. The United Nations seems determined to drag the secessionist northern region of Somalia back into the country. That attempt is almost certain to be resisted violently by the dominant Issak clan, as well as smaller groups that have proclaimed the independent republic of Somaliland.

Second, similar humanitarian crusades should be resisted in the future. Other Somalias will beckon the United States to intervene. The post–Cold War world is a turbulent place, and human tragedies abound from Angola to Yugoslavia. But the experience in Somalia should demonstrate that, despite the best of intentions, outside interference can often make bad situations even worse.

Finally, U.S. policymakers should resolve to use the armed forces only to protect the vital security interests of the American people. In particular, they should be wary of endorsing the dubious "world order" agenda of the United Nations. Protecting the security of the United States is a demanding enough task in the post–Cold War era. The nation's leaders should never again let American troops become the Hessians of the 1990s—the hired guns of the UN Security Council—as they have in Somalia.

This article appeared in the *St. Louis Post-Dispatch*, August 9, 1993.

50 Years of Failure

Fifty years ago, the United Nations was created with the expectation that it would be an effective organization to preserve world peace. But all the anniversary celebrations now taking place cannot conceal the reality that the United Nations has been an acute disappointment.

During the Cold War, the organization was largely irrelevant as the rivalry between the United States and the Soviet Union paralyzed the Security Council. Despite the widespread expectation that the Cold War's end would enable the United Nations to function effectively, its record in the post–Cold War period has been equally unimpressive. The UN nation-building project in Somalia produced a bloody fiasco. The UN "protection force" mission in Bosnia, essentially an attempt to manage a civil war, has merely prolonged the agony by preventing a decisive battlefield verdict.

Even on nonmilitary matters, the United Nations' performance is uninspiring. Much of its energy and funds have been devoted to pushing such pernicious measures as the Law of the Sea Treaty and holding pretentious summits on the environment, world population, and other issues. Delegates to those boondoggles invariably embrace the discredited notion that more government intervention and regulation is the solution to any problem.

A dose of realism about the United Nations is long overdue. Although it has limited utility as an international forum for the airing of grievances and a mediation service to resolve quarrels, the notion of the United Nations as a powerful global security body is unrealizable and undesirable.

The United States should drastically reduce its financial support for the United Nations, insist that the organization trim its bloated, corrupt bureaucracy and block efforts to have it undertake missions for which it is ill designed.

Most important, the United States should refuse to commit troops to UN peacekeeping missions, much less the more ambitious and dangerous Somalia- or Bosnia-style peacemaking ventures. Not only is it dubious wisdom to attempt to "globalize" civil wars and minor regional conflicts, but the lives of American military personnel should be put at risk only to defend the United States' vital security interests. Their lives should never be sacrificed on the altar of global collective security.

This article originally appeared in *USA Today*, June 26, 1995.

A World Court Not Fit for Us, or Anyone

An especially curious feature of the ongoing debate about establishing the United Nations' Permanent International Criminal Court is the enthusiasm of American liberals for the project. Card-carrying members of the American Civil Liberties Union—and, in some cases, former high-level officials of the organization—lobby in favor of the court and denounce critics as alarmists and isolationists, if not apologists for war criminals. Yet the court and the special tribunals already established to prosecute war crimes in Rwanda and the former Yugoslavia make a mockery of the due process standards that ACLU types supposedly hold sacred.

Such luminaries as Morton Halperin, former head of the ACLU's Washington office, and Amnesty International's Stephen Rickard seem unperturbed about the definition of crimes over which the international court will have jurisdiction or the rules of evidence and procedure under which it will operate. For example, the usual vigilance of American liberals about "overly broad" statutes is strangely absent. Yet consider some of the crimes the court will be empowered to prosecute. The definition of genocide includes such offenses as causing serious "mental harm" to members of any national, racial, ethnic or religious group. War crimes include "committing outrages upon personal dignity, in particular humiliating or degrading treatment." Compared to such vacuous definitions, even the vaguely worded domestic criminal statutes that habitually provoke the wrath of the civil liberties community are models of precision.

Even worse, protections that are considered core requirements for a fair trial in the United States are greatly diluted or absent entirely in the special war crimes tribunals and the proposed international court. Instead of having a right to trial by an impartial jury, a defendant faces the prospect of trial by a panel of judges appointed by majority vote of member-states. Most, sometimes all, of the judges on a panel could come from countries where there is no concept of an independent judiciary. A defendant might even face jurists who are representatives of regimes that are openly biased against his government or political movement. More generally, a defendant's fate could hang on the willingness of jurists from such bastions of civil rights as Angola, Saudi Arabia and Indonesia to render a fair verdict.

There is also no right to either a speedy or a public trial. The court would have the authority to hold defendants for months or even years before judicial proceedings commence. In the case of the tribunal for the former Yugoslavia, trial sessions have been held behind closed doors—ostensibly to protect the privacy of alleged victims of war crimes.

Perhaps most worrisome of all, the right of defendants to confront their accusers is highly conditional. The court would have the authority to conceal the identity of witnesses whenever it deemed that step

197

to be appropriate. Such restrictions have already marked some of the trials conducted by the special tribunals.

That is an especially pernicious dilution of due process standards. Frequently, the ability to rebut testimony depends on knowledge of the witness's identity and background. Such information may yield important clues about possible personal malice, a history of prevarication or a hidden financial or ideological agenda. Without that knowledge, cross-examination must be conducted in an informational vacuum and is likely to yield less than impressive results.

Liberals would never tolerate such perversions of due process standards in an American court. Why then do so many prominent liberals embrace the Permanent International Criminal Court, even though it will contain these and other appalling defects? One might justifiably ask Mort Halperin and his colleagues, "What are good civil liberties activists like you doing in an ethical sewer like the PICC?"

The answer appears to be that most liberals are also ardent disciples of Woodrow Wilson and his dream of international cooperation. To them, a multilateral institution—especially if it operates under the auspices of the United Nations—is presumed to be desirable. That multilateralism-uber-alles mentality has caused them to endorse the court, despite its abundance of warts.

It is a huge mistake as well as a betrayal of principle. Conservative and libertarian critics of the PICC should miss no opportunity to compel their liberal adversaries to confront the hypocrisy of their support for the court. Unfortunately, many conservatives often fail to emphasize the core problem with the court. They typically stress that we should not want to risk having Americans tried before such a tribunal. That is a valid but secondary point. People who believe in civil liberties should not want anyone tried before such a tribunal.

This article originally appeared in the *St. Petersburg Times*, August 7, 1998.

Anatomy of a Failure

Before President Bill Clinton sends a proposed 4,000 U.S. soldiers on a peacekeeping mission to Kosovo, he should consider this sobering reality: Peacekeeping operations all over the world are falling apart, despite the investment of billions of U.S. dollars and several dozen lives. Rather than continue pushing America's luck in regions irrelevant to the nation's security and well-being, Clinton should end this grandiose post–Cold War experiment in fixing failed states.

The list of failed peace missions is long and growing. Somalia remains a hotbed of chaos and clan warfare following ambitious United Nations and U.S. attempts at nation building. Five years after a U.S. invasion aimed at "restoring democracy in Haiti," yet another leader, President René Preval, just dissolved parliament, while the country's economy remains a basket case and political violence is on the rise: A prominent senator was assassinated on March 1.

Cambodia, once touted as the signature peacekeeping success, has descended into renewed dictatorship. In 1997, barely four years after UN-supervised elections, Second Deputy Prime Minister Hun Sen overthrew his rival, First Deputy Prime Minister Prince Norodom Ranariddh, in a bloody coup. Though Hun Sen tried to legitimize his rule by holding elections last July, the balloting was marked by fraud.

The United Nations has just beaten a hasty retreat from Angola, where a long-smoldering civil conflict has reignited. A multiyear UN mediation and peacekeeping effort collapsed last December, when Jonas Savimbi's National Union for Total Independence of Angola guerrillas attacked government forces. In fact, during the initial fighting, two UN aircraft were shot down, killing more than two dozen peacekeeping personnel. Secretary General Kofi Annan then conceded the mission was no longer viable, and ordered peace-keepers to leave.

The original UN mission in Bosnia floundered and its North Atlantic Treaty Organization–led successor has long exceeded its deadline. Yet, after three years of occupation by the world's most powerful military alliance, Bosnia shows few signs of becoming a viable country, as tacitly acknowledged by the administration's warnings that setting deadlines for final U.S. troop withdrawals could plunge the region back into chaos. In fact, supporters of extensive U.S. involvement in the Balkans now admit the United States may need a military presence in the region as long as it has had one in Korea, nearly a half century.

These dismal results should not be surprising. U.S. participation in peace operations was always a dubious policy. The failed states involved fit no traditional definition of vital or even significant U.S. interests. None is militarily strong enough to threaten America or its major allies. None is a significant market for U.S. goods or a major site of U.S. investment. None supplies any scarce raw materials. Those that were Cold War battlegrounds lost whatever strategic significance they may have had once the Soviet Union collapsed.

Nor, despite numerous warnings, have their troubles repeatedly spilled over to more important countries. Until the Asian financial crisis, most of Cambodia's neighbors boomed economically and cohered socially, despite that country's troubles. Interventionists portray the Kosovo crisis as the inevitable result of Bosnia's recent war, but the Albanian Kosovars' grievances against their Serb rulers long predate that conflict.

Indeed, Bosnia's continuing woes have not prevented Slovenia from prospering and flowering politically. Despite broader claims that Bosnia and the rest of the Balkans hold the key to stability in Europe, reform in the Continent's eastern half continues its uneven pace, while much of Western Europe has just established a common currency.

Where failed states' troubles have hurt their neighbors, as in Rwanda's effect on the Congo's continuing turmoil, the "victim" has been equally inconsequential to the United States.

Just as important, though the failed states themselves might be marginal to America, the costs of U.S. involvement in peacekeeping are anything but. The price tag of the Bosnia mission, for example, has already hit $12 billion, with no end in sight. Haiti has cost more than $2 billion. Washington has even spent $1.5 billion on tiny, remote Rwanda.

Moreover, as finally acknowledged by the administration, peacekeeping obligations have stretched U.S. combat forces dangerously thin and increased the tempo of military operations far beyond prudent norms. The new defense budget hikes supported by Clinton and Congress are mere Band-Aid fixes. Unless Washington's appetite for peace operations fades, the United States could find itself with a stressed-out force of armed social workers, hard-pressed to handle bona fide security threats that might emerge.

Interventionists have long emphasized America's alleged moral interests in helping failed states through peace operations. But how moral is it to risk U.S. lives in unnecessary and futile ventures? The record shows that outside forces haven't the vaguest idea how to fix failed states at any politically acceptable or strategically sensible price.

Tragically, the only lesson apparently learned by the administration from this growing list of peacekeeping failures is to tar domestic critics as isolationists. Moreover, the administration's policy guidelines for peace operations, issued in 1994, after the Somalia disaster, still define America's vital interests open-endedly. By emphasizing the reputedly tight links between America's fate and instability literally anywhere in the world, they create doctrinal pressure to act first and think later when crises erupt.

Nowhere is the obsession with peacekeeping more evident than in the administration's plans to expand NATO and "adapt" it to "new crisis management and peacekeeping missions," in Clinton's words. Indeed, the alliance's proposed new "strategic concept," which is to be approved at a summit this spring, has a large peacekeeping component. Such an orientation would practically guarantee the use of U.S. soldiers in civil and ethnic conflicts all over still shaky Eastern Europe and even in more volatile former Soviet republics.

Interventionists inside and outside the administration insist that America's superpower status requires actively supporting UN and NATO peace operations. Yet, the reality is just the opposite. Precisely because the United States is so strong, wealthy and substantially self-sufficient, it can afford to ignore tempests in local teapots, however tragic.

Prolonging the peacekeeping experiment can only needlessly expose Americans to greater risks and costs. It's time to pull the plug on these operations and focus our nation's attentions on higher international and domestic priorities.

This article, coauthored with Alan Tonelson, originally appeared in the *Los Angeles Times*, March 14, 1999.

Giving UN New Powers Would Create a Monster

Zealous supporters of the United Nations are again trying to give that organization powers it does not need and should not have. A new UN report asserts that imposing a global tax on "speculative" currency transactions is an idea that deserves consideration. Such "speculative" transactions—a term the report does not define—could easily net $150 billion a year for the United Nations' coffers.

The currency tax proposal is not new. A number of outspoken internationalists have floated the idea for years as a means to give the United Nations an independent source of revenue so the organization is not dependent on payments by member-states. The report is the first time the UN bureaucracy itself has sent such a trial balloon aloft.

That balloon should be punctured. Advocates of the tax assure skeptics that it would be imposed at a rate of only 0.1 percent—a minuscule burden on wealthy international currency speculators such as George Soros. The American people and the U.S. government must not succumb to such blandishments. We should remember that the federal income tax began as a small assessment on only the wealthiest Americans. Today, it is a voracious monster that devours a major part of the earnings of ordinary citizens.

The same thing is likely to happen if the United Nations ever gains the power to tax. Merely redefining what constitutes a "speculative" transaction a few years from now could net the United Nations additional hundreds of billions of dollars. Leaving aside the danger of escalating taxation, the United Nations should not have an independent taxing authority on general principle.

The United States and other Western countries that pay the bulk of the organization's expenses have precious little say over what the General Assembly or the corrupt and ill managed UN bureaucracy does. They would have nearly no input if the United Nations had its own source of funds.

The proposed taxing authority is one of several ideas advanced by those who want the United Nations to become more powerful. Other prominent schemes include creating a standing army, which the Security Council could use for peacekeeping and nation-building missions, and diluting or ending the veto power used by the United States and other permanent members of the Security Council.

Officials of the United States should put the United Nations and its enthusiastic boosters on notice that pushing such changes will endanger American support for the organization. Some conservatives advocate U.S. withdrawal from the world body. That step is premature. The United Nations has achieved some positive results. It helped facilitate the Soviet withdrawal from Afghanistan, orchestrated the transition to democracy in Namibia and helped effect a reconciliation between warring factions in El Salvador. Also, it is a good idea to have a place where governments can gather to air grievances.

At the same time, the extent of the United Nations' value must be kept in perspective. The United Nations is not "mankind's last best hope for peace" or the "conscience of humanity," as asserted by its supporters. It is merely an association of the world's governments created for a limited purpose. The United Nations is a minor player in the international system, and that is how it should remain. Kept within such confines it can do a modest amount of good; outside those boundaries it would be an embryonic superstate that would menace liberty.

It is not yet necessary for the United States to withdraw from the United Nations. But if the world body attempts to acquire a taxing authority, raise a standing army or dilute America's veto in the Security Council, the United States should end its membership. That is the message—indeed, the ultimatum—that needs to go to the United Nations without delay.

This article originally appeared in the *Houston Chronicle*, February 12, 2001.

9. The International Drug War

Introduction

It has been more than three decades since President Richard Nixon declared a "war" on illegal drugs. Since that time, the United States has waged a concerted campaign against narcotics trafficking at home and abroad. The "supply-side" portion of that campaign has focused on stemming the flow of illegal drugs from Latin America— the source of most drugs entering the United States.

The drug war has been no more successful than America's earlier crusade against alcohol during the Prohibition Era. More than $20 billion a year is now spent by the federal government (and another $20 billion by state and local governments) on the new prohibitionist venture. America's courts and prisons have been clogged with cases involving nonviolent drug offenders, and portions of our major cities have frequently resembled war zones as rival drug gangs vie for control of the lucrative black-market trade. In the course of waging the drug war, authorities have done irreparable damage to the Fourth Amendment and other portions of the Bill of Rights.

The situation is no better on the international front. Washington continues to pressure governments in Latin America and elsewhere to eradicate the commerce in illegal drugs. Responding to U.S. pressure, those governments have conducted aerial spraying campaigns against drug crops (further impoverishing hard-pressed farmers), shot suspected drug-carrying planes out of the skies, and attacked powerful drug-trafficking organizations. The positive results of those efforts have been meager. Even the U.S. government's own figures show that the quantity of illegal drugs coming out of Latin America is greater today than it was 20 years ago. An especially severe crackdown in a specific country may lead to a temporary decline of production in that country, but the traffickers merely relocate their operations. For example, in recent years the U.S. government has boasted about the reduction in the amount of coca (the raw material for cocaine) coming out of Peru and Bolivia. Yet at the same time the amount of coca being grown in neighboring Colombia has soared. That "push down, pop up" effect has been a prime characteristic of the supply-side component of the war on drugs since the beginning.

The international phase of the drug war has not only been futile, it has produced devastating side effects in many of the drug-source countries. The multi-billion-dollar illicit trade has fostered an enormous amount of corruption and violence. That process is most advanced in Colombia, where the democratic government is caught in a maelstrom of civil war involving leftist rebels, right-wing paramilitaries, and narcotics traffickers. A surge of corruption and violence is also now afflicting Mexico. In addition to those problems, Washington's pressure on the drug issue is contributing to a sharp upsurge of anti-U.S. sentiment throughout the hemisphere.

I began writing about the folly of the international phase of the drug war in the mid-1980s. Much of what I described then remains equally true today, although I did overestimate the willingness of U.S. policymakers to commit American military forces to combat the drug trade in Latin America. U.S. officials have continued to prefer more subtle and indirect forms of involvement. But there is little doubt the disruptions caused by Washington's crusade against drugs are mounting inexorably. The United States is asking its hemispheric neighbors to do the impossible: wage war on a multi-billion-dollar industry that has attracted the support of powerful political constituencies. Asking the people of Colombia or Mexico to eradicate the drug trade is akin to asking the people of Japan to eradicate their automobile or electronics industries. Not surprisingly, Washington's policy of alternately bribing and pressuring its neighbors to do the impossible continues to fail.

Foreign Anti-Drug Wars Carry a Hefty Tab

The Reagan administration has waged a war of unprecedented intensity against international narcotics trafficking during the past four years. Numerous agencies are involved in the effort, including the Drug Enforcement Administration, the State Department, the Agency for International Development and even the Central Intelligence Agency. Washington entices, cajoles and coerces foreign governments to eradicate drug crops and interdict supply routes. The United States' Third World allies are responding to this pressure with an unstable mixture of resentment and cynical exploitation.

Examples of resentment abound. The ugly confrontation between Mexico and the United States earlier this year over the abduction and murder of DEA agent Enrique Camarena is indicative of a larger problem. Government officials in several countries, most notably Bolivia, Jamaica and Panama, complain about the Reagan administration's coercive tactics. From their perspective, the United States is insisting that foreign countries assume onerous law enforcement burdens to solve what is essentially a U.S. domestic problem—epidemic drug use. A Bolivian general expressed this underlying antagonism succinctly when he resigned rather than conduct anti-narcotics raids, stating that he was not about to kill peasants merely to please Washington.

What's in It for Me?

Resistance to U.S. pressure is motivated in part by nationalist pride, but less savory motives also exist. Drug-related corruption is endemic in many Third World governments. The chief minister and two aides of the tiny Caribbean nation of Turks and Caicos Islands were recently convicted of conspiring to arrange a major drug deal in the United States. A Bahamian Royal Commission investigative report implicated three cabinet ministers in narcotics activities. Evidence has surfaced that officials in regimes as politically diverse as Nicaragua, Colombia and Bolivia are involved in drug trafficking.

Whatever the underlying motives, several foreign leaders have apparently decided to exact a substantial financial price for cooperating in the U.S. war against narcotics. When Peru's new president, Alan Garcia, announced a vigorous offensive against the cocaine trade, his interior minister quickly added that "a lot more help" was needed from the United States in addition to the $4.4 million in law enforcement funds now provided. Other Peruvian officials acknowledged that the campaign against drugs was spurred by the hope that the Reagan administration would respond with assistance to lift Peru out of its economic crisis. The implicit quid pro quo of economic aid for cooperation in the war on drugs was echoed by the new chief minister of Turks and Caicos, who repeatedly stressed his nation's "meager" financial resources.

Bolivian vice president Julio Garrett-Aillon made an even more audacious play for Western aid during an address before the United Nations General Assembly earlier this month. He proposed that the United States and other drug-consuming countries establish a fund to purchase coca leaves (the source of cocaine), thereby decreasing illicit supplies without damaging the economies of drug-producing nations. Mr. Garrett-Aillon likewise emphasized the impossibility of Bolivia devoting its limited resources to a campaign against narcotics without such incentives.

Third World governments are clearly playing diplomatic "hardball," seeing in Washington's obsession with the drug issue a device to secure foreign aid funds to alleviate pressing internal economic problems. But even if lucrative aid programs are forthcoming, those governments may find it a bad bargain to enlist in Washington's anti-drug crusade. Indeed, some of those regimes might be imperiling their own existence by acceding to Washington's demands. Throughout South America's Andean region, impoverished peasants have discovered in coca leaf cultivation an income source 5 to 10 times greater than any competing crops. Moreover, the coca leaf played a legitimate role in Andean cultures (the brewing of "coca tea," for example) long before cocaine use became a serious issue in the United States. Andean peasants do not appreciate efforts by their governments to coerce them into growing unprofitable "substitute" crops, and they react with anger to raids by U.S.-trained and U.S.-sponsored forces against coca fields.

By joining Washington's campaign against drugs, the governments of Colombia, Peru and Bolivia are antagonizing large portions of their own populations. It is an opportunity not lost on leftist guerrillas operating in those countries. Marxist insurgents in Colombia have formed a tacit alliance with narcotics growers. The situation in Peru is even more ominous as the Maoist "Shining Path" guerrillas exploit popular discontent toward the Lima government's drug crop eradication programs. Clyde D. Taylor, a high-ranking U.S. State Department official, concedes that when Shining Path recruiters "announce that they have come to protect the livelihood of growers against government interference, they find some ready listeners."

It would be a bitter irony indeed if U.S.-sponsored anti-narcotics programs helped foment radical left-wing revolutions in Latin America, but that danger is quite real. Moreover, such alarming developments are not confined to the Western Hemisphere. One of the more prominent repercussions of the U.S. campaign to eradicate opium poppy cultivation in Burma has been to expand the amount of territory controlled by the Burmese Communist Party, which is waging a guerrilla war against the socialist central government of Gen. Ne Win. Again, besieged growers flocked to the one political force offering them protection—even though any communist government would probably collectivize agriculture.

Demand Causes Supply

Washington's anti-drug crusade is creating a diplomatic morass for itself and its Third World allies. Even worse, this disagreeable situation is not even mitigated by discernible success in reducing the international supply of narcotics. The State Department's International Narcotics Control Strategy Report, issued earlier this year, underscores the futility of Washington's global policy. According to the report's own figures, small declines in marijuana and opium poppy production were offset by a comparable rise in cultivation of hashish. Most distressing of all was the data on the production of the coca leaf, which revealed a massive increase. The principal "accomplishment" has been a geographic dispersal of narcotics cultivation and trafficking to previously unaffected countries. Despite the usual amount of optimistic rhetoric from bureaucrats who have a vested interest in perpetuating the crusade, the U.S. war against international narcotics is being lost, not won.

The Reagan administration should finally acknowledge that extensive drug use in the United States is a domestic problem and, therefore, cannot be solved in the arena of foreign policy. A Panamanian official assessed the situation correctly when he stated that "if there weren't the frightening demand in the States, we wouldn't even have to worry about trying to eliminate the supply." In reality, the administration's global campaign is little more than a vain attempt to deflect public attention from the continuing failure of domestic efforts to stem drug usage. It is high time that Americans face up to their own problem and stop seeking external solutions. Washington's current international crusade against narcotics is an irredeemable failure that threatens to become a diplomatic catastrophe.

This article originally appeared in the *Wall Street Journal*, October 31, 1985. Reprinted with permission of the *Wall Street Journal* © 1985 Dow Jones & Company, Inc.

U.S. Foreign Policy Is Hooked on the Drug War

The global campaign against narcotics trafficking has become an increasingly prominent item on the Reagan administration's foreign policy agenda. John C. Whitehead, deputy secretary of state, stressed the depth of that commitment when he assured a Senate committee that the United States will "use every opportunity" to convince other nations of the need for more vigorous drug eradication programs.

Reagan administration officials fail to comprehend that Washington's preoccupation with halting the drug trade creates an insidious contradiction in U.S. foreign policy, especially with respect to Latin America. They assume that a successful crusade against narcotics will enhance the security, economic health, and political stability of Latin American countries. The reality is considerably more complex and disturbing.

The administration's hemispheric policy embraces four objectives. The first and most fundamental goal is to prevent the emergence of any more Cuban-style dictatorships. A closely related goal is to see civilian democratic governments become the norm, replacing authoritarian military regimes, while a third goal is to promote regional economic growth based upon free-market principles. All three objectives figured prominently in the report of the President's National Bipartisan Commission on Central America as well as in the much-touted Caribbean Basin Initiative.

Although one may quarrel with specific proposals in the administration's hemispheric policy statements, the first three objectives are compatible, even complementary. Communist insurgents have found stable democratic governments to be more difficult targets of opportunity than rigid, unresponsive military dictatorships. Similarly, economic prosperity strengthens incumbent democratic systems and eliminates an issue that is often exploited by Marxist revolutionaries.

Unfortunately, the fourth objective—intensifying the campaign against drug trafficking—is not necessarily compatible with the other three. Narcotics constitute the single most important export of Peru, and they equal or exceed the value of all legitimate Bolivian exports combined. The drug trade also plays a significant role in the economies of Mexico, Belize, Colombia, and Jamaica. Powerful constituencies committed to preserving the trade have emerged in all of the drug-producing states. But Washington seems only dimly aware that a successful campaign against narcotics would create severe economic, political, and social dislocations.

Assistant Secretary of State Elliott Abrams epitomized such myopia when he praised Bolivia for its increasing determination to confront coca growers even as he noted that members of that nation's anti-narcotics strike force, the Leopards, had been surrounded by "17,000 angry peasants" in one province. He either failed to understand or ignored what such an outpouring of hostility implies for the tenure of Bolivia's fragile democratic system.

When administration leaders do analyze the political ramifications of the drug trade, they habitually oversimplify. Linkages between narcotics organizations and leftist insurgencies, such as Peru's Shining Path and Colombia's M-19 guerrillas, are stressed, and it is asserted that drugs have become part of a Soviet-Cuban plot against the Western democracies. But that is only part of the picture. Rensselaer Lee, an expert on U.S. anti-drug policies in the Western Hemisphere, points out that narcotics organizations have also cultivated ties with key military elements in several countries, thereby intensifying a threat to democracy from that quarter.

It is increasingly questionable whether the United States should encumber its foreign policy with a crusade against international narcotics trafficking. That supply-side campaign has shown little promise of success. Even massive efforts such as last year's Operation Blast Furnace, in which U.S. troops helped Bolivian troops conduct raids against cocaine-processing facilities, have achieved only ephemeral gains. Indeed, the State Department's latest annual report on international narcotics control strategy, released in March, exhibits a pervasive sense of futility. Illicit production of coca leaf, marijuana, and opium all increased significantly in 1986.

Even if the campaign against narcotics should eventually prove effective, the geopolitical price for the United States may exceed any

211

benefit. Merely making the effort exacerbates economic, social, and political strains throughout the hemisphere. U.S. officials must confront the reality that the goal of eradicating narcotics often impedes more fundamental foreign policy objectives. It is a dilemma that the Reagan administration can no longer afford to ignore.

This article originally appeared in the *Orange County Register*, July 1, 1987.

Panama Smacks of Search for a New U.S. Enemy

The Bush administration has embarked on a new and dangerous phase of its drug war in Latin America by invading Panama. To be sure, President Bush stressed other reasons for the military action: The lives of American citizens supposedly were in danger (especially after the killing of a U.S. soldier on Dec. 16), the Panamanian government had issued blustering statements that a "state of war" existed with the United States, and there even were intelligence reports that Manuel Noriega might be planning to seize the Panama Canal. The administration also would have us believe that it launched the invasion to bring the blessings of democracy to the people of Panama.

All these considerations may have played a role in the U.S. decision, but another motive, mentioned less frequently, is crucial. There is unsettling evidence that the Bush administration regards the invasion of Panama as an initial foray in a strategy to use the U.S. armed forces against drug traffickers throughout Latin America. Washington clearly was determined to apprehend Noriega and return him to the United States to stand trial on drug charges. Drug czar William Bennett and other administration officials emphasized that goal, and the decision to offer a $1 million bounty for Noriega's capture attests to their seriousness. Less known but perhaps more revealing is the fact that agents of the Drug Enforcement Administration accompanied the initial wave of U.S. troops in an effort to snare other traffickers reported to be in Panama. Clearly, the invasion was not merely to protect American lives, defend the canal or advance the cause of democracy.

The context in which the armed intervention took place also suggests that it is the first military battle in Washington's international war on drugs. Just five days before the troops landed, the Justice Department confirmed that it had issued a legal ruling giving American military forces the authority to pursue drug traffickers in foreign countries—even without the consent of the host government. That decision followed the much-touted "Andean Initiative" announced in September, whereby the administration decided to send military advisers to Colombia, Peru and Bolivia to assist indigenous anti-drug forces. A few weeks before the adoption of the Andean Initiative, the president approved a new National Security Decision Directive greatly easing restrictions on the involvement of U.S. military personnel in anti-drug efforts overseas.

Thus there was a clear pattern of rapidly escalating American military involvement in the drug war even before the invasion of Panama. Moreover, some administration supporters now are portraying the intervention as an integral part of that struggle. Rep. Stan Parris (R-Va.) openly boasted, for example, that the U.S. action "is as much a victory in the war on drugs as it is a victory for the freedom of the Panamanian people."

Cynics who wondered what the $300 billion-per-year U.S. military establishment would find to do as the Cold War winds down may have their answer—it could be fighting drug traffickers throughout the mountains and jungles of Latin America. The international drug lords are becoming the new "necessary enemy," replacing the Soviet Union.

Those celebrating the "victory" in Panama ought to realize that a hemispheric drug war is likely to entail extremely unpleasant costs. The Panamanian invasion will reawaken memories of "Yankee imperialism" in Latin America—memories that are not slumbering too soundly to begin with—and may poison U.S. relations with those nations for years. It sets the stage for acrimonious confrontations concerning the issue of sovereignty. Even friendly governments can be expected to resist uninvited U.S. military incursions, and they may resist Washington's "requests" for permission to send in troops with nearly equal vigor. Peru already has withdrawn from the scheduled February drug summit in response to the attack on Panama—an indication that Lima is very uneasy about the direction Washington's drug war is taking.

In addition to the hostility of incumbent governments, the United States will have to confront drug cartels that are well armed and determined to protect their multi-billion-dollar enterprises. The casualties suffered in Panama will be only the first of many if the Bush administration continues its ill-advised strategy to employ the military in the war on drugs. American soldiers will come home in flag-draped coffins from yet another useless, ultimately unwinnable, crusade.

This article originally appeared in the *Army Times*, January 15, 1990.

Plan Colombia: The Drug War's New Morass

The United States is flirting with deep involvement in yet another murky, parochial conflict, this time in South America. Under the banner of launching a new offensive in the international war on drugs, Washington risks becoming entangled in Colombia's multi-sided civil war. There is still time for America to draw back from the abyss, but the Bush administration's policy is moving in the opposite direction.

The vehicle for U.S. involvement is Plan Colombia. As envisioned by Colombian president Andres Pastrana, Plan Colombia is an ambitious blueprint to solve many of the country's economic problems as well as combat narcotics trafficking. The United States became an eager participant from the beginning, although its focus was somewhat narrower than Pastrana preferred. Washington agreed to provide $1.3 billion to assist Bogotá combat drug trafficking. Most of the U.S. money goes to the Colombian military to purchase hardware, provide training, and otherwise fund drug eradication efforts. About 300 Green Beret troops are already in the country providing training for Colombian officers and enlisted personnel.

Colombia's Volatile Politics

Colombia's political setting is extraordinarily complex, as the government is involved in a struggle with no fewer than four factions. Explicitly arrayed against the government are two radical leftist insurgent movements, the Revolutionary Armed Forces of Colombia (FARC) and the National Liberation Army (ELN). Both of them have been designated as terrorist groups by the U.S. State Department. Violently opposed to FARC and ELN are the right-wing paramilitaries, most notably the United Self-Defense Forces of Colombia (AUC). And finally there are various narcotrafficking organizations. Most of them have no strong political allegiances; they are primarily profit maximizers who are willing to form tactical alliances with whatever faction seems to be dominant in a particular region and, therefore, is in a position to advance or retard their business prospects. At times, they have worked closely with the rebel forces and

214

paid "taxes" to FARC and ELN on drug crops and quantities of raw cocaine. On other occasions and in other places, they've cooperated with the AUC against the rebels.

Not surprisingly, this political witch's brew has produced chaos and violence. More than 2 million Colombians have fled their homes to avoid the fighting. Some 35,000 civilians have died in the fighting over the past decade, and according to Bogotá's official figures, more than 126,000 were made homeless by the war in 2000 alone. Some human rights groups place the latter figure at closer to 300,000. In addition, there are thousands of murders each year that may have a connection to either the ideological struggle or the drug trade. The economy is a shambles with an unemployment rate estimated at 20 percent. Capital flight is epidemic, and middle- and upper-class Colombians are beginning to leave the country in large numbers. In the past five years, more than a million Colombians—out of a population of 40 million—have emigrated.

The strength of the guerrilla forces has surged in recent years. In 1985, FARC had some 3,000 fighters and was active in 25 isolated sectors. Today, it has at least 20,000 better-armed fighters—the largest insurgent force in all of Latin America—and it launches strikes all over Colombia. It controls a swath of territory in the south nearly the size of Switzerland. The ELN is considerably smaller, but its forces dominate the territory in the northeast through which runs Colombia's economically crucial oil pipeline.

Meaningless Distinctions

Into this snake pit now wanders the United States with its participation in Plan Colombia. The lack of realism underlying U.S. involvement is illustrated by the Clinton administration's original assurance that the funds would be used only to fight drug trafficking, not support the government's struggle against FARC and ELN. Critics point out the obvious: that the military hardware purchased can and will be used for both purposes. Indeed, most of the military operations ostensibly directed against narcotraffickers take place in areas that also have a large guerrilla presence. In many cases, narcotrafficking organizations are allied with one or both of the guerrilla groups, and any action against the former will be considered by the latter as a blow against their cause. The functional distinction emphasized by liberal supporters of Plan Colombia is, therefore, ludicrously impractical.

That is a point conceded early on by some officials in the Bush administration. Robert Zoellick, a top foreign policy adviser to Bush during the 2000 presidential campaign and now U.S. Trade Representative, scoffed at the distinction that the Clinton administration had imposed. "We cannot continue to make a false distinction between counterinsurgency and counternarcotics efforts," Zoellick stated. "The narcotraffickers and guerrillas compose one dangerous network." Candidate Bush himself took a similar line, vowing that U.S. assistance "will help the Colombian government protect its people, fight the drug trade, [and] *halt the momentum of the guerrillas.*"

Actions in the field may be making the distinction between counternarcotics and counterinsurgency assistance moot in any case. In April 2001, Counter-Narcotics Battalion 1, an elite Colombian army unit that had specifically been trained by the United States to conduct anti-drug operations, clashed with FARC guerrillas in southern Colombia. Nine rebels and one government soldier were killed in the skirmish.

Whatever the initial intent, Plan Colombia inexorably draws the United States into Colombia's civil war. Pastrana clearly wants Washington to play a role in ending the insurgency as well as funding anti-drug efforts. During a visit to Washington in late February 2001, he urged the Bush administration to begin participating in peace negotiations between his government and the two rebel organizations. Initially, President Bush and other administration leaders firmly rebuffed that initiative. Within days, however, U.S. policymakers seem to have had second thoughts about a policy of noninvolvement in the peace process. Trial balloons began appearing in the news media suggesting that, perhaps, the United States could play a constructive, albeit supporting, role in the negotiations—if the rebels were serious about wanting peace.

Colombia probably would be a violent and turbulent place even without the drug factor. FARC and ELN arose because of widespread anger among the rural peasantry against the country's political system, and the insurgency would likely exist even if it did not derive funds from the drug trade. After all, similar left-wing insurgencies erupted in such countries as El Salvador, Guatemala, and Nicaragua in earlier decades even though drug revenues were not a major factor. Likewise, the rise of the AUC occurred because of the resistance of more conservative Colombians to the violent inroads made by leftist forces and the inability of the government in Bogotá to repulse those incursions and control the affected territory. Again, the parallel with the rise of right-wing paramilitary groups in Guatemala and El Salvador is striking.

But the lucrative illegal drug trade in Colombia makes an already bad situation even worse. Both rebel organizations (and to a lesser extent the AUC as well) derive much of their revenues from the drug trade. The bulk of the money appears to come from "tax levies" the groups impose on drug crop farmers and the drug-trafficking organizations. But there is evidence that FARC and ELN are sometimes directly involved in trafficking. The strongest evidence emerged from raids conducted by Colombian military forces in early 2001. Those raids uncovered documents, eyewitness accounts, and financial receipts showing that the rebels were directly engaged in the production and export of cocaine. One estimate places the revenue flow to FARC alone at more than $600 million a year. If that is true, it would make that group the most well-funded insurgency in the world today.

The massive flow of drug-related funds to the Colombian insurgent organizations should be somewhat embarrassing to drug warriors in the United States and Colombia. After all, when the Cali and Medellin drug cartels were broken in the early and mid-1990s, victories in that phase of the drug war were loudly proclaimed. In reality, the traffickers merely adapted to the new environment and adopted a more decentralized form of business organization. Today, some 300 loosely connected families control the drug trade, and Colombia still accounts for approximately 80 percent of all the cocaine produced in the world and two-thirds of the heroin consumed in the United States.

Human Rights

Human rights advocates in the United States and elsewhere have had grave reservations about Plan Colombia. They worry that Washington is crawling into bed with some of the worst abusers of human rights in the Western Hemisphere, especially given the ties between portions of the Colombian military and the AUC. Congress sought to deflect such criticism by attaching a number of conditions to the aid package, including a provision requiring the executive branch to closely monitor the behavior of Colombia's military and police forces.

As is often the case with congressionally imposed standards, those "requirements" have turned out to be little more than political window-dressing. Indeed, Congress itself gave the executive branch a spacious legal escape hatch. Although the implementing legislation officially conditioned aid on certification by the secretary of state that Colombia was taking specific, tangible steps to improve the military's human rights performance, it also allowed a presidential waiver on national security grounds. That shell game has a dreary familiarity, since it has characterized congressional restrictions with regard to many other foreign aid programs. The waiver provision effectively renders the so-called requirements meaningless. Sure enough, the first time the certification came due (in August 2000), President Clinton waived the requirement on the grounds of national security.

Even President Pastrana is alarmed at the growing strength of the right-wing paramilitary organizations, their continuing ties to elements of the Colombian military, and their willingness to commit horrific acts of violence. He has blasted the paramilitaries as a "veritable cancer spreading in our body politic," and accuses the AUC of being "responsible for 70 percent of the massacres."

The AUC fighters are hardly the only parties guilty of committing atrocities, though. In May 2001, FARC troops massacred more than two dozen farmers in northern Colombia. The FARC assault was characterized by acts of shocking brutality, with many of the victims being hacked to death by machetes. The apparent motive for the FARC offensive was quite revealing. Rebel forces invaded an area where a new coca crop had been used to generate income for the AUC. The massacre was also part of a larger FARC campaign to open a transportation corridor to the Caribbean and Panama to facilitate the flow of drugs and arms. To achieve that goal meant eliminating a stronghold that the AUC had seized more than five years earlier. The horrific episode is merely one example of how the issues of ideology, drug trafficking, and human rights abuses all interact in the complex Colombian morass.

Failure of Eradication Efforts

Human rights organizations are not the only critics of Plan Colombia. Governors in the coca-producing provinces, although strongly opposed to the Marxist guerrillas, condemn aspects of the plan. They reserve their harshest rhetorical fire for the aerial spraying campaign that Washington pushes with such enthusiasm. The governors warned in January 2001 that the operation would imperil the livelihood of thousands of poor peasants. Their worst fears were soon confirmed as the herbicide used in the spraying program killed acre upon acre of legal crops along with the coca plants.

Predictably, both Colombian and U.S. officials touted "spectacular" early successes from the aerial spraying campaign. Just as predictably, details soon emerged to cast doubt on those claims. *Washington Post* correspondent Scott Wilson, traveling in Colombia just weeks after the most massive phase of the spraying offensive in December 2000 and January 2001, noted Bogotá's claims that some 40,000 acres of coca crops had been destroyed in one province, Putumayo, alone. Yet "in interviews around this village [El Tigre] . . . farmers said many drug plantations remained untouched, protected from spray planes in hard-to-reach valleys by jungle cover and guerrilla troops. Valleys full of coca were evident from the main east-west highway. And on almost every farm hit by the herbicide since December, small tents protected young coca plants for future cultivation."

Evidence emerged in May 2001 that cast even more doubt on the effectiveness of the crop eradication strategy. A source within the Colombian government leaked information about revised estimates of the country's cocaine production. According to those revised estimates, Colombia is producing 800 to 900 tons of cocaine annually, not the 580 tons estimated by the U.S. State Department and the U.S. Drug Enforcement Administration. If accurate, the new estimates mean that Colombia is producing more cocaine than the earlier U.S. estimates of total world production (780 tons). Similarly, U.S. satellite data had suggested that Colombia had approximately 340,000 acres under cultivation with coca when the crop-spraying program got under way in December 2000. By May, about 75,000 acres had been fumigated.

But if the Colombian government study is correct, the actual acreage under cultivation is considerably higher—perhaps as much as 50 percent higher. In short, even if one accepts the notion that the spraying completely eradicated the coca plants in the 75,000 acres affected, the reality is that the amount of acreage still under cultivation is greater than the total previously estimated acreage when the campaign began. As the Colombian source put it, Plan Colombia has "not made a dent" in the country's output of cocaine.

Increasing Risks

As if the reports leaking out of Colombia were not enough to cast doubt on the effectiveness of Plan Colombia, Donnie Marshall, the head of the U.S. Drug Enforcement Administration, made a telling admission barely a week later. Marshall conceded that cocaine prices in the United States were not rising, despite the eradication efforts in Colombia. If those efforts were being effective, they should have produced at least a modest supply shortage in the United States. That, in turn, should have created upward pressure on street prices for the drug. Yet Marshall admitted that prices had remained steady since December 2000, when eradication efforts under Plan Colombia went into effect. Such is the fate of crop eradication "victories" in the war on drugs.

The risk exposure to those Americans waging the drug war in Colombia is also on the rise. Planes conducting the spraying have been fired on. In February 2001, an armed search and rescue team, working under contract with the State Department, was also fired upon as it plucked the crew of a Colombian police helicopter that had been disabled in a firefight with guerrillas trying to protect a coca crop. The search and rescue team included several Americans.

The negative effects of Plan Colombia are not confined to Colombia. Indeed, one of the great dangers of the scheme is that it will cause Colombia's troubles to spill over the border into neighboring countries. The neighbors certainly are worried about that risk. As soon as it became evident that the United States was financially backing Plan Colombia, and that Washington was primarily funding the military, anti-drug component, officials in other countries began to express concern and objections.

True, some of the warnings about Plan Colombia and the professed reluctance to endorse the scheme appear to be part of a cynical strategy on the part of various governments to extract more money from the United States. Ecuador's foreign minister, Heinz Moeller, was not exactly subtle when he warned that it would be impossible to prevent Colombia's war from spreading to Ecuador (and other neighboring countries)—unless the United States came up with additional financial assistance. He thought that another $400 million to $500 million over a five-year period might be appropriate.

Indeed, the lure of U.S. aid dollars eventually caused most Latin American leaders to embrace Plan Colombia, however reluctantly. By April 2001, even Venezuela's eccentric leftist president, Hugo Chavez, was on board. In contrast to his remarks a few months earlier warning of the "Vietnamization" of the Amazon Basin and the advent of a "medium intensity conflict," Chavez stated that doubts about Plan Colombia "have now been clarified." Coincidentally, his conversion took place barely two weeks after the Bush administration proposed to double the aid package to Colombia's neighbors.

But some influential Latin Americans have refused to mute their objections merely because their countries now hope to get U.S. aid funds. Even as Chavez and other politicians were announcing their conversion experiences, some 100 prominent Latin Americans, including Argentine Nobel laureate Adolfo Perez Esquivel, sent President Bush a letter calling U.S. military aid and forced coca eradication in Colombia "misguided and harmful," and warning that the policy "will [adversely] affect the entire Andean region." Ecuadorean congressman Henry Llanes, a prominent critic of his government's decision to allow the United States to run its anti-drug surveillance flights out of a big air base at Manta, cites as one reason for his opposition the fear of a dangerous entanglement. "We are compromising our neutrality in the Colombian conflict with the Manta base, dragging ourselves into a war between the Americans and their enemies in Colombia," Llanes warns.

His fears are not unfounded. A few days earlier, Ecuadorean troops killed six men at an illegal drug lab near the border with Colombia. Evidence at the scene indicated that they were members of FARC. That marked the first armed clash between the Ecuadorean military and the Colombian rebels. Other incidents were not long in coming. In early February, more than 500 Ecuadoreans fled their Amazon jungle homes after Colombian armed groups threatened their border hamlets. That incursion seemed to be in direct response to the earlier destruction of the labs. In early June, an Ecuadorean army unit clashed with ELN guerrillas some 13 miles inside the border.

Similar incidents have occurred along Colombia's border with Venezuela. In addition, Colombians fleeing fighting between rebels and government forces—or between the rebels and right-wing paramilitary units—have crossed into neighboring countries. In one such

221

incident in early February 2001, more than 400 people from four villages sought refuge in Venezuela after paramilitary forces pillaged their homes. Other victims have fled into neighboring countries to avoid outrages by the rebels. More than 100 refugees crossed the border into Panama after FARC guerrillas killed the mayor of their Pacific Coast village and terrorized them.

In addition to the spillover of violence from Colombia's civil war, there has been a spillover of the drug trade itself. Even as U.S. support for Plan Colombia got under way in 2000, U.S. officials were reporting a marked increase of drug trafficking in the upper Amazon River region in Brazil as well as in Panama. The spillover effects have become serious enough that U.S. and Colombian officials are now explicitly addressing that phenomenon as they assess the performance of Plan Colombia. By late 2000, U.S. officials promised that additional funding would be forthcoming. Undersecretary of State Thomas Pickering was surprisingly candid in his reasons for the policy change. "As we increase our efforts in Colombia, there will be a tendency [for the drug organizations] to find new areas, either in Colombia or outside Colombia, in which to move the cultivation and production of cocaine and heroin."

One would be hard-pressed to come up with a more concise description of the "push down, pop up" (or "balloon") effect and the inherent futility of the drug eradication component of the hemispheric war on drugs. But Pickering did not draw the obvious conclusion from evidence of the push down, pop up effect. Instead, he cited the phenomenon as a reason for a broader and better funded drug eradication program throughout the Andean region and beyond.

In March 2001 the Bush administration proposed a significant increase in funding for Colombia's neighbors in the 2002 fiscal year budget. As part of a $731 million "Andean Initiative" aid program, the administration earmarked $332 million for anti-drug efforts. (It is perhaps symbolic of the intellectual sterility of the war on drugs that not only are the policies periodically recycled, but even the names of the various schemes are recycled. "Andean Initiative" is the same name given to the grandiose regional anti-drug offensive waged during the administration of the elder Bush.) The new Andean Initiative request submitted to Congress included an additional $399 million for Colombia, $156 million for Peru, $101 million for Bolivia, and about $75 million for Colombia's four other neighbors—Brazil, Ecuador, Panama and Venezuela.

Trouble Ahead

For all the claimed successes, Plan Colombia is already showing signs of trouble. It was certainly not encouraging that, barely months after the program went into effect, Pastrana was already calling for a substantial additional infusion of financial support. In an interview shortly before his summit meeting with President Bush in February 2001, Pastrana asserted that perhaps as much as another $500 million a year was needed. Those funds, he argued, should go for economic development in the provinces where the aerial spraying programs were taking their greatest toll. He added ominously, "This is a long-term plan, maybe 15 to 20 years." That is not good news for Americans who worry that Plan Colombia was merely the first stage of what could become an endless U.S. entanglement.

And Plan Colombia already shows signs of creating a nasty, anti-U.S. backlash among portions of the Colombian population. When Pastrana visited Putumayo province in May 2001 to sell the "softer" (economic development) side of Plan Colombia, he was repeatedly confronted by groups of protesters. Many of them waved signs showing a Colombian flag being subsumed by the Stars and Stripes, with the caption "Plan Colombia's achievements." Other demonstrators greeted the president with chants of "Pastrana subservient to the gringos." "The United States thinks they're the boss here," one angry resident stated to a reporter. "We don't want fumigation, and we don't want money from Uncle Sam."

Given the long-standing history of anti-U.S. sentiment in Latin America, the resurgence of such attitudes in Colombia is cause for concern. Latin American paranoia about U.S. imperialism, a fear that never slumbers too soundly to begin with, is beginning to resurface. And that development could have widespread, very negative ramifications.

There is another troubling possibility in connection with Plan Colombia. If the effort fails to achieve its objective, pressure will mount on the United States to escalate its commitment. Even during these relatively early stages of the campaign, one can already hear arguments that America's credibility is on the line. In the cover letter accompanying the release of a June 2001 RAND Corporation report advocating an escalation of Plan Colombia, Edward R. Harshberger, director of the think tank's strategy and doctrine program, stated: "Should the Colombian government falter, the United States would be confronted with a strategic dilemma: whether to escalate its support of the Bogotá government or to scale it down, potentially at the cost of Colombia's tottering democracy. The latter approach would involve a significant loss of credibility and a degradation of the United States' ability to protect its interests in a critical region."

As we have seen in regions as diverse as Southeast Asia, the Persian Gulf, and the Balkans, once America's "credibility" is invoked, it is very difficult to stem the drive toward a major military commitment. In Colombia, another quagmire is beckoning.

This article originally appeared in *Cato Policy Report*, September/October 2001.

To Avoid Making Mexico the Next Colombia . . .

As President Bush prepares to travel to Latin America, one of the top issues for discussion will be the war on drugs. The Bush administration is especially alarmed at the situation in Colombia, fearing that the democratic political system in that country could collapse under an assault by leftist insurgencies allied with powerful drug traffickers.

Washington's nightmare scenario is the emergence of a Marxist/narcotrafficking state. U.S. leaders are so worried about that possibility that they are ready to expand America's military aid to Bogotá and eliminate the restriction that the aid must be used only for counternarcotics campaigns, not counterinsurgency campaigns.

The fears about Colombia are not unfounded, but U.S. policymakers have a serious problem brewing much closer to home. The prominence of the drug trade in Mexico has mushroomed in recent years. Just two years ago, Thomas Constantine, head of the Drug Enforcement Administration, told Congress that the power of Mexican drug traffickers had grown "virtually geometrically" over the previous five years and that corruption was "unparalleled." Matters have grown even worse in the past two years.

As is often the case with lucrative black markets, the illicit drug trade in Mexico has been accompanied by escalating corruption and violence. In a number of troubling ways, Mexico is beginning to resemble Colombia a decade or so ago. Indeed, Mexicans are beginning to refer to the trend as the "Colombianization" of their country.

True, Mexico does not face a large-scale insurgency like that afflicting Colombia, but the similarities of the two countries are greater than the differences.

U.S. policy seems to assume that if the Mexican government can eliminate the top drug lords, their organizations will fall apart, thereby greatly reducing the flow of illegal drugs to the United States. Thus, U.S. officials have rejoiced at the recent capture of Benjamin Arellano Felix—the leader of one of Mexico's largest and most violent drug gangs—and the apparent killing of his brother.

But that is the same assumption that U.S. officials used with respect to the crackdown on the Medellin and Cali cartels in Colombia during the 1990s. Subsequent developments proved the assumption to be erroneous. The elimination of the Medellin and Cali cartels merely decentralized the Colombian drug trade. Instead of two large organizations controlling the trade, today some 300 much smaller, loosely organized groups do so. The arrests and killings of numerous top drug lords in both Colombia and Mexico over the years have not had a meaningful impact on the quantity of drugs entering the United States. Cutting off one head of the drug-smuggling hydra merely results in more heads taking its place.

Of all the similarities between Colombia and Mexico, the most troubling may be the increasingly pervasive violence. It is no longer just the cocaine and heroin trade that is characterized by bloodshed. Even the marijuana trade, which traditionally had generated little violence, is now accompanied by horrific killings. Indeed, the biggest and bloodiest massacres over the past three years in Mexico have involved marijuana trafficking, not trafficking in harder drugs.

Mexico can still avoid going down the same tragic path as Colombia. But time is growing short. If Washington continues to pursue a prohibitionist strategy, the violence and corruption that have convulsed Colombia will increasingly become a feature of Mexico's life as well.

The illicit drug trade has already penetrated the country's economy and society to an unhealthy degree. The brutal reality is that prohibitionism simply drives commerce in a product underground, creating an enormous black-market potential profit that attracts terrorists and other violence-prone elements.

U.S. officials need to ask whether they want to risk "another Colombia"—only this time directly on America's southern border.

If they don't want to deal with the turmoil such a development would create, the Bush administration needs to change its policy on the drug issue—and do so quickly.

This article originally appeared in the *Houston Chronicle*, March 19, 2002.

10. General Strategy

Introduction

In various books and articles, I have outlined an alternative security strategy for the United States, coining the term "strategic independence" to describe that alternative. Some critics have charged that strategic independence is merely a sophisticated form of isolationism, but nothing could be further from the truth. In the first place, "isolationism" is a terribly vague concept; frequently it is nothing more than a pejorative that advocates of global interventionism use in an attempt to intimidate their opponents and foreclose debate. To the extent that the term has any meaning at all, it connotes an America that wants little or nothing to do with the outside world.

Strategic independence, on the other hand, specifically embraces economic, cultural, and diplomatic engagement with the rest of the world. It is only in the arena of security policy that it mandates a cautious approach, reserving the use of military force solely for the defense of vital American security interests. Rejecting the notion that the United States must subsidize the defense of wealthy allies, confront other countries' adversaries, and attempt to solve all manner of injustice in the world hardly constitutes isolationism. That kind of restraint merely reflects realism and basic prudence.

A policy of strategic independence would emphasize a number of subsidiary principles. It would place a premium on managing relations with Russia, China, the European Union, Japan, and other major players in world affairs. Strategic independence would also welcome (indeed, encourage) the development of balances of power in key regions of the world instead of vainly trying to maintain U.S. global hegemony. Thus, it would be alert to the opportunities afforded by an emerging democratic great power such as India. As I indicated in some recent articles, India could be an important source of stability in Central and South Asia and the Persian Gulf region as well as a strategic counterweight to an increasingly assertive China.

Another principle of strategic independence would be an avoidance of excessively close relations with repressive regimes. One of the most unfortunate aspects of U.S. foreign policy during the Cold War was the tendency to make common cause with repressive and corrupt dictatorships merely because they professed to be anti-Soviet. With the end of the Cold War, one might have hoped that such a practice would come to an end, and for a time it appeared that that was happening. With the advent of the war against terrorism, however, Washington is again acquiring a variety of rather unsavory "allies." Although some principles may have to be bent to wage an effective war against the perpetrators of the September 11 atrocities, care must be exercised to make sure that temporary alliances of convenience do not become long-term relationships. America must not again become an accomplice in repression by "friendly" autocrats.

Finally, strategic independence would avoid the error of substituting empty symbolism for effective policy. Nowhere is that distinction more important than with regard to the issue of economic sanctions. Washington has imposed comprehensive embargos on Cuba, Iraq, and other countries. As I noted in several pieces, economic sanctions have the unique quality of being simultaneously cruel and ineffectual. They devastate innocent populations in the target country while rarely achieving the removal of the offending regime or even altering the behavior of that regime. The embargos against Cuba and Iraq have been among the most misguided and counterproductive policies the U.S. government has ever pursued. They should be lifted immediately. Equally important, the United States should avoid the temptation to impose economic sanctions against other countries in the future.

Repression Is Repression

American leaders habitually regard any anti-communist government, however repressive and undemocratic it might be at home, as a "friend" whose excesses must be ignored or excused. Conversely, they view leftist regimes as little more than Soviet surrogates meriting unrelenting U.S. hostility. With only occasional exceptions, relations with China constituting the most recent and prominent example, a rigid dichotomy has characterized America's policy toward the Third World throughout most of the Cold War era.

Although defenders of current policy sometimes cite strategic and economic justifications for it, they stress that an underlying ideological kinship exists between democracies and right-wing "authoritarian" governments. Marxist dictatorships, on the other hand, are "totalitarian" and represent mortal threats to the democratic West. Henry Kissinger and Jeane Kirkpatrick are among the more prominent proponents of this thesis.

While acknowledging that rightist regimes sometimes engage in political repression, they insist that it is milder and less pervasive than that practiced by communist states. Moreover, authoritarian governments are supposedly susceptible to gradual liberalization, while totalitarian systems, more rigid in nature, are not. In this view, helping to preserve autocratic "friends" from Marxist onslaughts becomes something akin to a moral imperative.

The theory has a certain facile logic, but it ignores two crucial considerations. First, one may readily concede that left-wing regimes practice more virulent forms of repression than do their right-wing counterparts, but the issue of American complicity must be addressed. While the United States cannot eradicate oppression in the world, as the most powerful symbol of democracy America does have an obligation not to become a participant in acts of brutality.

Sponsorship of right-wing autocracies, especially through military aid and security training, violates that important tenet. Assisting dictatorial allies makes the U.S. government, and by extension the public that elects it, an accomplice in the suppression of other peoples' liberty. Worst of all, many victims of that repression—as recent events in South Korea and the Philippines demonstrate—are not communists but legitimate democrats. A betrayal of our own political values also does little to enhance America's reputation from a moral standpoint. A perception has emerged throughout the Third

229

World that the United States is the principal patron of reactionary dictatorships. Long-suffering populations see detested autocratic regimes as American clients, and they view the removal of such regimes as an eradication of U.S. hegemony. At the same time, they demonstrate a virtual reflex action to repudiate everything American—including capitalist economics and Western-style democracy.

Should we really be surprised at this result, when Washington routinely portrays corrupt tyrants such as Ferdinand Marcos, Mobutu Sese Seko and Chun Doo Hwan as symbols of the free world? The United States is paying a high price today in Iran and Nicaragua for its previous sponsorship of hated rulers. Similar cauldrons are now boiling in the Philippines, South Korea, Chile and elsewhere, with potentially disastrous consequences.

It is imperative that the United States alter its approach to Third World dictatorships. A change in policy does not mean that we should return to Jimmy Carter's inconsistent moral posturing, using American aid funds to bribe autocratic allies into making token gestures of respect for human rights. Nor should we replace the Reagan administration's conservative double standard with an equally hypocritical liberal version.

The United States has no holy writ to destabilize the governments of Cuba or Nicaragua because it finds them repugnant nor to preserve authoritarian systems in South Korea or Zaire because Washington considers them congenial. By the same token, no one has anointed America to overthrow the Pinochet regime in Chile or to coerce South Africa into implementing internal reforms.

The most constructive alternative is one of benign detachment toward all Third World dictatorships, whatever their ideological orientation. This approach appreciates the diversity of Third World societies, rejecting the simplistic categorization of right-wing regimes as friends and Marxist governments as Soviet surrogates. It stresses an even-handed approach, recognizing that rightist dictatorships are just as alien to our democratic values as their left-wing counterparts. A policy of benign detachment would encourage cordial diplomatic and commercial relations with any government willing to reciprocate. At the same time, it would avoid such embarrassing and dangerous entanglements as military aid and security training programs.

Benign detachment assumes a more passive strategy than America's current pretentious status as global gendarme, and it avoids the many lethal pitfalls of interventionism. More important, it is the policy that is most consistent with our own heritage and values.

This article originally appeared in the *St. Louis Post-Dispatch*, October 8, 1985.

Ill-Conceived Meddling in Angola

Rebel leader Jonas Savimbi's visit to Washington to lobby for American aid intensified a long-simmering debate regarding U.S. policy toward Angola.

Few men are more controversial than Savimbi. Conservative admirers in the United States hail him as a charismatic "pro-Western" leader and a dedicated "freedom fighter" against the Marxist regime in Luanda. Liberal critics castigate him as a "megalomanic," an "opportunist" and—because his UNITA organization accepts the friendship and assistance of South Africa's racist government—an "Uncle Tom."

This acrimonious debate needs an injection of realism.

Ideologically inspired portrayals of Savimbi as an unprincipled South African stooge or, conversely, as a noble, pro-American freedom fighter are caricatures and serve no useful purpose. Jonas Savimbi is simply the pragmatic leader of one faction in a power struggle that has convulsed Angola for more than a decade—a conflict as much tribal as it is ideological. Angola's misfortune is that outside elements—the Soviet Union, South Africa and the United States—have exploited the situation to advance their own political and strategic agendas.

A new Reagan administration policy toward Angola has emerged, but unfortunately it seems destined to increase rather than diminish interference in that nation's internal affairs. The administration this week made public its intention to provide aid to Savimbi's forces.

A statement last month by Chester Crocker, assistant secretary of state for African affairs, suggesting that American companies in Angola curtail their investments, also signals a stark reversal in U.S. policy. Previously, the administration encouraged such investment as a way to dilute Soviet influence.

This desire for economic accommodation was so extensive, in fact, that the Export-Import Bank provided loan guarantees totaling

231

nearly $230 million to the joint Gulf Oil–Angolan government enterprise in Cabinda province. As Sen. William Proxmire has pointed out, when the administration funds the UNITA rebels, American taxpayers will be subsidizing both sides in the civil war—a novel but not very intelligent strategy.

Rather than deepening U.S. involvement in Angola's strife, the administration should seek ways to reduce the level of outside interference. Previous State Department diplomatic initiatives designed to secure the withdrawal of Cuban and South African forces were commendable to the extent they were confined to that objective. Unfortunately, Washington also sought to promote allegedly vital U.S. interests in southern Africa and increase its "leverage" with the Luanda government through loan guarantees and vague offers of economic aid.

Conservative critics are justified in their complaints that those actions, especially the massive Export-Import Bank financing, strengthened a Marxist dictatorship and significantly enhanced its chances of retaining power.

The appropriate remedy for such ill-conceived meddling in Angola's affairs, however, is not to formulate an equally ill-advised military aid program for UNITA. Assisting UNITA entangles the United States further in a complex civil war, creating expensive and perilous possibilities. Even if Savimbi's forces emerge victorious, we may simply have helped replace one repressive regime with another, at considerable cost.

A more productive option would be for the United States to adopt a consistent noninterventionist posture while pursuing a diplomatic offensive to end Cuban and South African interference as well. America's objective ought to be an Angolan settlement achieved by Angolans—an outcome reflecting the internal dynamics and contending forces of that society. The United States can never attain that goal if it becomes a participant in the conflict.

This article originally appeared in the *Chicago Tribune*, February 22, 1986.

Secrecy and the Erosion of Democratic Values

Recent revelations that the Reagan administration orchestrated an elaborate disinformation campaign against Libyan dictator Moammar Gadhafi and is providing arms to Iran in return for the release of hostages should compel all Americans to consider the inherent ethical dilemmas whenever a democratic government employs covert activities to implement its foreign policy. These latest incidents represent one more symptom of an insidious condition that is undermining essential American values.

Concern about the Libyan project should go beyond the realization that once again an administration's foreign policy has become snared in a web of falsehoods. The bizarre distinction drawn by a senior administration official—that while the United States used foreign media news to deceive Gadhafi, there was no intent to mislead the domestic media or the American people—warrants both derision and anger. The notion that lying is acceptable so long as it is solely for overseas consumption betrays a moral agnosticism. Furthermore, the distinction makes sense only if one assumes that foreign and domestic news industries operate in hermetically sealed compartments—that deception in one arena would not inevitably contaminate the quality of information in the other.

But there are more troubling issues involved than a government's propensity to lie in order to advance certain policy objectives. A more serious shortcoming is demonstrated by the Iran caper. In that case, and in the case of the Libyan disinformation campaign, President Reagan and his top advisers chose to pursue a major foreign policy initiative in arrogant isolation from Congress and the American public. Moreover, they were risky, if not reckless, undertakings that involved calamitous possibilities for the entire nation.

The official rationale for the disinformation campaign was that it would keep Gadhafi "off balance." Erroneous fears that the United States contemplated further military action against Libya might finally impel his domestic opponents to oust the mercurial dictator. In the same fashion, U.S.-generated rumors that key aides were plotting against Gadhafi might cause him to take action against them, thereby possibly precipitating a coup in response.

The logic behind this strategy was dubious at best. Rather than the sanguine administration scenarios, it was just as likely that such alarming rumors would cause Gadhafi to lash out in a spasm of violence against American targets. A new round of terrorist incidents was certainly a serious danger, and even a preemptive strike against the U.S. fleet operating in the Mediterranean, an action that would mean war, was not outside the realm of possibility.

The danger inherent in provoking a political leader who has previously demonstrated—to put it charitably—some emotional instability should be obvious to any prudent policymaker. To engage in such provocation needlessly is the height of folly. Yet, the administration's own internal memos at the time of the disinformation strategy was adopted apparently conceded that Gadhafi has been "quiescent" on the terrorist front since the U.S. air strikes in mid-April. Why then the insistence upon renewing his paranoia?

One especially ominous cloud now hangs over this entire operation. Some evidence implicates Libya in the bloody highjacking incident aboard a Pan American jet in Karachi on September 5th—three weeks after the disinformation campaign began. If that proves to be the case, 21 innocent passengers, including several Americans, may have paid the ultimate price for the administration's clever strategy.

Disinformation campaigns and similar covert operations inherently corrode democratic societies. The essential features of a democratic political system include free and vigorous debate on policy, respect for the rights of individuals and accountability to the electorate. A foreign policy conceived and executed in secret, employing massive deception and needlessly endangering the lives of citizens is antithetical to all those values.

If the Reagan administration believes that the Gadhafi regime represents a serious threat to American security (and there is a respectable case to be made for that proposition), then it should take its case to Congress and the American people. The federal government has a constitutional obligation to protect the lives and safety of American citizens. If the Gadhafi government is implicated in the murders of Americans traveling abroad, as the administration contends, then action is warranted—perhaps even including a declaration of war.

Before such momentous steps are taken, U.S. policy should be formulated in the light of day with explicit justifications for the chosen course of action. It should not be formulated by a handful of executive branch officials operating under a cloak of secrecy in the National Security Council.

If a free society is to survive, its foreign policy must embody the fundamental values of that society. Covert activities such as the disinformation operation against Libya and the undercover dealings with Iran clearly violate this standard.

This article originally appeared in the *Baltimore Sun*, November 13, 1986.

Afghanistan—A New Lebanon?

Reagan administration officials are eagerly anticipating a moral and geopolitical triumph for U.S. policy in Afghanistan, as agreement nears on terms for continued aid to rebels that could set the stage for a withdrawal of Soviet troops by 1989.

But an attitude of caution, or even apprehension, would be more appropriate. Although the Soviet Union's brutal aggression against its tiny neighbor will apparently go unrewarded, the outcome of that struggle may well be as unappealing to Washington as it is to Moscow.

In some conservative circles, to be sure, there is a lingering fear that Moscow may be executing a devious maneuver—that is, lull the United States and Pakistan into terminating military aid to the Afghan mujahideen on the mere promise of a Soviet withdrawal. Most observers, though, believe the Kremlin's desire to escape the Afghan quagmire after eight costly years is genuine.

Proponents of the Reagan Doctrine—assisting insurgents who battle pro-Soviet forces in the Third World—are already boasting that Afghanistan demonstrates the wisdom and cost-effectiveness of that strategy.

The Reagan administration and its supporters have portrayed the Afghan war as a morality play pitting noble "freedom fighters" against a diabolical Soviet invader and its quislings in Kabul. The implicit message is that a rebel victory would mean the emergence of a democratic, pro-Western government.

But that outcome has always been improbable, and the emerging accord, if it continues the flow of arms to the region, would make it especially so. The mujahideen are a fractious coalition of seven organizations tenuously linked by their hatred of the Russians. Four of those groups embrace versions of the virulent Islamic fundamentalism practiced in neighboring Iran, and Gulbuddin Hekmatyar, the leader of the most powerful faction, openly denounces the United States while accepting American military aid.

The three "moderate" groups differ from their fundamentalist brethren only in degree. They certainly do not advocate secular democracy. In the unlikely event that all seven factions could unite to form a government following a Soviet withdrawal, the resulting regime would likely be not only anti-Soviet but also authoritarian and anti-Western.

235

Although there is a danger that Afghanistan will turn into another Iran, it is more likely to become another Lebanon. Already there are reports of bloody skirmishes among the rival factions. That internecine fighting has erupted before the enemy has even begun to withdraw from Afghanistan is an ominous development. One could anticipate a fierce struggle for power—not just between the insurgents and the communists but also among the insurgents.

Schisms within the mujahideen reflect the myriad divisions in Afghan society, which comprises at least 10 major linguistic and ethnic groups. Before the communist coup in 1978 and the Soviet invasion in 1979, Afghanistan enjoyed a precarious unity at best. It never possessed a sense of nationhood in the Western conception of that term. Thus, a probable scenario after a Soviet withdrawal is the creation of regional enclaves, each dominated politically and militarily by one of the mujahideen factions.

Most Americans would regard the emergence of either an anti-Western Islamic theocracy or a South Asian Lebanon with extreme distaste, neither having been worth the expenditure of nearly $2 billion.

By overselling the ideological purity of the Afghan resistance, the Reagan administration has created prime conditions for a domestic backlash. The administration portrayed the conflict in stark moral terms and effectively minimized opposition to its Afghan policy in the short run. The American people were led to believe that they were assisting "freedom fighters" who would restore Afghanistan to the "free world."

Yet the result will probably be far different, in which case proponents of the Reagan Doctrine are going to be hard-pressed to explain the discrepancy. They are likely to discover that this much-touted triumph is a Pyrrhic victory. Having been deceived once, the American people will be justifiably skeptical about commitments to other alleged freedom fighters.

This article originally appeared in the *New York Times*, April 7, 1988. Reprinted with permission.

Going It Alone: U.S. Foreign Policy

Americans are exhibiting considerable uncertainty and uneasiness about what foreign policy course Democratic nominee Michael Dukakis would chart as president. The Bush camp has exploited that apprehension by frequently caricaturing the Massachusetts governor as a weakling and a charter member of the "blame America first" club.

Notwithstanding such unfair accusations, there are reasons to be concerned about Dukakis's foreign policy orientation. One trait is especially disturbing: an obsession with multilateral mechanisms for pursuing U.S. objectives.

The alleged virtues of multilateralism abound in Dukakis's speeches and are increasingly evident in the comments of other liberal Democrats as well. Democratic godmother Pamela Harriman characterized her party's approach as an effort to "replace the go-it-alone posturing of the last eight years with the hard work of peacetime cooperation among sovereign nations." Dukakis touts his "conventional defense initiative" as a way to enhance America's military collaboration with its European allies and refute allegations that NATO is a vehicle for U.S. hegemony. He advocates working in tandem with nations in Central America to implement the Arias peace plan for Nicaragua. Finally, the Massachusetts governor wants to revitalize the United Nations as an international peacekeeping organization.

Many conservatives suspect that the Dukakis Democrats embrace multilateralism merely to provide an excuse for the United States to abdicate its role as leader of the free world. According to such critics, a Dukakis administration would allow an assortment of timid allies to exercise veto power over vigorous U.S. efforts to defend the Republic's security interests.

There is some merit to their indictment, but there is another, more subtle danger. Under certain conditions, multilateralism could seriously increase the prospect of unwise U.S. entanglements. Because our allies and clients have their own foreign policy agendas, they may wish to draw the United States into controversies that are important to them but tangential or detrimental to America's well-being. The skill with which Kuwait and other Persian Gulf states maneuvered the United States into steadily escalating its naval commitments and becoming a de facto ally of Iraq in the war against Iran is a recent textbook example of that process. The Dukakis Democrats' infatuation with multilateralism could well lead to a proliferation of such episodes.

The central effect of the Dukakis wing's foreign policy is that it would allow other countries to dictate America's security interests.

Dukakis and his followers have concluded that the problem with the nation's Cold War strategy—especially as it has been applied during the Reagan years—is an excessive unilateralism. That is a colossal misdiagnosis. The actual problem is the chronic failure of U.S. leaders to distinguish between essential security interests and less important or even largely irrelevant ones. Too often the United States has acted as though it has interests everywhere in the world that must be defended at all costs. Its foreign policy has been not only promiscuously interventionist but costly and dangerous.

There is unquestionably a need for an alternative to the Cold War global interventionist strategy developed by Harry Truman and his successors. But the Dukakis doctrine would bring about the worst of all possible worlds. It would give the diverse and unstable governments of the Caribbean Basin the power to obstruct U.S. efforts to prevent a proliferation of Soviet satellites in the region. It would also give NATO's European members the power to prolong the presence of U.S. troops on the Continent—a commitment that benefits the Europeans but represents a severe drain on American taxpayers.

Finally, it would render the United States a compliant agent of the United Nations and a partner in furthering that organization's warped conception of peace and justice in the world. Under the multilateralism of the Dukakis Democrats, we would retain the over-extended global commitments we have borne since the dawn of the Cold War but have less control over how to fulfill them. That is a blueprint for disaster.

A unilateral approach would be eminently workable if the Republic's security interests were defined in a more discriminating and sophisticated manner than they have been throughout the Cold War. It is the task of defining those interests and minimizing the costs and risks of defending them, not the seductive snare of multilateralism, that merits the attention of the next administration.

This article originally appeared in the *Orange County Register*, October 26, 1988.

Hostility toward Japan Reminiscent of Fears of a Stronger Germany

As the Cold War between the United States and the Soviet Union ebbs, there is growing apprehension about the status of West

Germany and Japan in a more complex international political environment. Observers as diverse as *New York Times* columnist A. M. Rosenthal and Singapore prime minister Lee Kuan Yew recently have emphasized the undesirability of having Bonn and Tokyo assume more vigorous political and military roles in their respective regions.

Rosenthal assailed the suggestion that West Germany acquire an independent nuclear deterrent, recalling that Germany twice had plunged the world into war. In a similar vein, Lee observed that the Japanese "were greater warriors than they were merchants" and rejected the notion that "they have lost those martial qualities." He urged other countries to press Japan to abide by its "peace" constitution, whose provisions Tokyo already had breached, he said, by creating its modest Self-Defense Forces.

Rosenthal and Lee are only a little more direct than most critics of increased responsibilities for West Germany and Japan. Those who wish to maintain America's extensive and costly military presence in NATO commonly assert that the alliance is needed, not only to thwart any lingering Soviet expansionist aims, but to prevent a revival of Europe's internecine conflicts. There is reason to be suspicious about the emphasis that such Atlanticists now place on the U.S. role in "preserving European stability." That phrase frequently is little more than code for "stopping the Germans from running amok."

An early NATO official described the alliance as a European arrangement designed to "keep the Russians out, the Americans in, and the Germans down." That attitude appears to be alive and well nearly four decades later, despite the incongruity of arguing that an important function of NATO in the 1990s should be to constrain its most important European member.

Critics of a more vigorous role for Germany typically focus on countering proposals for its reunification and its acquisition of nuclear weapons. (The question of a West German conventional force was decided more than three decades ago, although not without great controversy and only within NATO's multilateral structure.) The hostility toward Japan is more comprehensive. Many prominent Americans and East Asians regard any increase in Japan's military role as undesirable. Their attitude approximates that of the most intense Germanophobes in France toward rearming the Federal Republic in the early 1950s.

Such hostility toward Germany and Japan is objectionable for two reasons. First, it is based on the fallacious doctrine of collective guilt. The German and Japanese leaders who were responsible for plunging humanity into World War II long have been in their graves. An overwhelming majority of the populations of both countries were not even born when the war began. The contention that modern-day Germans and Japanese somehow are tainted by that tragedy, and that their nations therefore cannot be entrusted with significant global political and military power, is—however elliptically phrased—a form of bigotry.

The hostility toward Germany and Japan also is objectionable from a geopolitical standpoint. As the stark bipolar contest between the United States and the Soviet Union continues to erode, major regional powers inevitably will become more assertive. Among the most important powers are Germany, which has the world's fourth largest economy, and Japan, which has the second largest. It is unrealistic to expect such economic giants to continue being diffident in the political and military realms.

Indeed, instead of attempting to constrain Germany and Japan (and keep the former nation divided), the United States should encourage both nations to play more active roles in defending their regions. A strong Germany as the keystone of a self-reliant Western Europe's effort to counterbalance the Soviet Union militarily would relieve America of NATO burdens that currently consume more than $160 billion of the $300 billion U.S. military budget. The United States also would realize more modest but substantial savings if Japan assumed wider security responsibilities in the western Pacific.

There is little doubt that neighboring nations are uneasy about the prospect that Germany and Japan will re-emerge as significant political and military actors. Many of them, as Prime Minister Lee indicated, would prefer that the United States continue serving as a benevolent protector of the two regions. But America must not jeopardize its economic health in an attempt to sustain an increasingly burdensome network of security commitments merely to reassure the neighbors of Germany and Japan.

World War II ended nearly four and a half decades ago, and it is time to put its ghosts to rest. Even if we accept the odious concept of collective guilt, we should apply a statute of limitations. No one suggests that France, for example, be restrained because of Napoleon's expansionist binge.

It would be increasingly difficult for the United States to prevent Germany and Japan from pursuing their own political and security interests in any case—as the Bush administration discovered during its dispute with Bonn over short-range nuclear missiles. Persistent efforts to keep those nations subordinate politically and militarily would serve only to poison America's relations with them. The United States must not permit its security strategy for the 1990s to be distorted by the assumption that the Germans and the Japanese are afflicted with a double dose of original sin. Germany and Japan can and should undertake more extensive security responsibilities in their regions.

This article originally appeared in the *Army Times*, December 4, 1989.

America Can't Police the Planet

The Bush administration's response to Iraq's invasion of Kuwait demonstrates an unmistakable intention to preserve America's hyperactivist Cold War strategy in a post–Cold War era despite vastly altered world conditions. That attitude has emerged on other occasions. In his 1990 report to Congress, Secretary of Defense Dick Cheney argued that the United States must strive to "attain the same basic strategic objectives with a somewhat smaller defense budget." The president himself has sought to justify the preservation of venerable Cold War alliances by stressing a new U.S. mission to prevent "instability and unpredictability."

Making the United States the guardian of global stability is a blueprint for the indefinite prolongation of expensive and risky U.S. military commitments around the world. The international system has always been characterized by instability and unpredictability, and there is little evidence that the future will be materially different. Struggles between status quo and revisionist powers are nothing new, and territorial adjustments (frequently by force) have been the norm in international affairs for centuries. Iraq is not the first, nor will it be the last, nation to expand its territory and influence or to exploit regional power vacuums. When policymakers invoke simplistic comparisons of a mundane Third World tyrant like Saddam Hussein with Adolf Hitler and reflexively cite the overused Munich analogy as policy guidance concerning Iraq's absorption of Kuwait, they ignore that lengthy historical record.

241

Instability per se in distant regions does not threaten America's security. Indeed, in a post–Cold War world there may be many local or regional disputes that are (or at least should be) irrelevant to the United States. U.S. leaders must learn to distinguish between vital and peripheral security interests, unlike the Cold War tendency to regard even the most trivial geopolitical assets as essential. To be considered a threat to a vital interest, a development should have a direct, immediate and substantial connection with America's physical survival, its political independence or the preservation of its domestic freedoms. The possibility of higher oil prices arising from a stronger Iraqi position in the Middle East does not meet that standard. Threats to truly vital interests are relatively rare and should be even less common in a post–Cold War setting, in which no potential adversary is capable of making a bid for global domination.

In that context, the preservation of America's Cold War system of alliances and commitments is ill-advised. Not only are such entanglements expensive, they are profoundly dangerous. As one defense expert has noted, alliances are lethal "transmission belts for war," converting what should be minor, localized conflicts into wider confrontations between great powers. There are various flash points around the world where obsolete Cold War–era commitments could entangle the United States. In addition to the volatile Persian Gulf, the tense situations involving Pakistan and India, Syria and Israel and the two Koreas are the most visible examples.

With the decline of the Soviet threat and no other would-be hegemonic power on the horizon, a global network of U.S.-dominated alliances makes little sense. The rationale for undertaking such expensive and risky obligations throughout the Cold War was to prevent Soviet global domination. Because even minor conflicts frequently involved Moscow's clients, U.S. policymakers believed that an adverse result would automatically strengthen the Soviet Union and correspondingly weaken the United States. It was always a questionable assumption, but with the end of the Cold War even that rationale for U.S. engagement on a global scale has disappeared. Perpetuating extensive obligations merely to prevent vaguely defined "instability" or discourage the outbreak of local quarrels comes perilously close to having clients simply for the sake of having clients. If the United States insists on policing the planet as the self-appointed guardian of the status quo, it may need an even larger and more expensive military establishment than it maintained throughout the Cold War.

The Persian Gulf crisis is symbolic of a fundamental choice confronting U.S. leaders and the American people: Shall this country define its vital security interests less expansively now that the Cold War has ended, or shall it bear the costs and risks of intervening in a multitude of conflicts around the globe? Americans have borne great risks and burdens throughout the Cold War period, and they now deserve to reap the benefits from the end of that long, difficult struggle.

This article originally appeared in the *Washington Post*, August 30, 1990.

We Are Not the World's Social Worker

Those members of the U.S. foreign policy establishment who favor a global interventionist strategy have viewed the demise of the Cold War with at least a twinge of regret. For more than four decades they used the existence of the Great Soviet Threat as the principal justification for maintaining a vast array of U.S. political and military commitments around the globe. The sudden collapse of Moscow's East European empire and the adoption of more conciliatory policies by the leaders of the Soviet Union deprive them of that justification.

Bush administration officials and their allies in the foreign policy community have been scrambling for alternative rationales to justify U.S. interventionism in a post–Cold War world. They have exhibited an astounding degree of creativity in formulating new missions, but two have emerged as the leading candidates: preserving an elusive stability of the international system, and leading a movement to bring democracy to all portions of the planet.

At first glance, those two objectives would seem inconsistent if not fundamentally incompatible, and indeed there is a certain amount of inherent tension between the two camps. Nevertheless, the two goals have one important feature in common: They would entangle the United States in a morass of regional, local, and even internecine conflicts throughout the world. More often than not those conflicts would have little or no relevance to America's own vital security interests.

America would become either the social worker or the policeman of the planet—or in a worst case scenario, seek to play both roles. Instead of a peace dividend emerging from the end of the Cold War, there would be a de facto "peace penalty." The United States would find itself with even more political and military burdens than it endured throughout the Cold War. It would be unable to concentrate on its own pressing domestic problems, and the political and economic distortions that afflicted American society during the Cold War would continue unabated.

For all of those reasons, the American people should resist the temptation to follow the foreign policy Pied Pipers who would lead America on fruitless and debilitating post–Cold War campaigns either to impose stability on a fractious international community or to achieve universal democracy at the point of American bayonets.

Bush administration leaders typically stress the need for continuing U.S. leadership to prevent global instability. President Bush himself has argued that NATO, as well as the U.S. troop presence on the Continent, will be needed for decades to forestall the twin dangers of "instability and unpredictability" throughout Europe.

He conveniently ignores the reality that NATO's original purpose was to deter a Soviet attack on Western Europe—a mission that quite clearly has been accomplished now that the Warsaw Pact has disintegrated and Moscow has released its East European vassals. Attempts to preserve other hoary but increasingly irrelevant Cold War security arrangements, such as the U.S. military commitment to South Korea, have been based on a similar obsession with stability.

Indeed, for the Bush administration the goal of global stability has become the post–Cold War equivalent of the search for the Holy Grail. The president has justified the dispatch of U.S. forces to the Persian Gulf in response to Iraq's invasion of Kuwait on the basis of such "world order" objectives. Portraying Saddam Hussein as a modern-day Adolf Hitler, he contends that it is necessary not only to demonstrate that aggression does not pay but that the United States is prepared to lead a global effort to enforce collective security. America's mission in the post–Cold War era, according to Bush, must be nothing less than to protect the "sovereignty and freedom of nations."

The administration's commitment to stability, as well as its respect for national sovereignty, is quite selective, however. Washington displayed little reluctance about interfering in the internal affairs of Panama and overthrowing the incumbent government when that step served other U.S. objectives. Administration leaders responded

244

to allegations of inconsistency and hypocrisy expressed by Latin American critics by insisting that such interference was justified because it advanced the cause of democracy. The invasion, U.S. policymakers noted, helped install the Panamanian government that had been duly elected in May 1989 but had been prevented from taking office by dictator Manuel Noriega's armed thugs.

The selectivity of the Bush administration's enthusiasm for stability makes a tacit alliance possible with the more ardent advocates of an American campaign for global democracy. But it is an uneasy alliance. A variety of journalists, pundits, and think tank scholars have embraced their own version of a holy crusade for America in the post–Cold War era—a mission that would keep the United States busy for decades. They are less concerned about stability in the international system than with bringing the blessings of political democracy to all nations. Indeed, most of them are quite willing to risk or sometimes even create instability to make democracy a universal system.

Their enthusiasm for secessionist movements in the Soviet Union is a case in point. Several of the most prominent members of the global democracy crowd, including columnists William Safire and Charles Krauthammer, and think tank gurus Frank Gaffney, Michael Ledeen, and Joshua Muravchik, have urged the U.S. government to assist those movements in a variety of ways.

During the Lithuanian crisis earlier this year, for example, they pressured the Bush administration to extend full diplomatic recognition to the secessionist regime. Some of the more enthusiastic types suggested that the United States break the Soviet economic embargo on the break-away republic by sending in supply ships or organizing an airlift like the one that broke the Berlin Blockade. They seemed strangely oblivious to the fact that the latter actions would have created the grave risk of a direct military clash between the United States and the Soviet Union.

That they would risk such a conflict between two nuclear-armed states merely over the issue of Lithuanian independence underscores the pervasive recklessness of the global democracy crusaders. One of the prime characteristics of their enthusiasm for democratic revolutions, and especially their determination to involve the United States in those struggles, is a blissful disregard of possible adverse consequences.

245

Indeed, that is a trait that proponents of America as the guardian of global stability and proponents of America as the leader of a second democratic revolution typically share. They apparently believe that the foreign policy of the United States should be a wish list of desirable objectives.

But America's foreign policy, if it is well conceived, must take into account the probable domestic and international constraints and dangers. Unless they have a direct connection to the nation's vital security interests, it is not enough that goals be objectively worthwhile. The crucial issue is whether they are attainable, and equally important, whether they are attainable at an acceptable level of risk and cost. That assessment is especially important for the government of a free society. The lives, freedoms, and financial resources of the American people are not—or at least should not be—at the disposal of the national government to be used in whatever manner suits the whims of political leaders. The U.S. government has a fiduciary responsibility to protect the security and liberties of the American people. It does not have a writ to implement the political elite's conception of good deeds internationally any more than it has one to do so domestically.

Both the global stability and the global democracy goals fail the basic tests that must govern an effective foreign policy. It is not that either objective is undesirable; quite the contrary, both are highly desirable. The world would undoubtedly be a better place if all nations settled their differences by peaceful means rather than resorting to military force. It would likewise be a better place if the remaining communist regimes, as well as the assortment of military dictatorships, one-party states, and feudal autocracies that dominate the Third World, gave way to freely elected governments.

But it is unlikely that either objective is attainable, and it is even less likely that a hyperactivist U.S. role can bring about such utopias. It is far more probable that an American attempt to do so will entangle this country in a multitude of conflicts that will result in a massive hemorrhage of wealth and lives.

The international system has always been characterized by instability and there is little evidence that the future will be materially different. Struggles between status quo and revisionist powers are nothing new, and forcible territorial adjustments have been the norm in international affairs for centuries. Iraq's invasion of Kuwait may be an omen of the post–Cold War world, with a proliferation of local or regional conflicts. Iraq is not the first, nor will it be the last, country to expand its territory or seek to exploit regional power vacuums.

But instability per se in distant regions does not threaten America's security. In a post–Cold War world there are likely to be numerous quarrels that are (or at least should be) irrelevant to the United States. Interfering in such imbroglios in a vain effort to maintain stability poses far greater dangers than the remote possibility that a limited conflict might spiral out of control and ultimately threaten our well-being.

The observation of one defense analyst that alliances and other security commitments are lethal "transmission belts for war," converting minor local or regional struggles into potentially lethal entanglements for the United States, applies with special force to U.S.-led collective security enterprises.

In addition to the volatile Persian Gulf, the tense situations between Pakistan and India, Syria and Israel, and the two Koreas are the most visible examples of arenas where U.S. efforts to preserve stability could involve the United States in disastrous conflicts.

Longer term, the unresolved ethnic problems of Eastern Europe and the disintegrating Soviet empire could pose dangerous snares. It is difficult to see how America's best interests would be served by placing American soldiers in harm's way in an attempt to suppress a conflict between, say, Hungary and Romania over the status of Transylvania. Yet such dangers will be quite real in a post–Cold War setting if the United States becomes the self-appointed guardian of global stability.

The law of unintended consequences would also apply to an American-led crusade for global democracy. Proponents look to the U.S. interventions in Grenada and Panama as a model of how Washington can oust dictatorial regimes and replace them with democratic governments. But the situations in Grenada and Panama were atypical. Both countries were small and geographically situated where the United States could bring its military power to bear with maximum effectiveness, and neither target regime had a shred of legitimacy with its own population.

Those conditions would rarely apply in other cases where the United States might decide to intervene. It is pertinent to recall that at the same time Washington achieved its much-touted success in Grenada, it endured a spectacular failure to impose democracy in Lebanon. And that unsuccessful effort cost more that 250 American lives. Long before the Lebanon episode, the United States experienced the most disastrous failure at democratic nation building in South Vietnam, an effort that cost more than $150 billion and 58,000 American lives. What the democracy crusaders do not comprehend is that there are far more potential Lebanons and Vietnams than Grenadas.

Efforts to support democratic movements without the direct participation of American forces are also unlikely to achieve the desired goals. Proponents of an American-led global democratic revolution frequently envisage large-scale economic assistance programs to friendly regimes. Aside from the fact that such schemes unfairly bleed American taxpayers, the record of economic aid programs is a dismal one. They have repeatedly financed counterproductive economic policies in recipient countries, thereby retarding rather than stimulating economic growth.

Moreover, it scarcely enhances the reputations of fledgling democratic governments and their claims to legitimacy if they are perceived as U.S. puppets kept in power by an infusion of Yankee dollars. In the long run, such a suffocating embrace is likely to undermine, not strengthen, those governments.

Finally, there is the danger that the goals of international order and democratic revolution will be used as facades to conceal less savory objectives. That was all too often the case during the Cold War. Those who view that long twilight struggle between the United States and the Soviet Union exclusively or even primarily as a clash of values betray an astounding naivete. That is not to say that there was a moral equivalence between the two superpowers; the pre-Gorbachev Soviet Union was by far the more evil system. But U.S. policymakers frequently stressed a commitment to freedom, democracy, and national self-determination when U.S. actions actually undermined those values.

It was not a commitment to democracy or a respect for national self-determination that led to the U.S.-orchestrated coups against the elected government of Iran in 1953, the elected government of Guatemala in 1954, or the repeated efforts to undermine Chile's elected government in the early 1970s.

It was not a love of freedom that caused Washington to support such Third World dictators as the shah of Iran, Anastasio Somoza, Park Chung Hee, Ferdinand Marcos, etc., etc., ad nauseam. Washington may have had economic or strategic reasons for its actions, but the officially cited motives were little more than hypocritical propaganda.

There is a danger that the new noble sounding objectives will serve a similar purpose. Already the Bush administration's goal of restoring stability in the Persian Gulf includes a demand to return the autocratic emir of Kuwait to power. The president has repeatedly described the emir's regime as the "legitimate" government of Kuwait, although how it acquired its "legitimacy" remains a mystery. A U.S.-led effort to preserve international stability according to such standards will be viewed by revisionist nations with their lengthy set of (frequently legitimate) grievances as a cynical effort by Washington to protect an unjust global status quo that happens to benefit the United States.

The global democracy advocates also run the risk of embracing unsavory clients and causes. Merely because movements around the world employ the rhetoric of democracy does not mean that they adopt the underlying concepts. Despite a vigorous propaganda effort by his American supporters, there is evidence that Angolan rebel leader Jonas Savimbi would impose a dictatorship not noticeably different from the one he seeks to oust. Even many leaders of the Baltic independence movements seem more concerned with narrow nationalist agendas—including depriving the Russian minority of political rights—than they do with establishing a system of limited, democratic government.

Instead of embarking on quixotic crusades for global stability or global democracy, the United States should use the end of the Cold War as an opportunity to adopt a less interventionist role.

America can encourage greater respect for international law and the peaceful resolution of disputes through its diplomacy and by setting a good example. But while a greater degree of international order is desirable, it is not crucial to America's own security and well-being. Likewise, the promotion of democracy is a worthwhile objective, and, in this case, the power of example is even more potent. But the distinction made by John Quincy Adams nearly two

249

centuries ago is still valid. He stressed that America "is the well-wisher to the freedom and independence of all. She is the champion and vindicator only of her own."

It is especially important that the use of American military power be reserved for the defense of vital American security interests. And vital interests must not be defined in the casual, promiscuous manner that they were throughout the Cold War.

This article originally appeared in the *Orange County Register*, October 7, 1990.

An Independent Course

The sudden collapse of the Soviet Union's Eastern European empire at the end of the 1980s seems to have been nearly as traumatic for members of the Cold War foreign policy elite in the West as it was for Leninist true believers the world over. American policy experts who had grown accustomed to viewing global developments through a Cold War prism for more than four decades are now having to confront entirely new issues and contemplate a markedly different role for the United States. For the most part, they have not made the intellectual adjustment. In the months since the opening of the Berlin Wall, there has instead been a frantic search for new rationales and alternative missions to justify the perpetuation of Cold War policies and institutions.

Underlying such efforts is the assumption that although the Cold War may be ending, the United States must continue to play an activist role—especially a security leadership role—throughout the world. Michael Mandelbaum of the Council on Foreign Relations was only a little more candid than most of his colleagues in expressing that view when he told Thomas Friedman of the *New York Times* that although the Cold War is over, "we can't just pick up our chips. We have to stay at the table and get involved in a new game."

That is a distressingly myopic approach. Instead of reflexively clinging to a strategy of global interventionism, U.S. leaders need to define an entirely new role for the United States in a post–Cold War world. America must position itself to take advantage of opportunities that may arise from the breakdown of the bipolar Cold War system while avoiding the pitfalls that are also likely to emerge in what will be a more diverse and, at times, disorderly global environment. What is needed is a policy of strategic independence—

an independent course free from the dangerous and expensive burdens of obsolete security commitments.

Several principles should guide that new strategy. Perhaps the most essential is that policymakers must overcome the belief that America lacks the luxury of choice, that it must continue to play the role of Atlas, carrying all the world's security burdens on its shoulders. That attitude is a product of the early years of the Cold War when the global balance of power lay in ruins and the United States seemed to be the only nation that possessed the economic and military strength to thwart Soviet (or more broadly, communist) expansionism. Today the assumption that only a U.S.-dominated network of alliances can prevent global catastrophe represents egregiously retrograde thinking.

Several major centers of power have emerged or re-emerged over the last 40 years. The nations of Western Europe long ago ceased to be war-ravaged waifs incapable of defending the security of the Continent. Japan now has the world's second largest economy and is capable of playing a more active political and military role in the Far East. China, India, and other nations have become significant regional actors with their own political, economic, and security agendas. Not only does the United States no longer have to police the planet, it is increasingly unlikely that it can do so without intruding on the interests of other powers, thereby creating needless frictions and confrontations.

A related principle is that in a post–Cold War world, U.S. leaders must learn to define American interests, especially security interests, with greater precision. Throughout the Cold War, there was a tendency to define "vital interests" far too broadly and casually—with the vast overcommitment to Vietnam as the quintessential example. The concept of vital interests should be reserved for those geopolitical assets that have a direct, immediate, and substantial connection with America's physical survival, its political independence, and the preservation of its domestic freedom.

Not all adverse developments in the world automatically impinge on vital American interests, thereby becoming national security imperatives that justify the use of force. Indeed, in a post–Cold War setting there may be many local or regional quarrels that are—or at least should be—of little relevance to the United States. It will require a major conceptual adjustment to restrain the interventionist impulses of policymakers who have been accustomed to viewing even the most obscure conflicts as possible Soviet expansionist probes carried out by political surrogates.

There is a danger that the United States will inject itself into such imbroglios even if the Cold War rationale for doing so no longer applies. The Bush administration's obsession with preventing "instability" in the world is especially ominous. It seems intent, for example, on converting NATO from an anti-Soviet alliance into an arrangement with the amorphous objective of preserving European stability. That approach creates a multitude of unwarranted risks. The ethnic cauldron of Eastern Europe in particular may well be a prolific source of future conflicts. It was one thing for the United States to risk war to prevent the Soviet domination of Europe (however improbable that danger seems in retrospect); it is quite another to undertake such risks to curtail ethnic bloodletting among newly independent components of the Yugoslavian federation. The stakes simply do not justify the expenditure of American resources or the sacrifice of American lives.

Instead of regarding local conflicts as matters of wider concern involving the United States, Washington should seek to avoid such entanglements. That objective would require America to phase out its system of alliances. Even during the Cold War, alliances had become, in Earl C. Ravenal's apt phrase, "transmission belts for war," converting otherwise minor conflicts into potential superpower confrontations. Indeed, both the United States and the Soviet Union have frequently found themselves in the midst of quarrels between clients, usually involving issues that were at most of marginal relevance to the patrons. The tense confrontations between India and Pakistan, Syria and Israel, and the two Koreas are examples. The prospect of being drawn into unwanted and unnecessary conflicts by irresponsible clients will persist in the post–Cold War era. At the same time, without the Cold War rivalry even the most theoretical benefits to the United States of maintaining patron-client relationships will recede to the vanishing point.

An effective post–Cold War strategy for the United States would involve a more limited definition of vital security interests and the adoption of a more independent approach to world affairs. The shedding of alliance burdens could reduce America's defense costs by nearly two-thirds, producing a sizable peace dividend for the

American people. Even more important, a policy of strategic independence would materially reduce the level of risk in what promises to be a dangerous and disorderly world.

The third principle that should guide American policymakers is that the necessary curtailing of security commitments must not lead to a headlong plunge into economic autarky or intolerant nationalism. The proliferation of protectionist trade proposals, the hostility to foreign investment in the United States, the drive for more restrictive immigration laws, and the ugly tone of many alliance "burden-sharing" debates show that the danger of such insularity is not imaginary. It is both possible and desirable for America to play active economic, cultural, and diplomatic roles in the world without being the planetary gendarme, and it is essential for the people of the United States to make that crucial distinction. The challenge for American leaders will be to avoid the extremes of either the promiscuous interventionism that has characterized U.S. policy since World War II or the storm shelter isolationism that immediately preceded it.

Ironically, many of those who seek to preserve the strategy of compulsive global activism are employing arguments that could eventually play into the hands of chauvinists and advocates of economic autarky. Secretary of Defense Richard Cheney, for example, insists that "the United States needs a military presence in Europe to maintain political ties with Western Europe" (the *New York Times*, February 13, 1990). That is a crabbed view of America's influence, measuring it in only the most narrow military terms. Such reasoning fails to take into account the weight of the common democratic heritage, extensive cultural links, and pervasive economic ties between the United States and Europe. It demeans both the Europeans and ourselves to argue that estrangement will automatically occur without a large U.S. troop presence on the Continent.

The notion that unless the United States virtually occupies a region militarily it cannot have productive economic and diplomatic ties with the nations there is fallacious. Other countries, most notably Japan, have been able to establish such ties without an overbearing military presence, and America did so throughout most of its history. Americans must relearn how to operate in a multipolar environment.

In fact, the United States enjoys some enviable advantages in a multipolar world. Unlike other major powers, it does not have large, potentially hostile neighbors. Its security problems are therefore less pressing than those of Japan, China, the Soviet Union, and the nations of Western Europe. America's economy is by far the world's largest, and with the manifest failure of centralized planning in the communist bloc as well as the Third World, societies around the world are looking with renewed interest at the free-market values that have made that prosperity possible. Likewise, America's political values are a source of considerable influence. From Tiananmen Square to the Berlin Wall, those who sought to bring a greater measure of freedom to their societies openly cited the American example of individual rights and limited government.

It is essential that a post–Cold War strategy contain an element of idealism as well as a more rigorous, realistic assessment of America's security interests—as important as the latter may be. Throughout the history of the Republic, most Americans have wanted their nation to stand for enduring principles, not merely practice a calculating realpolitik. It is that subtle but important point that Pat Buchanan and other advocates of a conservative national approach to world affairs fail to comprehend.

The challenge for policymakers in the 1990s is to formulate a strategy that leaves room for the promotion of values without embarking on an interventionist binge that will entangle the United States in dangerous and unnecessary conflicts. Long ago, John Quincy Adams made the correct distinction when he stressed that America "is the well-wisher to the freedom and independence of all. She is the champion and vindicator only of her own." A policy of strategic independence would make that same distinction in a post–Cold War setting. It would reserve the use of military force for the defense of vital American security interests while emphasizing the potent example of America's economic and political values. Such a strategy offers the best hope for minimizing the risks and maximizing the opportunities for America in the emerging multipolar international system.

This article originally appeared in the *National Interest*, Fall 1990. Reprinted with permission.

Let's Not Risk U.S. Soldiers: We Could Repeat Lebanon Disaster

The Bush administration's offer to support a United Nations' military intervention in Somalia with up to a division of American troops underscores the intellectual bankruptcy of U.S. foreign policy in the post–Cold War era. It was possible to make the case that tangible American security interests were threatened in the Persian Gulf crisis. It is even possible to contend that the fighting in Bosnia impinges on American interests (although the argument strains credulity to the breaking point).

No one, however, can argue that Somalia is relevant to the security of the United States. With the possible exception of Antarctica, it would be difficult to find a place that is less relevant. It is a telling point that even the most dedicated advocates of intervention do not raise the issue of U.S. security as a justification for sending in troops. Instead, they rely solely on appeals to humanitarian concerns.

It is impossible not to deplore the terrible human suffering taking place in Somalia. Nevertheless, we should think long and hard before embracing the doctrine of humanitarian intervention, which would mean risking the lives of American soldiers in any number of global hot spots. Although it is a tragedy that bodies are piling up in Somalia, it is hardly an intelligent solution to add American bodies to the pile.

A military intervention to pacify Somalia risks repeating the Lebanon disaster of the early 1980s when the United States led a multinational force that attempted to restore order to that politically fractured country. American troops were soon targeted by disgruntled factions, and more than 250 Marines perished before Washington abandoned the futile campaign in 1984. The parallel with the anarchic situation in Somalia is ominous.

Even worse, Somalia is likely to be only the first opportunity for humanitarian military crusades in the post–Cold War period. Former U.S. ambassador to Somalia Frank Crigler—an outspoken proponent of intervention—conceded that chaos, such as we now see in Somalia, is probably going to be the norm in many regions of the world. Events already confirm Mr. Crigler's point. Aside from the conflicts raging in Somalia and Bosnia, there is plenty of bloodletting from civil wars in Afghanistan, Moldova, Nagorno-Karabakh and the Republic of Georgia—not to mention the continuing low-intensity fighting in such places as Kashmir, Sri Lanka, Kurdistan and East Timor.

If the United States no longer regards its own security interests as the standard by which to decide whether to use military force, there is literally no limit to the possible arenas in which American lives may be sacrificed. Washington will have a rudderless policy buffeted by the unpredictable winds of emotionalism. Where and when we intervene will be determined by the quantity of television images of suffering and the lobbying skills of foreign political factions, not the relevance of the stakes to the security of the American republic.

Accepting the costs and risks of intervening in internal or regional conflicts during the Cold War to thwart allies and surrogates of the Soviet Union was bad enough—especially since that strategy led the United States into Vietnam. Doing so in the post–Cold War period when there is no need to counter the threat posed by a rival superpower is far worse. In the absence of a compelling strategic rationale, meddling in an assortment of parochial struggles would be masochism.

The primary responsibility of the U.S. government is to guard the security and liberty of the American people. Washington has neither a constitutional nor a moral writ to play the role of Don Quixote and attempt to correct all the ills of the world. American lives and resources must not be sacrificed in international military crusades waged in the name of humanitarian intervention. The Bush administration should reconsider its ill-advised impulse to send U.S. troops to Somalia.

This article originally appeared in the *Arizona Republic*, December 8, 1992.

United States Should Adopt Policies Minimizing Nuclear Threat

Proliferation of nuclear weapons will be one of the most difficult security problems confronting the Clinton administration. The U.S.-led international nonproliferation system, symbolized by the 1968 Nuclear Non-Proliferation Treaty (NPT), is showing signs of serious strain. Ukraine's delay in carrying out its pledge to become a nonnuclear state—and the mounting domestic opposition to that step because it would give Russia a regional nuclear monopoly—is only the most recent indication of trouble.

Instead of ignoring the emerging multipolar nuclear environment, the new administration should initiate a comprehensive reassessment of U.S. strategy. Three options are available: a "status quo–plus policy," coercive nonproliferation, and adjustment to proliferation.

The status quo–plus approach favors a redoubled diplomatic effort to strengthen the existing nonproliferation regime.

But the NPT is producing increasingly perverse results. Although it has persuaded the Italys, Japans, and South Koreas of the world not to acquire nuclear weapons, it is less and less able to dissuade the Irans, Libyas, and North Koreas from doing so. That, along with Washington's adherence to extended deterrence, commits the United States to shielding an assortment of nonnuclear allies from nuclear-armed adversaries.

Some foreign policy experts, sensing that the old nonproliferation system is breaking down, advocate a new, more coercive form of nonproliferation based on Washington's willingness to launch pre-emptive military strikes against emerging nuclear weapons states. Proponents see the "Osirak option"—the Israeli air raid against an Iraqi reactor in 1981—as the appropriate model.

Using military force to preserve the crumbling nonproliferation system has several serious drawbacks. The most obvious is that the attacked nation might seek revenge. Bombing North Korea's nuclear facilities, for example, could easily trigger a general war on the Korean peninsula. Even if a target regime did not resort to military action, there would always be the possibility of terrorist reprisals. A coercive strategy might prevent some proliferation, but it would be unlikely to halt the overall trend, and it would create a host of new problems for the United States.

Washington should instead adopt a strategy that adjusts to the reality of nuclear proliferation and insulates America from the most harmful consequences. The policy on which that strategy is based must recognize the importance of maintaining a credible deterrent despite the demise of the Soviet adversary. The need for air defenses and at least a "thin layer" anti–ballistic missile system is clear.

A policy of adjustment also requires the exercise of extreme caution about meddling in regional conflicts. The threshold for concluding that a vital U.S. security interest is involved in such disputes should be extremely high. The only thing worse than becoming needlessly entangled in a conflict between belligerents armed with conventional weapons would be to do so when one or more parties have nuclear weapons.

Equally important, the United States will need to abandon extended deterrence. Without the threat of global domination posed by a superpower challenger, assuming the risks entailed by extended deterrence is unwarranted. Removing the U.S. nuclear umbrella would, of course, mean that some major allies might decide to acquire independent arsenals. Although that is hardly a pleasant prospect, it is better than the alternative.

Finally, instead of automatically treating nuclear aspirants as international pariahs, the United States should seek ways to mitigate the harmful effects of proliferation. An especially worrisome prospect is that many new nuclear states will lack the technical expertise to establish reliable command-and-control systems or to guard their arsenals from theft or terrorism. Inadequate safeguards greatly increase the danger of an accidental or unauthorized launch.

Washington can help to minimize such problems by disseminating command-and-control technology and assisting in the creation of crisis management hotlines and other confidence-building measures among emerging nuclear powers. The United States can also encourage regional adversaries to engage in strategic dialogues to delineate the kinds of provocations that might cause them to use nuclear weapons and outline the doctrines that would govern their use. A dialogue of the sort that helped to stabilize the dangerous superpower rivalry would at least reduce the chances of a nuclear conflict erupting because of miscalculation or misunderstanding.

A policy of adjusting to proliferation is not a panacea, but it is superior to the present policy and the dangerous alternative of coercive nonproliferation. The United States cannot halt the spread of nuclear weapons, but it can make adjustments that minimize danger to the American people.

This article originally appeared in the *Christian Science Monitor*, February 22, 1993.

Defense Cuts Are Too Timid

The defense plan outlined by Les Aspin is marginally better than the Bush administration's version, but it is still based on obsolete assumptions about the U.S. role in the world. It is a "cheap hawk" strategy that would have us continue subsidizing the defense of prosperous allies and attempting to police the planet, albeit with smaller military forces. A more prudent security strategy would enable us to make far deeper cuts in force levels and military spending.

According to Aspin's blueprint, the U.S. defense budget would remain wildly excessive compared to the budgets of all other major nations. Washington's military expenditures are more than eight times those of Japan or Germany, the world's second- and third-ranked economic powers. Indeed, the USA spends nearly as much on the military as the rest of the world combined.

That disparity cannot be justified when the USA faces no great-power challenger such as Nazi Germany or the Soviet Union. There is certainly no reason to continue stationing 100,000 troops in Europe and another 100,000 in East Asia to defend allies that are fully capable of defending themselves.

With the demise of the Soviet Union, the USA enjoys a massive surplus of military power. It can focus on the defense of its vital security interests without reacting to every political hiccup in the world.

If the USA confines itself to defending its vital interests, military spending can be reduced to $129 billion. That budget would support an active-duty force of 725,000 personnel. Although such a force would not be large enough for the Clinton administration's grandiose strategy of "assertive multilateralism," it would be more than sufficient for America's legitimate security needs.

This article originally appeared in *USA Today*, September 2, 1993.

Lift the Embargo, Clinch Democracy

For more than three decades, Washington has sought to bring down the regime of Cuban dictator Fidel Castro through a strategy of economic coercion. Various administrations, Republican and Democratic, liberal and conservative, have steadfastly refused to lift the embargo imposed in 1961, despite its manifest failure to achieve the original goal. The trend, in fact, has been in the opposite direction; congressional passage of the Cuban Democracy Act in the fall of 1992 tightened the economic screws on Castro's Stalinist enclave.

Except for a few leftist ideologues, Americans eagerly await the demise of communism in Cuba. But the pertinent question is whether maintaining the embargo is the best way—indeed, whether it is an effective way at all—to attain that objective. There are ample reasons to believe it is not. A strategy based on encouraging trade, tourism, investment and an array of cultural and political contacts has far greater potential to hasten the departure of Castro's dictatorship. A

259

growing number of conservatives now advocate that course, including William Ratliff, a senior research fellow at the Hoover Institution, and Roger Fontaine, a member of the National Security Council staff during the Reagan administration.

Defenders of the current strategy insist that abandoning economic coercion would snatch defeat from the jaws of victory. The communist regime is already tottering, they contend, as the Cuban economy spirals downward, largely because of the embargo. According to that reasoning, establishing normal U.S.-Cuban relations would bolster Castro's sagging political prestige and dishearten a growing internal opposition. Even worse, lifting the embargo would cause an influx of hard currency, giving the beleaguered dictatorship the economic relief it needs to survive.

Proponents of the embargo must account for the disconcerting fact that their strategy has failed for more than 30 years to dislodge Castro. Their standard explanation is that during most of that period the Soviet Union frustrated Washington's policy by purchasing Cuba's sugar exports at above-market prices and providing cheap oil supplies—a subsidy that exceeded $5 billion a year by the late 1980s. The emergence of a noncommunist government in Moscow has fundamentally changed the context in which the embargo operates, insist its defenders. Because Cuba can no longer look to a communist patron for relief, economic sanctions now should succeed.

That argument is plausible, but hardly compelling. U.S. officials and leaders of the Cuban exile community in the United States repeatedly have predicted the imminent demise of the Castro government since the early 1960s. There is no certainty that their latest predictions will prove any more accurate than the previous ones. Although economic deprivation sometimes has been a factor in the collapse of repressive regimes (for example, in the Philippines in 1986), it frequently fails to produce that result. If economic calamity were a sufficient condition for successful revolts, tyrants such as Zaire's Mobutu Sese Seko, Iraq's Saddam Hussein and Serbia's Slobodan Milosevic would have been out of power years ago. Indeed, historians have documented that revolutions usually occur when bad economic and political conditions are improving, not deteriorating. Sclerotic dictatorial systems are at greatest risk when they belatedly attempt to reform. The Gorbachev era in the Soviet Union is the latest confirmation of that phenomenon.

Defenders of the Cuban embargo, like defenders of such sanctions generally, also overrate the effectiveness of economic coercion in bringing about political change in other countries. In their book *Economic Sanctions Reconsidered*, the definitive study of that tactic during the 20th century, Gary Clyde Hufbauer, Jeffrey J. Schott and Kimberly Ann Elliott show that embargoes fail more often than they succeed. That especially is true when the objective is as ambitious as the wholesale transformation of the political system of the target country. Trade policy expert Joseph G. Gavin casts doubt on even the modest claims of success made by Hufbauer, Schott and Elliott. Gavin notes that even when sanctions are apparently successful, there frequently are other factors present that more plausibly account for the result.

Gavin's point may be pertinent to the current situation in Cuba. Supporters of the embargo are exceedingly quick to attribute nearly all the island's economic woes to the supposed effectiveness of the embargo. But a significant portion of the economic distress is simply the consequence of the inherent defects of Leninism. A system devoted to suppressing market forces, eradicating the concept of private property and extinguishing the entrepreneurial spirit of the people predictably produces massive economic dislocation and stagnation. That would be true, embargo or no embargo.

Americans need to be more realistic about what embargoes can and cannot accomplish. Applied in a comprehensive fashion, those measures have considerable ability to damage the economy of the target country. But they seldom inflict enough pain on political and military elites to induce either a change of policy or a successful revolt. Typically, economic sanctions devastate the least powerful segments of society, driving the already poor to the brink of destitution while causing the governing class little more than minor inconvenience.

In no case is that perverse result more apparent than the embargo imposed on Haiti by the United States, the Organization of American States and, subsequently, the United Nations. As foreign policy analyst Ian Vásquez has documented, the sanctions have destroyed more than 50 percent of Haiti's private-sector jobs. Fuel blockades have forced Haiti's poor to burn scarce wood, causing massive deforestation and soil erosion. Malnutrition, disease and famine throughout the country are approaching epidemic levels. Meanwhile, the soldiers and political elites who are the supposed targets of the embargo profit by hoarding and selling smuggled goods. The sanctions have exacerbated the suffering of Haitian civilians but have not caused the regime to capitulate or be overthrown.

The effectiveness of U.S. embargoes against several other countries, including China in the 1950s and 1960s, Panama in the late 1980s and, until President Clinton rescinded it recently, against Vietnam for more than two decades, has been equally meager. Given that uninspiring record, there is little reason to assume that the embargo against Cuba will succeed. Persisting in that strategy is more likely to cause Castro and the Communist Party to adopt a bunker mentality, claiming for themselves an undiminished portion of a shrinking economic output while deflecting the wrath of the Cuban people by continuing to use the United States as a scapegoat for their troubles.

A better strategy would be to exploit the indications that Castro and his cohorts finally may be recognizing economic realities and be willing to open Cuba to the capitalist world. U.S. policymakers should have learned some relevant lessons from the events leading to the collapse of the Soviet empire.

Conservatives insist that Ronald Reagan's policies—especially the massive buildup of military forces—caused the implosion of the Soviet Union and the communist regimes in Eastern Europe. According to that thesis, the Soviet Union could not compete in an intense arms race, particularly in such high-tech areas as ballistic missile defense, and the futile attempt to do so caused its economy to crumble.

Although the Reagan factor cannot be dismissed entirely, other, more important reasons for the collapse of the Eastern bloc are evident. One of the most crucial is the massive expansion of trade and other contacts with the West, especially the nations of Western Europe, beginning in the early 1970s. Led by West Germany's policy of Ostpolitik—Bonn's strategy to normalize economic and political relations with East Germany and other members of the Soviet empire—such contacts increased dramatically during the 1970s and 1980s. For example, trade between the members of the European Community and the Warsaw Pact countries more than quadrupled from 1972 to 1988, reaching some $37.9 billion.

Among other effects, the more open relationship enabled thousands of Western businesspeople and tens of thousands of tourists to travel throughout Eastern Europe and the Soviet Union. Families received visits from relatives in the West—who gave them graphic descriptions of life in the capitalist world. Although the communist regimes attempted to restrict contacts between their citizens and Westerners, that became increasingly difficult as the numbers grew.

Moreover, as part of the more open East-West relationship, VIPs from the communist countries increasingly traveled to the West. Efforts by the Eastern bloc regimes to confine such travels as much as possible to trusted members of the Communist Party elite failed; even the people commonly expected to resist the contagion of Western values frequently succumbed. Western scholars who studied the Gorbachev era note that many of the strongest supporters of perestroika were members of the foreign ministry, the external branch of the KGB, and the universities—precisely those segments of Soviet society that had the greatest exposure to the West. Such respected Russian scholars as Andrei Kortunov and Peter Gladkov of Moscow's Institute of the USA and Canada confirm that expanded contacts with the West played an important role in creating the conditions that produced the upheavals of the late 1980s and early 1990s.

America's experience with the other communist giant, China, has been similar. For a quarter century after the 1949 communist revolution, Washington labored to isolate China politically, diplomatically and economically. Beginning with Richard Nixon in the early 1970s, the United States instead aimed at establishing a normal relationship between the two countries. Among other results have been burgeoning U.S. investments in China and a rapidly expanding U.S.-China trade that exceeds $30 billion a year.

China is not yet a free society, as the Beijing regime's continuing human rights violations remind us. Nevertheless, during the last 16 years China has pursued a course of market-oriented reform that has produced one of the world's highest rates of economic growth. The beneficiaries of reform now constitute assertive and influential constituencies that seek additional economic reforms and a more open, pluralistic political system.

One need only compare the current situation with the suffocating totalitarianism of Mao Tse-tung's "great leap forward" in the 1950s (which may have cost as many as 30 million lives) or the Orwellian horrors of the Cultural Revolution in the 1960s to realize how far

263

the country has progressed. Although it certainly would be too much to attribute all of the worthwhile changes to Washington's abandoning its strategy of isolating China, that move did create incentives—including access to the American market—that were irresistible and conducive to reform.

Such experiences suggest an important lesson for U.S. policy toward Cuba. Attempts to transform or overthrow repressive regimes through a strategy of isolation generally prove futile. Conversely, encouraging economic and cultural relations—especially people-to-people contacts—maximizes the prospects for meaningful economic and political change.

Castro undoubtedly hopes that the inflow of hard currency from an economic relationship with the United States would save his decrepit regime. Soviet and East European leaders probably indulged in similar fantasies during the initial years of expanded contacts with the West. But no amount of hard currency can save inherently defective economic systems, nor will it offset the subversive effects of capitalist influences. It is no accident that communist rulers prefer to keep their countries isolated and that they begin to open to the outside world only when economic conditions leave them little choice. Competing ideas and values pose a mortal threat to the stability of their systems, and they instinctively recoil. When Castro or any other Leninist dictator becomes desperate enough to risk such outside contamination, U.S. leaders should recognize a superb opportunity and exploit it.

Ending the embargo would not be a panacea. Many painful and difficult issues would have to be postponed for a post-Castro government to address, including the property claims of American businesses (and Cuban exiles) whose assets were stolen by Castro's regime. Nevertheless, lifting the embargo would have several beneficial effects. It would ease the suffering of the Cuban people, with whom the United States has no quarrel. It also would facilitate the emergence of a new commercial class in Cuba and help create political and economic sectors that would have a vested interest in reforms and be likely to grow increasingly impatient with the retrograde policies of the communist hierarchy. The development of such new leadership personnel could prove crucial in preventing a future power vacuum, thereby minimizing the disorder and dislocations that are likely to accompany the eventual collapse of the Castro regime.

Washington has pursued a strategy of isolating Cuba for more than three decades without discernible success. It is time to break from that sterile policy and adopt a new approach. We should poison Castro's totalitarian system with a lethal dose of American tourism, trade and investment.

This article originally appeared in *Insight*, April 25, 1994. Reprinted with permission.

Feels Our Pain

With Bill Clinton spending his time listening to children recite *The Little Engine That Could* and Bob Dole pontificating about the quality of Hollywood movies, it is difficult to remember that the president's primary responsibility as set forth in the Constitution is to conduct America's foreign policy. Yet that clearly was the intent of the Founders. Not only is the president made commander in chief of the armed forces, but he also has the task of receiving the representatives of foreign governments, appointing America's own diplomatic envoys, and negotiating treaties and other agreements.

How did we get from the president as steward of foreign policy to the president as crusader for literacy or guardian of public morals? It has been a gradual, almost insidious, process. Ambitious chief executives increasingly sought to play the dominant role in setting the domestic policy agenda, especially on economic issues. Throughout the 20th century, voters have tended to elect presidents because of their apparent domestic rather than foreign policy expertise, sometimes with horrific results. Woodrow Wilson, elected to implement an economic "reform" program at home, ended up leading the nation during World War I and its aftermath. An utter neophyte in international affairs, Wilson pursued a disastrous foreign policy, the naivete of which was exceeded only by its arrogance.

In the past few decades, however, we have gone beyond expecting our presidents to have extensive domestic agendas. Increasingly, the chief executive is playing the role of tribal chieftain, seeking to reassure Americans when they are insecure, comfort them when they suffer a natural disaster or other calamity, and instruct them in how to live upright and constructive lives. Few voices speak out against such saccharin paternalism and ask what relevance such activities have to the president's constitutional role.

265

We are now witnessing the emergence of a full-blown therapeutic presidency. Candidates are obligated to show that they have an abundance of "compassion" and the solution to every imaginable social problem, from finding a cure for AIDS to raising happy and well-adjusted children.

The therapeutic presidency is unhealthy on several levels. First, it is symptomatic of a trend toward not merely intrusive but virtually unlimited government. Even the architects of the New Deal and the Great Society generally confined their schemes for government activism to issues that were at least arguably matters of public policy. The current presidential aspirants seem reluctant to concede that there is any aspect of human behavior that is not a subject of government concern or responsibility.

Second, the therapeutic presidency creates unrealistic expectations about the effectiveness of political leadership. It is a dubious enough assumption that the election of a particular president will determine the destiny of the huge, dynamic American economy. (Several other factors, especially the monetary policy pursued by the Federal Reserve Board, are probably more important.) But many of the issues emphasized by Clinton and Dole involve extraordinarily complex social and psychological factors—areas in which there are no conceivable governmental solutions. Creating the impression that the occupant of the White House has the answers to such problems merely fosters public disillusionment when, by the time of the next election, it is evident that he did not.

Perhaps worst of all, the requirements of the therapeutic presidency distract the president from his legitimate responsibilities. Dole's views on movies or the Clintons' theories on child rearing should not matter—and one would hope, do not matter—to most Americans. But how the president conducts the nation's foreign policy during the next four years can matter a great deal.

It will be small comfort if the president seizes every photo opportunity to demonstrate compassion at home but causes the Republic to blunder into war abroad. The president's proper focus should be on dealing with terrorism, assessing such adverse geopolitical developments as the emerging Moscow-Beijing axis, encouraging allies and clients to take greater responsibility for their own defense, and extracting American troops from the Bosnian morass. That is an exceedingly full agenda for even the most competent chief executive.

Instead of looking for a comforting father figure, voters need to place greater importance on the foreign policy views and the expertise of presidential candidates. Constitutionally, the president is America's steward of foreign affairs, not the national therapist.

This article originally appeared in the *Winston-Salem Journal*, September 28, 1996.

Clinton's Bogus Allegations of "Isolationism" Bear Watching

The latest example of the current administration's foreign policy spin control was Clinton's allegation that the recent U.S. Senate vote against ratification of the Comprehensive Test Ban Treaty (CTBT) signaled "a new isolationism" in the United States.

The new isolationists, the president contended, "are saying that the United States does not need to lead" and believe that "we should bury our heads in the sand behind a wall."

Clinton's comments were not simply an ill-considered emotional outburst. In a major address to the Council on Foreign Relations, the president's national security adviser, Sandy Berger, also warned of a growing isolationist threat and stated that isolationists "believe in a survivalist foreign policy—build a fortified fence around the United States and retreat behind it."

Nor is the recent campaign of vilification the first time that administration officials have sought to caricature the views of their opponents. In the summer of 1998, U.S. Secretary of Defense William Cohen stated that Americans should not act "as if we could zip ourselves up into a continental cocoon and watch events unfold on CNN."

Such caricatures stifle—and undoubtedly are intended to stifle—debate on the real U.S. foreign policy options at the dawn of the 21st century.

No American of any prominence is suggesting that the United States cut itself off from the world and create a Fortress America or a hermit republic. Instead, critics of the current policy are making two serious, substantive points.

The first is that the United States should not place excessive faith in paper agreements (such as the CTBT) or cumbersome multilateral institutions (especially the UN) to protect and advance important U.S. interests.

The second, and even more important, point is that Washington should focus its foreign policy resources, energy and attention on

267

those relatively few developments in the international system that can have a direct and substantial impact on America's own security and well-being.

Critics worry that the Clinton administration is unwilling or unable to set priorities and distinguish between essential and nonessential matters. The administration's record of pursuing military interventions in such strategically and economically marginal places as Haiti and Kosovo confirms their worst fears.

Administration leaders prefer to engage in name-calling rather than address such criticism. Equally troubling, the administration's description of its own foreign policy approach is fuzzy at best. Berger reiterated the tired formulation that U.S. policy must be one of "engagement" in world affairs. But engagement is a term that is so vacuous that it can mean almost anything.

The most serious attempt to define the substance of engagement was a speech Clinton delivered in San Francisco earlier this year. In that address, Clinton outlined five "great challenges" requiring U.S. leadership: spreading peace; helping Russia and China achieve greater prosperity and political pluralism; combating terrorism, drug trafficking, environmental degradation, and proliferation of weapons of mass destruction; expanding international trade; and promoting democracy around the world.

That is a breathtakingly broad agenda, and it implies U.S. omnipotence. An intelligent and sustainable foreign policy, however, must consist of something more than a wish list of desirable objectives. There are distinct limits to the ability of any nation—even one as powerful as the United States—to shape the global political, economic and strategic environment. Indeed, such objectives as the promotion of democracy and "spreading peace" are so amorphous that they beg the real questions. Spread peace how? where? and at what level of cost or risk to the American people?

To take just one example, is it really wise for the United States to spend billions of taxpayer dollars, risk the lives of U.S. military personnel, damage its relations with both Russia and China, and put its credibility on the line by meddling in civil wars in the Balkans? Perhaps there is a compelling rationale for that mission, but if so, the administration ought to rebut the substantive objections rather than dismiss opponents as knuckle-dragging isolationists. It also must provide a coherent strategic analysis instead of resorting to preposterous clichés about geopolitical dominoes toppling throughout the Balkans and triggering another world war if the United States fails to take preventive action.

The administration's handling of the Balkans issue illustrates an overall tendency to use hyperbole and distortions when portraying America's post–Cold War foreign policy options. All too often, the argument is that if Washington does not exercise leadership to ensure peace and justice in virtually every region, chaos will ensue and eventually require U.S. intervention at greater cost and under less favorable conditions.

That thesis ignores the possibility of other strategies and outcomes.

A more selective global political and military role by the United States would exert inexorable pressure on other significant regional powers to do more, on the basis of self-interest, to stabilize the security environment in their respective regions.

It is both puzzling and troubling that, more than a half century after the end of World War II, Japan and its neighbors in East Asia are incapable of containing a smallish rogue state like North Korea but must instead rely on the United States.

Similarly, Americans have a right to ask why the European Union, with nearly 400 million people, a collective GDP of some US$8 trillion, and more than a million active-duty military personnel cannot deal with instability in the Balkans or problems of similarly modest magnitude.

Is it really in America's best interest to continue tolerating—and in some cases, encouraging—such pervasive dependency? Or would it be better for the United States to insist that major democratic powers take primary responsibility for their own defense and the stability of their neighborhoods? It can at least be argued that fostering multiple centers of power in the world would lead to the creation of security buffers that would reduce America' s risk exposure and provide other important indirect benefits to the United States.

Whatever the merits of that theory, it is the kind of issue that should be at the center of a meaningful discussion about America's role in the 21st century.

Prolific use of the isolationist slur to intimidate and discredit opponents may postpone an honest foreign policy debate, but it does not reduce the urgent need for one.

This article originally appeared in the *Taipei Times*, December 7, 1999.

Debunking Clinton's Foreign Policy

President Clinton's extensive overseas travels in recent months highlight his determination to leave an impressive foreign policy legacy.

The pursuit of that goal is not surprising. Unless something changes dramatically, future generations are more likely to associate the Clinton presidency with the Monica Lewinsky affair (and the chief executive's reprehensible personal conduct in general) than any substantive accomplishments. Moreover, his prospects for a significant domestic policy legacy are not good since Congress is controlled by the opposition party.

The president doesn't generally receive credit even for the unprecedented economic boom of the 1990s; Federal Reserve chairman Alan Greenspan usually gets the applause. Almost by default, foreign policy provides the only opportunity for the Clinton presidency to leave a positive historical record. If one believes the president and his advisers, that record is already impressive and rapidly becoming more so. Unfortunately, those claims of success are more spin than substance.

Several points become apparent from an examination of U.S. foreign policy during the Clinton years. First, the administration has demonstrated an "instinct for the capillaries." It has expended an enormous amount of time, energy, money and diplomatic (and sometimes military) resources on problems in strategically marginal countries and regions. The notorious record of Warren Christopher, secretary of state during Clinton's first term, in visiting Damascus, Syria, more than 30 times while setting foot in Beijing just once— and other major capitals scarcely more often—was an appropriate symbol of the administration's distorted priorities.

A second conclusion, related to the first, is that the administration's foreign policy successes have rarely come on issues that are significant to the health and stability of the international system. Yes, brokering a peace in Northern Ireland is beneficial to the people in that strife-torn land, but it is of little importance except to the parties directly involved.

Even the much-touted Middle East peace process deals with a quarrel that is indistinguishable from dozens of other petty tribal disputes elsewhere in the world. In the absence of the Cold War rivalry between the United States and the Soviet Union, the spat between Israel and its Arab neighbors does not have wider strategic ramifications.

The third conclusion is that most of the administration's claimed foreign policy successes have been both murky and ephemeral. Although U.S. forces ousted Haiti's military dictatorship and restored the elected president to power, that did little to alter the long-term economic or political dynamics in that country. Haiti's economy remains a shambles, and the president has dissolved parliament, choosing to rule by decree. Thus, Haiti has merely gone from having a military dictatorship to having a presidential dictatorship.

Washington's nation-building experiment in Bosnia has not fared much better. True, the Dayton Accords ended the bloodletting, but Bosnia is no closer to being a viable multiethnic country today than it was when the accords were signed in December 1995. Three feuding ethnic groups run the respective regions they control as ethnically pure ministates, and the United States and the other intervening powers have resorted to increasingly undemocratic means (including dismissing elected officials) in a frantic effort to preserve the fiction of a unified, cooperative Bosnia.

The reality is that Bosnia is a divided, impoverished, Potemkin state run by a swarm of international bureaucrats backed by NATO troops. Not dissuaded by that depressing outcome, the United States and its allies have undertaken an equally futile mission in Kosovo.

Finally, and most disturbing of all,, the administration's foreign policy "successes" have frequently come at the cost of damage to far more important U.S. interests. For example, Washington's decisions to push for the enlargement of NATO and to make the Balkans a NATO sphere of influence have badly damaged U.S. relations with Russia.

U.S. political maneuvering on Russia's western and southern flanks through, respectively, the expansion of NATO's membership and joint military exercises with Ukraine, Kazakhstan and other former Soviet republics had created tensions between Moscow and Washington even before the Balkan war erupted. But the U.S.-led attack on Serbia made matters far worse. The bombing campaign discredited Washington's soothing assurances that Russia had nothing to fear from NATO's enlargement because NATO was a purely defensive alliance.

Whatever else one might conclude about the intervention in the Balkans, it showed conclusively that NATO was now a proactive, offensive military association. Kremlin leaders denounced the assault on Serbia with the kind of shrill rhetoric not heard since the worst days of the Cold War.

Nor was the harsh response confined to the political elite. Large anti-NATO and anti-U.S. demonstrations erupted in several cities. Russian anger was further inflamed when, despite Moscow's crucial diplomatic assistance in bringing the Balkan war to an end, the United States and its NATO allies refused to give Russia a separate peacekeeping zone in Kosovo.

Pro-democratic Russian political leaders have told their friends in the United States that the Balkan war caused an unprecedented degree of genuine anti-American sentiment among the Russian people. The comments of former prime minister Anatoly Chubais are typical of the dismay and despair expressed by pro-democratic Russian figures. "I have not in all my life seen such a scale of anti-Western sentiments as exist in Russia today." The communists and nationalists, "could not have imagined a present of this scale."

It was an extraordinarily myopic policy to jeopardize America's relations with a nuclear-armed great power to pursue a humanitarian crusade in the Balkans. That approach should not have survived even a cursory cost-benefit calculation. Indeed, to endanger the relationship with Russia merely for the emotional satisfaction of dictating the political status of an obscure province in a small Balkan country was akin to a chess player sacrificing a queen to capture a pawn.

Indeed, Washington's Balkan adventure managed to damage relations with not one but two great powers. The accidental bombing of China's embassy in Belgrade was the catalyst for a nasty chill in the relationship between the United States and China, but Beijing's anger was not solely the result of that episode. Chinese leaders objected—as did the leaders of Russia, India and many other countries—to the so-called Clinton Doctrine of humanitarian intervention that was used to justify the U.S.-led war in the Balkans. They saw it as a facade for a U.S. policy of global domination.

The willingness to risk damaging the relationship with yet another great power merely to pursue goals in a geopolitical backwater like the Balkans is not, however, the main problem with the Clinton administration's policy toward China. A deeper problem is that there has been no consistency to that policy.

The early years of the Clinton presidency were marked by a frosty relationship. Clinton had denounced President George Bush during the 1992 presidential campaign for being "soft" on Beijing and pledged that his administration would take a firm stand on human rights and other issues, if necessary linking them to China's continued access to the American market. He then backed away from such linkage barely a year after taking office.

Despite that retreat the relationship remained tense, reaching an alarming point when Beijing's provocative military exercises and missile tests in the Taiwan Strait in late 1995 and early 1996 caused the administration to dispatch two aircraft carrier battle groups to the area. That episode unnerved U.S. officials enough to have them place a high priority on an improvement in relations. Indeed, critics in Asia and the United States soon concluded that the administration had overshot the mark in its courtship of Beijing.

By 1998, Clinton and Secretary of State Madeleine Albright were describing the U.S.-China relationship as a "strategic partnership"— a term that sent political tremors throughout the region. The increasingly cozy ties between Washington and Beijing alarmed Taiwan, unsettled Washington's long-time ally Japan, and provided India with a reason to take the wraps off its nuclear program.

India's initiative was yet another example of how the Clinton administration habitually fails to anticipate an adverse reaction by a major power to one of Washington's policies. The pinnacle of the U.S.-China strategic partnership came during Clinton's visit to China in the summer of 1998, when the president issued his infamous "three no's" statement in Shanghai.

Clinton's attempt to construct a strategic partnership began to collapse, however, almost as soon as he returned from his trip. A cascade of criticism in Congress and throughout America's opinion elite caused the president and his advisers to beat a hasty retreat. Administration spokesmen rushed to assure critics that there was no substantive change in U.S. policy on the Taiwan issue, and within weeks the president dispatched Secretary of Energy Bill Richardson to Taipei—the highest ranking official to visit Taiwan in years. Those actions, in turn, infuriated China leaders, who suspected that Washington was professing one policy in discussions with Beijing while presenting another, entirely different, policy to domestic audiences.

The administration's clumsy and inconsistent China policy has managed to confuse and antagonize virtually everyone concerned, from U.S. allies and other friendly powers to the Beijing government.

Unfortunately, such ineptitude is all too typical of the Clinton administration's conduct of foreign policy on most of the truly important issues. And ultimately the president's foreign policy legacy will rest on how well he dealt with those issues—not peripheral matters like the mediation effort in Northern Ireland.

Perhaps the most pertinent way to judge the Clinton administration's stewardship of foreign policy is to assess the state of America's relations with the other major powers in the international system today compared with 1993. On that basis, future historians are not likely to treat the Clinton years kindly. Even America's Cold War–era allies have grown increasingly irritated at Washington's swaggering attitude as the "sole remaining superpower"—as well as the inconsistency and unpredictability of U.S. policies. France and other leading members of the European Union, for example, resent Washington's sniping at their efforts to create an independent European defense capability. Its insistence on a NATO-centric security policy for Europe, combined with the demand for more burden sharing, appears to many Europeans to be nothing more than a self-serving effort to get European taxpayers to fund transatlantic security policies controlled by Washington.

America's reputation with great powers outside the U.S. system of alliances is even more frayed. In addition to the increasingly wary U.S.-China relationship and the burgeoning animosity between Russia and the United States, the administration has stumbled in its conduct of relations with India. When New Delhi unveiled its nuclear weapons program in 1998, U.S. leaders responded with the foreign policy equivalent of a temper tantrum, imposing sanctions and insisting that India abandon its quest for a strategic deterrent. That demand was about as realistic as expecting a teenager who has just become sexually active to return to celibacy. Although Washington subsequently abandoned its shrill condemnations of India's behavior, the initial policy both angered New Delhi and rekindled Indian suspicions that the United States was intent on global domination.

Worst of all, concern about Washington's overbearing behavior during the Clinton years has caused Russia, China and India to begin forming a coalition to contain and balance U.S. power. The extent of Russian-Chinese cooperation—including several prominent sales of sophisticated Russian weaponry to Beijing—is especially worrisome. Although the creation of a Sino-Russian (and perhaps a Sino-Russian-Indian) coalition directed against the United States may not pose an immediate threat to U.S. security—given America's vast military superiority—it could result in a disastrous shift in the balance of global power a decade or two from now. If that occurs as a result of the Clinton administration's bungling, it will be small consolation to point to diplomatic achievements in the Middle East and Northern Ireland.

The verdict on the Clinton foreign policy legacy will likely be a harsh one. Although the administration has managed to do reasonably well on some secondary matters, it has stumbled into an assortment of unnecessary and impractical commitments in the Balkans and elsewhere. And most damning of all, it has presided over a disastrous deterioration in America's relations with the countries that really matter.

This article originally appeared in the *Taipei Times*, December 24, 1999.

Quiet Coups and Democracy

The scene was eerily similar to one that occurred nearly 15 years ago. Thousands of angry but peaceful demonstrators marched through Manila demanding the ouster of a corrupt president. The military elite administered the coup de grâce when it decided to back the insurgents.

But there was one important difference between the two events, and it should cause those now cheering the latest manifestation of "People Power" to have second thoughts. In 1986 a dictator was ousted. This time it was a democratically elected leader, albeit one charged with assorted wrongdoings.

The Philippines may be better off without Joseph Estrada as president, yet the "quiet coup" took place while the senate was still conducting impeachment proceedings against Mr. Estrada. Acquittal was likely, but the demonstrations—and especially the military's intervention—short-circuited the legal procedures mandated by the Philippine constitution. The senate had yet to vote; legislators backing Mr. Estrada could have been removed in the next election. More important is that Mr. Estrada, too, could have eventually faced the electorate.

Adhering to constitutional processes may produce frustrating, even unpalatable, results. As much as Republicans, and many others in the United States, wanted President Bill Clinton tossed out of office, no one suggested turning to public demonstrations, backed by Secretary of Defense William Cohen and the joint chiefs of staff, to leapfrog the Senate acquittal. The long-term political price would have been far too great.

However, Philippine columnist Paul Rodrigo complains that "Westerners are holding us to standards that simply do not apply. As a young democracy, we have to do things differently." But in doing so, the Philippines risks never becoming an old democracy.

Many of the nearly 10 million people who voted for Mr. Estrada in 1998 continue to support him. The newly anointed president, Gloria Macapagal Arroyo, enjoys only dubious legitimacy and has had to respond to numerous coup rumors with threats to "crush" her enemies. The military leadership says it supports her, but it could easily grow dissatisfied with Ms. Arroyo and back another change in government.

Using extralegal means to oust an elected leader isn't confined to the Philippines. Nearly four years ago Turkey's military staged a "quiet coup" against then–prime minister Necmettin Erbakan. Less than two years ago, the Pakistani military more forcefully overthrew Prime Minister Nawaz Sharif.

Several features were common to all three countries: the leaders of each were controversial but duly elected; the military played the decisive role; much of the public applauded the military's intervention; and the transfer of power did little or nothing to solve the country's underlying problems.

A similar process appears to be under way in Indonesia, where the military has never fully accepted civilian rule. Demonstrations against President Abdurrahman Wahid have been growing larger and coup rumors have been circulating more frequently. Some of his own ministers have criticized him; Vice President Megawati Sukarnoputri has publicly attacked him. He might become the next elected leader to lose power in a "quiet coup."

Though Mr. Wahid is barely governing, his forced departure, like Mr. Estrada's, would be a blow against democracy. Troubling is the question, who would follow him? The vice president's performance generates scant confidence in her ability to lead. And Assembly Speaker Amien Rais has irresponsibly fomented Islamic fundamentalism.

Admittedly, stable democracy requires the means to remove errant officials. But more fundamental is respect for the rule of law, even when the rules don't yield desired outcomes. Without respect for the rule of law, democracy risks disintegrating into mob rule, with the military becoming the ultimate arbiter—and imposing its will ever more loudly over time.

Creating democratic political systems after decades of authoritarian rule isn't easy. Apparently many Filipinos, like many Turks, Pakistanis and now Indonesians, believe that they must ignore democracy to save it. Let us hope that they don't end up destroying it.

This article, coauthored with Doug Bandow, originally appeared in the *Asian Wall Street Journal*, February 19, 2001. Reprinted with permission of the *Wall Street Journal* © 2001 Dow Jones & Company, Inc.

A Passage to India

American policymakers often display a suspicious attitude toward India, but Secretary of Defense Donald Rumsfeld apparently wants to outdo all of his predecessors. None of them managed to group democratic India with the likes of Iran and North Korea. But Rumsfeld did, according to the *Daily Telegraph*.

The offending comments came during the secretary's criticism of Russia as "an active proliferator." Rumsfeld accused the Russians of selling weapons to and assisting "countries like Iran and North Korea and India which are threatening . . . the United States and Western Europe." Russia's transfer of military technology to Iran and North Korea is a matter of concern. But what could have possessed Rumsfeld to include India in the same breath?

At the least, his comments suggest a familiar (and unhealthy) attitude toward India. Indeed, they are much more in tune with the policy pursued by the Clinton administration than that signaled by George W. Bush during the presidential campaign.

Under Clinton, the United States treated India primarily as a problem. American leaders saw India's feud with Pakistan as a potential threat to peace, and they viewed New Delhi's close ties to

277

Moscow with suspicion. Most of all, India was considered an obstacle to Washington's goal of preventing the proliferation of nuclear weapons.

When India tried to acquire a strategic deterrent by conducting a series of nuclear tests in 1998, the Clinton administration responded by imposing economic sanctions.

Candidate Bush seemed to hold a different attitude. In a foreign policy speech in 1999, he described India as a rising great power and stressed the potential for economic and political cooperation between the world's most powerful democratic country and the world's most populous democratic country.

Rumsfeld's gaffe may damage the prospect for improved relations—at least in the short term. But the instincts Bush showed in his speech are sound. Indeed, Washington should give the highest priority to cultivating ties with New Delhi. India has the potential to be a major American economic partner.

Equally important, India has the potential to be a major strategic player and alleviate some of the security burdens the United States is bearing throughout the long arc from the Persian Gulf to East Asia.

Economically, India appears to be about where China was in the mid-1980s: it is abandoning the command economy policies that retarded its economic growth since the country became independent. Privatization and deregulation steps are going forward. Growth rates have been 6 percent to 7 percent the last two years. Given its larger reservoir of educated citizens and its niche in high technology, India's economic progress in the coming years may well equal or surpass the torrid pace that China has set since the onset of reforms in that country more than two decades age.

India is also on its way to being a great power militarily. New Delhi increased its military budget 27 percent in 2000 and intends to raise spending nearly an additional 14 percent this year. A large part of that spending is going to modernize the air force and navy, including building aircraft carriers and submarines. In short, India is determined to have a first-rate military and is putting money behind that objective.

The United States should exploit rather than resist such developments. India has indicated its intention of being the leading power throughout the South Asia–Indian Ocean region. Among other things, that would mean taking an interest in the stability of the

Persian Gulf—a thankless and frustrating task now undertaken by the United States.

India is also a logical strategic counterweight to China in East Asia. There is little doubt that New Delhi frets about China's rising power and worries about possible PRC expansionism a decade or two from now. Indeed, Indian officials cited concerns about China as the principal reason for the decision to acquire a nuclear capability. Since then, Indian naval vessels have sailed into the South China Sea to participate in joint anti-piracy missions with the navies of various Southeast Asian countries.

American leaders need to get past the obsolete images of India as the home of sclerotic socialism, feckless pacifism or anti-American mischief-making. Whatever the truth of those images in the past, they do not resemble today's India—much less the great power that it is becoming. Bush administration policymakers need to treat India with respect and recognize that Indian and American economic and strategic interests are likely to coincide far more often than they conflict. Rumsfeld's comments aside, India is not an adversary of America—unless shortsighted U.S. actions turn it into one.

This article originally appeared in the *Newark Star Ledger*, March 26, 2001.

Major Powers Start to Pay Attention to India

India is being courted by several great powers.

One graphic sign of U.S. intent was the recent visit to New Delhi by Deputy Secretary of State Richard Armitage. During that visit, Armitage spoke warmly of India's growing economic strength and its significant political and moral influence in world affairs.

He indicated in every manner possible that the United States took India seriously as a rising great power. Armitage also hinted that the Bush administration was likely to lift the remaining economic sanctions, imposed when India conducted a series of nuclear tests in 1998, within the next few months. For its part, New Delhi seemed surprisingly receptive to Washington's position on ballistic missile defense.

Armitage's conciliatory approach was consistent with the overall attitude of the Bush administration. Indeed, Bush himself signaled an interest in India as a possible U.S. strategic partner in his first major foreign policy address as a presidential candidate in late 1999.

There is good reason for viewing India in that fashion. Not only is India the world's second most populous country, but in recent years it has begun to discard the shackles of socialist economic planning and adopt the market reforms that have spurred economic growth in several other countries.

India's economic growth rate the past two years has hovered near 6.5 percent, and according to International Monetary Fund estimates, India may have the world's fourth largest economy by 2020.

India is also rapidly emerging as a serious military player. It is already a member of the exclusive global club of nations with nuclear weapons. India's conventional forces are being rapidly modernized as well. Last year, New Delhi increased its military budget by some 27 percent and followed with another 14 percent this year. Much of that additional spending is going into the air force and navy with the goal of developing a credible force projection capability.

New Delhi is showing a growing interest in matters outside the subcontinent to match its expanding military capabilities. Last year, for example, it dispatched a naval contingent to the South China Sea to participate in maneuvers with a number of Southeast Asian countries. The official reason was to help battle the scourge of piracy in those waters, but a clear underlying motive was to show the Indian flag in a region that Beijing has increasing regarded as being within its sphere of influence.

The United States is wise to be interested in India as a de facto strategic partner. India has the economic and military potential to be part of an important balance of power in Asia. In particular, it could help serve as a strategic counterweight to China if Beijing should ever begin to pursue expansionist ambitions.

Unfortunately, some obstacles stand in the way of the Bush administration's goal. During the Clinton administration, America's actions often made New Delhi nervous. The U.S.-led NATO attack on Serbia (especially when combined with the decision to bypass the UN Security Council) raised fears among Indians that someday the United States might give New Delhi an ultimatum regarding the Kashmir dispute.

One important reason for the recent surge in India's military spending is to make certain that Washington can never treat Kashmir as it did the Kosovo problem. Washington's imposition of economic sanctions in response to India's nuclear tests also annoyed Indians across the political spectrum.

Those sanctions, reflecting the influence of the arms control faction in the United States, were a monumentally bad way to treat a rising great power. The United States also has competition for winning India's favor. After a brief lapse following the disintegration of the Soviet Union, Moscow is again cultivating economic and strategic ties with New Delhi. Indeed, the two countries just recently concluded a major arms sale agreement.

More important, Russia apparently sees India as an important component of a coalition of major powers to thwart U.S. global hegemony. Three years ago, then–foreign minister Yevgeny Primakov openly proposed that India join a "triangular alliance" with Russia and China to promote a "multipolar world."

Even China has sought to improve relations with India. The previously serious tensions along the disputed border between the two countries have noticeably eased over the past three years. When India and Pakistan became embroiled in an armed skirmish over Kashmir in 1999, Beijing gave surprisingly weak support to its Pakistani ally.

And just a few weeks ago, Indian and Chinese naval forces engaged in joint maneuvers.

India is clearly keeping all of its options open. The George W. Bush administration would be wise to overrule the arms control fanatics in the middle ranks of the State Department and lift sanctions against India immediately.

It should also enthusiastically support India's ambition to gain a permanent seat on the UN Security Council. Finally, the administration should make clear to New Delhi that it has no intention whatsoever to interfere in the Kashmir dispute.

India should be a natural de facto strategic partner for the United States. With wiser diplomacy on Washington's part, there are no serious issues on which the interests of the two countries are in conflict. Conversely, there are numerous areas in which Indian and U.S. interests coincide. Chief among them are stability in the Persian Gulf and placing a limitation on China's ambitions. A continuation of the inept diplomacy of the Clinton years, however, could drive India into the waiting arms of Russia and China.

This article originally appeared in the *Taipei Times*, June 16, 2001.

11. Foreign Policy and Domestic Liberty

Introduction

A major underlying motive for my work on defense and foreign policy has been to minimize America's risk exposure in the world. A global interventionist policy automatically entails the likelihood of entangling the United States in an assortment of irrelevant conflicts. The various missions during the 1990s—the Persian Gulf War and the interventions in Somalia, Haiti, Bosnia, and Kosovo—were prime examples of the problem. A policy of promiscuous meddling also always carries with it the likelihood that one or more adventures will turn into a full-blown disaster. Moreover, global interventionism increases the probability of terrorist attacks on the United States.

Those reasons alone would be sufficient for me to criticize the policy that the United States pursued during the Cold War and continued to pursue during the initial post–Cold War decade. But there is another important reason. A global interventionist strategy is antithetical to the values of a constitutional republic. America was not designed to be an empire, and it will prove increasingly difficult to maintain (much less expand) liberty at home if U.S. leaders insist on conducting an imperial policy abroad. (Many of the advocates of global interventionism no longer even shy away from embracing the term "imperial.")

Robert Higgs and other historians have noted that governmental power in the United States expanded dramatically during the two world wars and the Cold War. That is hardly surprising. War and preparation for war inevitably enhance the power of the political state. Power flows from the private sector to the governmental sector during periods of crisis. Within the governmental sector, power flows from state and local governments to the federal government. And within the federal government, power flows from Congress and the judiciary to the executive branch.

That phenomenon is not the result of machinations by evil people in government. The process would be roughly the same even if the most high-minded people were in charge. A global interventionist foreign policy requires secrecy, unity of purpose, and efficiency of execution. All of those requirements push inexorably for the concentration of power in the hands of the president and his advisers. Policy debate by Congress and the public becomes a luxury that can undermine the nation's foreign policy.

But America's constitutional system is predicated on federalism (the division of governmental power between the federal government and the states), checks and balances among the three branches of the federal government, and the legitimacy of debate on all policy issues. There is, therefore, a severe inherent tension between the requirements of a global interventionist foreign policy and the values embodied in the Constitution. That consideration alone should impel Americans to demand a more restrained and focused security strategy for the American republic.

Global Interventionism and the Erosion of Domestic Liberty

There is a tendency of many people to separate domestic and foreign policy issues. For instance, many supporters of the free market advocate government activism abroad. But categorizing issues as "foreign policy" or "domestic policy" can be artificial and misleading. Developments in one arena frequently interact with and affect developments in the other. Most analyses of this phenomenon have focused on how domestic attitudes and interests influence the style and substance of foreign policy. Less attention has been paid to the opposite phenomenon—the impact of foreign policy aims or requirements on domestic institutions and practices. Yet that feedback may ultimately have a more important impact on the health of American liberties.

The foreign policy of the United States has obviously changed dramatically since "isolationism" held sway at the end of the 1930s. Over the past half century, the Republic has acquired and maintained a host of global political and military commitments. Washington has linked America's security to that of the other hemispheric nations through the Rio Treaty and has done the same with Western Europe through NATO. It has negotiated multilateral pacts such as ANZUS (with Australia and New Zealand) and concluded bilateral security treaties with such nations as Japan, South Korea, and Pakistan.

Such formal arrangements, however, do not fully measure the extent of U.S. obligations in the world. The Truman Doctrine, promulgated in March 1947, pledged the United States to assist other nations confronting either external aggression or subversion by "armed minorities." Washington attached no discernible geographic limits to that promise of assistance, and it served as the explicit or tacit basis for U.S. involvement in numerous Third World struggles throughout the Cold War. In the late 1950s, the Eisenhower Doctrine committed the United States to "secure and protect the territorial integrity and political independence" of Middle Eastern nations from "any nation controlled by International Communism." The so-called Carter Doctrine, proclaimed in early 1980 following the Soviet invasion of Afghanistan, made the United States the gendarme of the Persian Gulf. That commitment, which was fulfilled on a grand scale during the Persian Gulf crisis of 1990–1991, remains in effect. In addition to the presidential doctrines, the United States has informal but real security arrangements with Israel and several other countries.

All told, the United States is committed to help defend dozens of nations. Moreover, growing U.S. involvement in peacekeeping operations authorized by the UN Security Council (most notably in Somalia) and "out-of-area" operations conducted by NATO (as in Bosnia and Macedonia) is likely to increase the total. That expansion of obligations is most evident in the Clinton administration's plan to enlarge the membership of NATO to include several Central European nations—and perhaps someday most East European nations as well. Five decades after the dawn of the Cold War, and more than six years after the end of that bitter rivalry, U.S. foreign policy remains interventionist on a global scale.

This policy has had a pervasive impact on the Republic's domestic affairs. In ways both obvious and subtle it has transformed the nation economically, socially, and politically. Some of those changes are unarguably positive. Concern about how America was perceived throughout the world—especially in the emerging nations of Asia and Africa, in which the United States was competing with the Soviet Union for influence—was a significant factor impelling political leaders to abolish the legal framework of racial segregation in the 1950s and 1960s. The odious Jim Crow system probably could not have endured in any case, but the fact that it was a liability to American foreign policy undoubtedly hastened its demise.

Other domestic changes caused or at least facilitated by Washington's policy of global interventionism, though, have been far less benign. The early 20th-century social critic Randolph Bourne observed that "war is the health of the state," by which he meant that governmental power inexorably expands at the expense of individual freedom during periods of armed conflict. Robert Higgs's seminal work, *Crisis and Leviathan: Critical Episodes in the Growth of American Government* (1987), documented that observation, showing how many of the powers now routinely exercised by the federal government were not acquired during such spasms of domestic "reform" as the Progressive Era, the New Deal, and the Great Society. Instead, they emerged because of national mobilizations to fight the two world wars. Moreover, the New Deal and the Great Society were explicit attempts to replicate in peacetime the mobilization of human talent and natural resources that had occurred during wartime.

Enhanced State Power Remains

Even when the nation terminated its war mobilizations, a sizable residue of enhanced governmental power always remained. Manifestations of that "wartime" authority would later surface during peacetime—often in unexpected ways. For example, President Richard Nixon based his 1971 executive order imposing wage and price controls on an obscure provision of the Trading with the Enemy Act of 1917, enacted during the early days of World War I but still in effect decades later.

These surviving wartime powers have also been an important factor in the permanent expansion of the size and scope of the political state. One "temporary" measure enacted during World War II was the withholding provision of the federal income tax. That device has had the insidious effect of disguising the true tax burden on most Americans by "painlessly" extracting the money from their payroll checks before they get an opportunity to see (and use) those funds. For such taxpayers the category of gross salary or wages is little more than a meaningless bookkeeping entry on their payroll check stubs.

One suspects that citizens would be decidedly less willing to carry their current bloated tax burden if they had to write annual or quarterly checks to the IRS. Indeed, it is likely that there would have been a massive tax revolt long before the federal government began consuming more than a quarter of the nation's gross domestic product. It seems more than a coincidence that the two groups that are not subject to the anesthetic of withholding taxes (sole proprietors and independent contractors) have most militantly opposed high taxes. A wartime innovation has thus become an important permanent building block of the leviathan state by continuing to conceal the real tax burden from most Americans.

Perpetual Crisis

Bourne's observation about war being the health of the state is not sufficient, however. It is not only an actual state of war that creates the regimentation and massive violations of civil liberties he feared. An atmosphere of perpetual crisis and preparation for war can produce the same result. The creation of a national security state to wage the Cold War produced many of the same domestic problems and distortions associated with periods of actual combat in earlier eras. America has been essentially on a war footing for more than half a century, and the result has been a significant erosion of liberty. Perhaps most ominous, the end of the Cold War has not produced a retrenchment in either the nation's foreign policy or pervasive garrison-state mentality.

There are numerous examples of undesirable changes in America's domestic system brought about by Washington's global interventionist foreign policy. Waging the Cold War led to the creation of a large and expensive military establishment. Despite the end of the Cold War, military spending (currently $268 billion a year) consumes nearly 4 percent of America's GDP. U.S. military outlays dwarf those of other industrialized countries. For example, Japan spends just $45 billion and Germany a mere $30 billion. Each American must pay more than $1,000 a year to support the military; the burden for each German is about $260 and for each Japanese about $240. That huge disparity is one tangible measure of the financial costs of sustaining a foreign policy based on maintaining U.S. global "leadership" and responsibility.

In addition, government continues to guide the American economy in the name of national security, much as it would during a wartime mobilization. In marked contrast to the pre–World War II era, the national security apparatus wields considerable economic power. The emergence of multi-billion-dollar defense firms whose principal (and, in some cases, sole) customer is the Pentagon is testimony to that fact. There are also restraints on commerce that would have been unthinkable only a few decades ago. Embargoes have been imposed on trade with certain countries deemed to be adversaries of the United States—including such a mortal threat to American security as Burma. In addition to such formal sanctions, there exists a variety of restrictions on the export of technologies that the government decides (often arbitrarily) could have military applications or national security implications. The tug of war between the Clinton administration and the business community over encryption policy is only the most recent example.

An interventionist foreign policy has not only facilitated the expansion of federal governmental power at the expense of the private sector, but has also produced ominous changes within the federal government itself. The conduct of foreign affairs during the Cold War enhanced the power of the executive branch to an unhealthy degree. Fulfilling global obligations placed a premium on the reliability of Washington's commitments as well as the speed (and often the secrecy) of execution. The procedural demands of an interventionist foreign policy are fundamentally incompatible with the division of responsibilities and powers set forth in the Constitution and generally adhered to throughout America's history. Extensive congressional participation in the foreign policy process involves the possibility of delay, the disruption of national unity, and the creation of doubts about the nation's constancy.

The Imperial Presidency

Maintaining a global interventionist policy has led inexorably to the emergence of an "imperial presidency." Chief executives have grown accustomed to using the military according to their personal definitions of the national interest, frequently without even the semblance of congressional consent. The congressional war power, stated in clear and concise terms in the Constitution, has become moribund. Harry Truman's unilateral decision to commit more than 300,000 U.S. troops to the Korean conflict in 1950 remains the most brazen episode of the imperial presidency, but it was hardly the only one during the Cold War. Nor has such executive usurpation of the congressional authority over matters of war and peace abated now that the Cold War is over. The Clinton administration's dispatch of 20,000 U.S. troops to Bosnia as part of a multilateral peacekeeping and nation-building mission confirms that the imperial presidency is alive and well.

The consequences of interventionism are not confined to changes in the nation's political and economic systems. Individual citizens find their liberties circumscribed in a variety of ways. Throughout most of our history, Americans routinely exercised the right to travel outside the country without having to beg permission from Washington. That has changed dramatically during the past half century. Foreign travel and participation in events held in other nations are no longer an inherent right of American citizenship; such activities are often used as pawns to serve foreign policy objectives. Certain countries are declared off-limits to U.S. citizens if Washington deems it in the national interest, and ostensibly nonpolitical events such as the Olympic Games have become tools of diplomacy. Americans whom the government brands as threats to national security are subjected to passport revocations and various forms of harassment.

Undermining Foreign Policy Debate

The garrison-state mentality fostered by an interventionist policy leads to practices that undermine both the legitimacy and the feasibility of debate on defense and foreign policy issues. Indeed, policymakers habitually regard public or congressional scrutiny as an obstacle to be avoided or removed. To thwart such oversight, they have sought to maintain a monopoly of information by misusing the secrecy classification system. Information that contradicts official versions of events or might cast doubt on the wisdom, legality, or morality of a presidential policy is kept from the prying eyes of potential critics. The cult of secrecy surrounding defense and foreign policy issues has evolved as an indispensable corollary of global interventionism. As Washington's overseas commitments have grown, so too has the scope of information—including much that is essential to any public debate on foreign policy options—concealed from the American people and even their congressional representatives.

Interventionism has not only encouraged foreign policy elitism and secrecy, but has also promoted a pervasive intolerance of alternative views on national security issues. Too often, dissent has been viewed as synonymous with disloyalty. The McCarthy era in the early and mid-1950s was the most infamous example of an intolerant loyalty crusade, but it was hardly unique. Precedents for what became known as McCarthyism were established during and immediately following World War I as well as the period just before American entry into World War II. Moreover, the Truman administration utilized the politics of loyalty even during the earliest stages of the Cold War to quash dissent.

The practice of smearing and harassing foreign policy critics did not expire with the junior senator from Wisconsin. The FBI, the CIA and other intelligence services, and even elements of the military conducted sophisticated programs to spy on, disrupt, and discredit opponents of the Vietnam War. And they usually did so with the full knowledge and approval of high-ranking officials in the Johnson and Nixon administrations. Disclosure of such tactics led to reforms designed to prevent a repetition, but events during the Reagan years indicated that those changes were largely ineffectual. Evidence surfaced that opponents of the administration's Central America policy were routinely harassed by agents of the Customs Service and the

FBI upon returning from trips to that region. Even more disturbing were revelations that the FBI secretly investigated the Committee in Solidarity with the People of El Salvador (CISPES) for more than two years despite a dearth of evidence that the group was engaged in any unlawful activities. Congressional allies of the Bush administration smeared critics of the Persian Gulf War as apologists for Saddam Hussein.

Managing the News

Because dissent is often equated with disloyalty, the national security bureaucracy has waged a determined effort to co-opt, intimidate, and exclude the press on foreign policy issues, since members of the news media who question the logic of policy decisions or the veracity of officials raise doubts about the wisdom of U.S. globalist strategy, thereby sowing division among the American people. That is especially true of those individuals who dare to penetrate the veil of secrecy and reveal evidence that might discredit that strategy.

During both world wars and the first two decades of the Cold War, the government primarily sought to enlist the press as an instrument of the nation's foreign policy, and did so with considerable success. (Although officials preferred to stress co-option, even in those periods the threat of intimidation, exclusion, and outright censorship lurked in the background.) As the press became more critical of U.S. policy during the Vietnam War, confrontation increasingly replaced co-option. During the Nixon administration, reporters who published stories based on leaked classified information were threatened, together with their sources, with prosecution for espionage. The alleged authority for such prosecutions was a statute, passed in the initial stage of World War I, that was aimed at preventing spies from giving militarily relevant information to enemy governments. A campaign to treat embarrassing disclosures as a form of espionage re-emerged during the Reagan and Bush administrations, and the government scored an ominous legal victory by successfully prosecuting defense analyst Samuel Loring Morison for the "crime" of leaking classified information, not to a foreign government, but to *Jane's Defence Weekly*.

In addition to resurrecting that technique of intimidation, the national security bureaucracy found an ingeniously effective method of stifling hostile press coverage of military operations. When the

United States invaded the tiny Caribbean nation of Grenada in the autumn of 1983, the Pentagon simply barred the media. For more than 48 hours, the government enjoyed the luxury of exercising absolute control over information about a significant and controversial military operation. In so doing, it established a tempting precedent for an exclusionary policy to be invoked in similar—and perhaps far larger and more prolonged—interventionist enterprises. Indeed, when U.S. forces invaded Panama in December 1989, the techniques used in Grenada were applied again, albeit in a slightly more subtle fashion. Reporters were delayed and kept away from the scenes of military action and were instead given guided tours of such important sights as Panamanian dictator Manuel Noriega's pornography collection.

Government manipulation of the media reached its apogee during the Persian Gulf War. Military officials herded reporters into organized pools monitored by "public affairs" personnel and barred them from attempting to reach front-line areas on their own. Meanwhile, correspondents were fed a steady diet of briefings (i.e., propaganda) by the military, replete with videotapes showing the clean-kill capabilities of smart bombs and other high-tech U.S. weaponry. The press corps became little more than a transmission belt for the Pentagon's version of events. Consequently, the American public saw astonishingly little of the bloody reality of the war (especially the extent of Iraqi casualties) and learned even less about the complex roots of the gulf crisis.

The politics of loyalty, the pervasive cult of secrecy, and governmental attacks on the press all have one thing in common. They have the effect (and perhaps the intent) of hobbling public debate on both the substance and the execution of U.S. foreign policy. A strategy of global interventionism, to be effective, requires domestic unity and conformity. Those requirements run directly counter to the values of political pluralism and unfettered debate so essential to the maintenance of a democratic system. An interventionist foreign policy promotes the growth of a centralized and remote political structure, creates economic regimentation, and undermines a variety of civil liberties, especially freedom of expression.

Another ugly manifestation of interventionism was the policy of conscripting young Americans into the military and sending them off to fight in distant wars. That infringement on their liberty was exacerbated by the fact that most of those struggles were murky geopolitical conflicts that bore little if any relevance to America's vital security interests. Many of the unfortunate conscripts returned home maimed in body or mind; many others failed to return at all.

The military draft became an important device to sustain an interventionist strategy in both world wars and throughout the most virulent stages of the Cold War. It also became the quintessential symbol of the domestic regimentation that global interventionism promotes. It is no coincidence that ardent global interventionists are usually among the most relentless supporters of efforts to restore conscription, either directly or in the guise of a more comprehensive national service system.

"For the Security of the Nation"

Perhaps the most corrosive domestic effect of Washington's interventionist foreign policy has been on national attitudes. Americans have come to accept governmental intrusions in the name of "national security" that they would have ferociously opposed as blatant power grabs in earlier eras. Politicians gradually learned that the fastest way to overcome opposition to schemes to expand the state was to portray initiatives as necessary for the security of the nation. Sometimes such reasoning has been exceedingly strained. The statute that first involved the federal government in elementary and secondary education was titled the National Defense Education Act. Similarly, the legislation funding the interstate highway system was the National Defense Highway Act. It is surprising that the sponsors of Medicare didn't fashion their bill as the "National Defense Elderly Care Act."

Not only has the national security justification been cynically used to defuse opposition to mundane welfare-state and traditional pork-barrel initiatives, the rhetoric of war has come to dominate the national discourse to an unhealthy degree. We have seen the "war" metaphor used promiscuously, including Lyndon Johnson's War on Poverty, Jimmy Carter's Energy War, the war on drugs, and more recently "wars" on cancer and illiteracy. Language matters, and the fondness for such rhetoric is a revealing and disturbing indicator of how deeply the garrison-state mentality has become entrenched.

The adverse domestic consequences of global interventionism raise serious questions about the future of individual liberty in the

United States. At the dawn of the Cold War, social commentator Garet Garrett warned that America could not indefinitely remain a republic at home while taking on the trappings of empire abroad. He noted a fundamental contradiction between the desire to play the role of global policeman and the objective of maintaining long-standing American traditions of limited government, free enterprise, and individual liberty. Garrett's warning is even more applicable today. Americans are rapidly reaching the point where they must confront a stark choice. Either the United States will adopt a more circumspect role in the world in order to preserve domestic freedom, or that freedom will continue to erode (perhaps beyond the point of recovery) to satisfy the requirements of a globalist foreign policy. That choice will determine not only how the United States is defended but whether this country retains the values and principles that make it worth defending.

This article originally appeared in *The Freeman*, November 1997. Reprinted with permission.

INDEX

295

*Bush (1) is George Herbert Walker Bush. Bush (2) is George W. Bush

About the Author

Ted Galen Carpenter is vice president for defense and foreign policy studies at the Cato Institute. Dr. Carpenter is the author or editor of 14 books and the author of more than 250 articles on international affairs. His books include *Bad Neighbor Policy: Washington's Futile War on Drugs in Latin America* (forthcoming, 2003), *The Captive Press: Foreign Policy Crises and the First Amendment* (1995), *Beyond NATO: Staying Out of Europe's Wars* (1994), and *A Search for Enemies: America's Alliances after the Cold War* (1992). Carpenter is a frequent guest on radio and television programs in the United States, Latin America, Europe, East Asia, and other regions. He received his Ph.D. in U.S. diplomatic history from the University of Texas and serves on the editorial boards of the *Mediterranean Quarterly* and the *Journal of Strategic Studies*.

Cato Institute

Founded in 1977, the Cato Institute is a public policy research foundation dedicated to broadening the parameters of policy debate to allow consideration of more options that are consistent with the traditional American principles of limited government, individual liberty, and peace. To that end, the Institute strives to achieve greater involvement of the intelligent, concerned lay public in questions of policy and the proper role of government.

The Institute is named for *Cato's Letters*, libertarian pamphlets that were widely read in the American Colonies in the early 18th century and played a major role in laying the philosophical foundation for the American Revolution.

Despite the achievement of the nation's Founders, today virtually no aspect of life is free from government encroachment. A pervasive intolerance for individual rights is shown by government's arbitrary intrusions into private economic transactions and its disregard for civil liberties.

To counter that trend, the Cato Institute undertakes an extensive publications program that addresses the complete spectrum of policy issues. Books, monographs, and shorter studies are commissioned to examine the federal budget, Social Security, regulation, military spending, international trade, and myriad other issues. Major policy conferences are held throughout the year, from which papers are published thrice yearly in the *Cato Journal*. The Institute also publishes the quarterly magazine *Regulation*.

In order to maintain its independence, the Cato Institute accepts no government funding. Contributions are received from foundations, corporations, and individuals, and other revenue is generated from the sale of publications. The Institute is a nonprofit, tax-exempt, educational foundation under Section 501(c)3 of the Internal Revenue Code.

CATO INSTITUTE
1000 Massachusetts Ave., N.W.
Washington, D.C. 20001